Human Character and Behavior
~ An Islamic Perspective ~

Human Character and Behavior

AN ISLAMIC PERSPECTIVE

DR. MUHAMMAD A. HAFEEZ

amana publications

First Edition
(1432AH/2011AC)

© Copyright 1431AH/2010 AC
amana publications
10710 Tucker Street
Beltsville, Maryland 20705-2223 USA
Tel: (301) 595-5777 / Fax: (301) 595-5888
E-mail: amana@igprinting.com
Website: www.amana-publications.com

Dr. Muhammad A. Hafeez
docmhafeez@hotmail.com

Library of Congress Cataloging-in-Publication Data

Hafeez, Muhammad A.
  Human character and behavior : an Islamic perspective / Muhammad A. Hafeez. -- 1st ed.
    p. cm.
  ISBN 978-1-59008-067-2
  1. Theological anthropology--Islam. 2. Muslims--Conduct of life. I. Title.
  BP166.7.H337 2011
  297.2'2--dc22
                                2011012352

PRINTED IN THE UNITED STATES OF AMERICA

International Graphics
10710 Tucker Street,
Beltsville, Maryland 20705-2223
Tel: (301) 595-5999
Fax: (301) 595-5888

Website: igprinting.com

Dedicated to Humankind

By your Lord's Grace, you are not afflicted with madness,
And surely yours shall be a never-ending reward,
And you are certainly on
the most exalted standard of moral excellence.

(The Qur'an, Surah al-Qalam: 2-4)

ACKNOWLEDGEMENT

THE IMPORTANCE OF LEARNING what God commands in the Qur'an is such that people should exert all their efforts to accomplish this task, and no one is exempt from this duty. Although the Messenger was illiterate, God commanded him to read, "Read in the name of your Lord Who created—created man from a clot. Read, and your Lord is Most Honorable..."[1] Knowledge of the Arabic language is preferable in learning the Qur'an, and in the past this was the only way to learn the Qur'an, due to a limited availability of books in other languages on the Qur'an and Ahadith. Since translations and interpretations of the Qur'an are now available in almost every widely known language, one can also learn to understand the Qur'an in a language known to the readers. It is so important to learn what God commands in the Qur'an that nothing should stand in its way; not even the lack of ability to understand Arabic. I am, therefore, highly indebted to those religious scholars, editors, translators and commentators whose works, even in other than the Arabic language, have been instrumental in my learning process.

In understanding the Qur'an, I have benefited from the Urdu and English translations and Tafsir (commentary) by Syed Abul Ala Maududi, as well as from English translations by 'Abdullah Yusuf Ali, Zafar Ishaq Ansari, Muhammad Marmaduke Pickthall, M. H. Shakir, and Dr. M. M. Khan and Dr. M. T. Al-Hilali. I am indebted to the scholarly writings of Dr. Malik Ghulam Murtaza, Adil Salahi, Sheikh Ali Tantavi, Sheikh 'Abdullah Bin Muhammad Al-Muhtaj, M. Al-Ghazali, and Hamza Yusuf, and I acknowledge that their contributions have greatly helped me in my pursuit of knowledge. I am grateful to Dr. Taqiuddin Ahmed, Imam/Director of the Islamic Society of Central New York, and to Mirza Iqbal Ashraf, author of Introduction to World Philosophies and Islamic Philosophy of War and Peace, for their invaluable review and comments.

The Qur'an was revealed for the benefit of all humankind, and God thusly enjoined Adam in Paradise: "We said: 'Get you down all from here; and if, as is sure, there comes to you guidance from me, whosoever follows My guidance, on them shall be no fear, nor shall they grieve."[2] God has also promised that, "As for those who were led to the guidance, Allah increases them in their guidance and causes them to grow in their piety."[3] Every human being is divinely blessed with a capacity to comprehend God's guidance. This has indeed encouraged me and will encourage whoever wants to learn his/her obligations as God's trustee on earth. God has reminded us in Surah Al-Qamar that, "We have indeed made the Qur'an easy to understand and remember; then is there any who will receive admonition?"[4] As members of humanity, for our own good both in this life and in the Hereafter, we should say, "Yes," to God's invitation to His guidance.

Dr. Muhammad A. Hafeez

NOTES

1. Qur'an 96:1-3.
2. Qur'an 2:38.
3. Qur'an 47:17.
4. Qur'an 54:17.

CONTENTS

FOREWORD

ISLAM, LIKE JUDAISM AND Christianity, consists of two dimensions, each of which is represented by an axis. The vertical axis defines what should be man's relationship to God Almighty, while the horizontal axis defines what should be man's relationship to the world around him and to his fellow man. In Human Character and Behavior, Dr. Hafeez focuses our attention squarely on the horizontal axis and argues quite passionately that we Muslims have for far too long been giving short shrift to our responsibilities as God's trustee on earth. Oh, we may think that we are good Muslims by fulfilling our responsibilities on the vertical axis by saying our five daily prayers at their appointed times, by attending the Friday prayer in a mosque, by fasting during Ramadan, etc. However, if we are neglecting our responsibilities and duties on the horizontal axis by failing as God's trustee on earth to care fully and appropriately for the rest of God's creation, how can it be said that we are adequately fulfilling our responsibilities to God? Do not our prayers and other acts of worship become empty rituals devoid of spirituality and meaning if we are failing to carry out God's commands regarding our duties to our fellow human beings and to the rest of God's creation?

How do we cure this malady within our individual selves and within the Muslim community? For Dr. Hafeez, the answer is straightforward: we must develop our human character and behavior to the point that we truly actualize our potential as God's trustee on earth. This is no easy assignment, for the distractions, temptations, and hardships of this world too frequently divert us from our higher calling as God's trustee. Far too often, we fall victim to petty racism, nationalism, tribalism, and ethnocentrism. Likewise, our own personal and selfish desires frequently prevent us from truly wanting for our brothers and sisters in humanity what we want for ourselves. Nonetheless, Dr. Hafeez notes that we each have the potential to fulfill our role as God's trustee. Drawing heavily on the Qur'an and Sunnah of Prophet Muhammad (peace be upon him), Human Character and Behavior offers us a chance to review our obligations along Islam's horizontal dimension, as well as a blueprint for how to grow and develop our spiritual selves to the point where we can begin fulfilling those responsibilities. The added benefit is that our growth on the horizontal axis simultaneously enhances our worship of and relationship to God along the vertical dimension.

Abu Yahya (Jerald F. Dirks), M.Div., Psy.D.
July 2, 2010

In the name of Allah, the Compassionate, the Merciful

PREFACE

DIVINE KNOWLEDGE HAS BEEN revealed to guide humanity through its journey towards its destiny. It tells what is expected from us, what our character should be, and how we are to behave in this world. Lack of knowledge could corrupt people. God (Allah) tells us in Surah Al-Rum, "Nay, the unjust people follow their selfish desires without any knowledge; so who can guide them whom Allah lets go astray (due to their own free will)? Such shall have no helpers."[1] It is narrated by Abu Huraira that God's Messenger said, "No child is born except in Islam (the nature in which God created humankind), and then his/her parents make him/her Jewish, Christian or Magian..."[2] The Prophet then recited the verse from Surah Al-Rum, "Then turn your face single-mindedly to the true faith and adhere to the nature in which Allah created humankind. Let there be no change in Allah's religion. That is the True Faith, although most people do not know."[3]

In Human Character and Behavior, I have expounded that according to the Qur'an, learning to manage our affairs on earth is the first obligation of humanity as God's trustee on earth. Though the importance of knowledge and learning is very hard to overstate, God has also given humanity a mind to think. It is quite natural that He expects us to use it, particularly in the most important issue of our existence, which is the knowledge of how and by whom we are created and for what purpose. With knowledge comes understanding, then obedience. God commands in Surah Al-Alaq, "Read in the name of your Lord Who created—created man from a clot. Read, and your Lord is Most Honorable, Who taught (man to write) with the pen—taught man what he knew not."[4] From the Qur'an we learn that:

° God created humankind and gave us wisdom, free will, and guidance. He appointed each one of us, male or female, rich or poor, as a trustee on earth to serve Him by implementing His commandments in managing our affairs, to the end that we build just human societies in the world. Such societies are built on hard work, truth, justice, and charity, and they run without corruption, discrimination, exploitation, and oppression.

° God commands humanity to believe in Him, His Messengers, His revelations, the resurrection, and the eventual accountability for our behavior and deeds. God expects us to acknowledge our mistakes, reform ourselves, do good deeds, and establish justice under all circumstances. Life in this world is a test to prove that we live our lives to their best purpose and potential.

° Divine guidance equips humankind with the desired character and behavior of a believer, which, in turn, helps build a just human society on earth. Our prayers and fasting remind us of our duties, teaching us the self-discipline needed to guard against the temptation to sin or to do evil and spread corruption.

° Happiness in the life hereafter greatly depends on the efforts of the believers to improve the life in this world. As individuals, irrespective of our situation or status in life, each one of us should improve our behavior and try to help others in their struggle in life.

° It is our acts and deeds that make us suffer or bring us happiness. God administers absolute justice to all. Our actions determine our present and our future. It is our choice, not chance, that determines our destiny - the choice one makes, knowing that all actions either good or bad have appropriate consequences.

There are as many ways of learning as there are human beings, and each may be adequate, depending on the emotional and intellectual makeup of an individual and on the availability of opportunities. The best is an educational system where the moral values of human character and behavior are developed along with competency in professional fields. Such an educational system is not available in contemporary secular schools. Since both the religious and secular aspects of human life need to be addressed to nurture an honest, hardworking, and competent individual, attending merely religious schools is not going to help. The most prevalent route to acquire knowledge that helps build the required human character and behavior, as it exists today, is through self-study and understanding of the Qur'an and Ahadith in consultation with religious scholars and their writings. Knowledge of the Arabic language is preferable in learning the Qur'an, and in the past this was the only way to learn the Qur'an, due to the limited availability of books on the Qur'an and Ahadith in other languages. Since translations and interpretations of the Qur'an are now available in almost every widely known language, one can now also learn to understand the Qur'an in a language familiar to its readers. The importance of learning what God commands in the Qur'an is such that nothing should stand in its way, not even the lack of ability to understand Arabic.

The Qur'an is a book of guidance for the humankind in general and for the believers in particular. It is the textbook of Islam. For better understanding, the Qur'an should be read with concentration, at least a chapter at a time, taking notes for easy reference and highlighting God's commands that need to be remembered for implementation. People should try their best to understand and implement God's commands individually, as well as jointly in the community. Since individual abilities vary, a person should not be discouraged in the pursuit of learning and implementing God's commands. God tells people, "As for those who believe and do good deeds, We do not impose on any person a duty except to the extent of his ability; they are the dwellers of the Paradise; in it they shall abide."[5]

Human Character and Behavior explicates that guidance from the Qur'an and Sunnah is to equip people with the desired character and behavior of a believer. Our prayers and fasting remind us of our duties and teach us the self-discipline needed to guard ourselves against the temptation to sin or do evil and spread corruption. Happiness, in this worldly life and the life hereafter, greatly depends on the efforts of the believers to improve the life in this world. As individuals, irrespective of our situation or status in life, each one of us should improve his behavior and try to help others in their struggle in life. The life of the Messenger of Islam is an excellent example to follow and emulate. Merely teachings and commands of "do and don't do" do not form the foundation of a good moral character in a society. The fruitful teaching of good conduct requires long training and constant watch. It also requires role models for nourishing and continually developing more and more excellent character among people. The Messenger of God has, by his practice, presented the best example of good moral character. During his lifetime, even before advising people to adopt a moral life by giving sermons and counsels, he sowed the seeds of high standard of ethics and morality by actually living that kind of life.

The Messenger stated that the foremost purpose of his being sent to this world was for the purpose of perfecting human moral character and behavior. In the translation of Malik's Muwatta, it is mentioned that, "Yahya related to me that he had heard that the Messenger of Allah, may Allah bless him and grant him peace, said, 'I was sent only to perfect good character.'"[6] This has been testified to in Surah Al-Qalam, in which God, addressing the Messenger, says, "You are certainly on the most exalted standard of moral excellence."[7] As narrated by 'Abdullah ibn Amar: "The Messenger of Allah was neither ill-mannered nor rude. He used to say that the better people among you are those who are best in their moral character."[8]

Regarding the habits and traits of the Messenger, he was known for his extreme generosity, and he was never miserly in anything. He was very brave and courageous. He never turned away from truth. He was just and loving. In his own decisions, he never committed any excesses or injustice. In his whole life, he was truthful and an honest trustee. God tells us in Surah Al-Jumuah that, "It is He Who has sent amongst the unlettered a messenger from among themselves, to rehearse to them His Signs, to sanctify them, and to instruct them in Scripture and Wisdom—although they had been, before, in manifest error"[9] In Makkah, we see the Messenger teaching verses of the Qur'an, purifying people, and imparting knowledge and wisdom. The core of human values developed among the early followers of Islam was a prerequisite to the establishment of a just community at Madinah. The end result of these efforts was what God declared: "You are the best community ever raised for humankind. You enjoin what is right, forbid what is wrong, and you believe in Allah."[10] Inculcation of such moral values among the followers of Islam is a prerequisite to the establishment of just communities even now, as well as in the future.

In *Human Character and Behavior*, God's commands, as revealed in the Qur'an, are propounded to motivate people to reform and to inculcate good moral character and behavior. Knowledge and, most importantly, application of what God commands help humanity to overcome its weaknesses and to reform the character and behavior of individuals in particular and of society in general. This is very important because only individuals of good moral and ethical character will help build a just human society on earth as is desired and expected by God from His trustees on earth. Efforts are required to improve the character and behavior of people, as well as the character and working of the state.

Human Character and Behavior, in the light of the Qur'an and the Sunnah of the Messenger, explicates that it is an individual's responsibility to elect honest and trustworthy people to the government, individuals who should be ready to face accountability for their actions and behavior, both to God and to His trustees, the people. Muslims should not permit themselves to be ruled by corrupt people or corrupt governments. It is obligatory upon all Muslims to resist corruption, both on individual and collective levels. We all are responsible within our own sphere of influence for the development, implementation, protection, and improvement of core human values. Our efforts should be continuous and simultaneous to ensure that the education to develop personal integrity and professionalism, inculcation of moral and social values, availability of opportunities for the honest earning of basic necessities, protection of individual and state rights, and protection of society and its institutions are being taken care of under all circumstances all the time.

Dr. Muhammad A. Hafeez

NOTES

1. Qur'an 30:29.
2. Sahih Bukhari 6.60.298.
3. Qur'an 30:30.
4. Qur'an 96:1-5.
5. Qur'an 7:42.
6. Malik, Muwatta 47.1.8.
7. Qur'an 68:4.
8. Sahih Bukhari 4.56.759.
9. Qur'an 62:2.
10. Qur'an 3:110.

INTRODUCTION

HUMAN DEVELOPMENT DURING ITS life on earth consists of two equally important aspects. These are its physical development and the development of its moral character. To be worthy of God's trust, humankind needs a human character in addition to its normal physical development. There is no difference between human physical development and the physical development of other creatures on earth. It is the development of human moral character and behavior that makes people human. The guidance to develop various aspects of human character and conduct is given in the Qur'an. These guidelines educate, and their implementation makes us disciplined. God invites people to be human and has addressed people directly by name twenty-one times in the Qur'an. God, in Surah al-Fatihah, the first Surah of the Qur'an, has acquainted humankind with a rejoinder of whatever we invoke in our prayers. These rejoinders have been summarized in the table below and elaborately discussed in the light of God's commands in the first chapter of this book.

O PEOPLE! BE CAREFUL OF (YOUR DUTY TO) YOUR LORD [1]

1	2	3	4	5
All praise is due to Allah, the Lord of the Worlds (1:2)	The Beneficent, the Merciful (1:3)	Master of the Day of Judgment (1:4)	You do we serve, and You do we ask for help (1:5)	Show us the straightway (1:6)
Worship your Creator so that you may learn righteousness (2:21)	Surely Allah has honored the children of Adam (17:70)	Serve only Allah Who will cause you to die (10:104)	Satan is your enemy, so take him as such (35:6)	There has come to you a clear proof from your Lord (4:174)
Following the guidance is for your good (10:108)	Eat lawful and good things and do not (be extravagant) follow Satan (2:168)	Those people who associate with Allah cannot even create a fly (22:73)	Your rebellion is only against yourselves (10:23)	Messenger has come with the truth from your Lord (4:170)

1

People stand in need of Allah (and His guidance) (35:15)	Remember Allah's grace toward you! (35:3)	Guard against the punishment from your Lord (22:1)	Do not make mischief in the earth (7:56)	Believe in Allah and His Messenger (7:158)
Believers who do good deeds: for them is forgiveness and honorable provision (22:50)	None knows what one will earn and where one will die (31:34)	If you doubt the Hereafter, (then consider your own creation and birth) ... (22:5)	The noblest person is the one who is best in conduct (49:13)	The Qur'an is guidance and a mercy for believers (10:57)

Human character and personality are shaped by individual efforts. Believers are God-fearing people who are most careful of their duties. They are also most righteous and the best in conduct. God tells us that only good deeds make people honorable.[2] Doing good deeds requires both human efforts in the right direction and good intentions. Generally, people think that a believer is simply the one who regularly performs all religious rituals. This is not so. If the performance of rituals by a believer does not help the person to be humble, virtuous, and truly God-fearing, then he or she is not a true believer. Similarly if a person, no matter what religion he/she follows, is not good and just in dealing with others and does not care to keep away from shameful and sinful acts that God has forbidden, then that person is not truly human. To be a human is to believe in humanity with all human values and be an embodiment of all that is good. Since people have to live together and deal with each other, they need to have a specific social behavior.

To be human is also an attitude that leads to continual improvements in individual character and behavior. Since people are liable to make mistakes due to their inherent weaknesses, selfish desires, surrounding temptations, and so on, absolute perfection of character and actions is not humanly possible. If people are conscious of their weaknesses and genuinely seek God's forgiveness, they are guided towards the perfection of their character and behavior. Human character is improved with every step of acknowledgment, regret, and effort not to repeat the mistakes again. Various aspects of human personality and attitude that impact moral development are reflected in the second chapter.

The third chapter expounds upon human vulnerabilities? and development. People should understand that all righteous activities are worship of God. The Islamic faith has, perhaps, the strongest leverage on the lives of its followers as compared with other religions of the world. Whatever a believer does, he must first make sure that it is not contrary to the teachings of Islam. If such a contradiction exists, then he must abandon every act that is against the teachings of his religion. This applies to matters that are universally recognized to be within the religious influence, as well as to matters that most people believe to be of no concern to religion. This is due to the fact that Islam is not merely a relationship between an individual and God. It is also a code of living that organizes human life in such a way as to make the pleasure of God their goal, something that is achieved only by living their lives as God's trustees on earth. The Qur'an consists of the true moral and socio-political code that helps people to achieve their status as God's trustee, which is a much higher status and calling than what is achieved by those who live only to fulfill their selfish needs. Only people devoid of wisdom reject God's guidance, while people who adopt obedience to divine guidance and lead a life of piety and righteousness become worthy of God's mercy and friendship. Various weaknesses of human character and behavior, the need to reform ourselves by following divine guidance, and what motivates us to improve our character and behavior are discussed in this chapter.

Since people have freedom of choice and a number of emotional weaknesses and physical desires, they are liable to make mistakes. Therefore, divine guidance is needed to reform humankind and to elevate its stature above other creatures. A person is made responsible for his behavior and deeds, and one should know one's shortcomings or weaknesses before one can desire and make efforts to overcome these. The environment and the nature of various human weaknesses demand that humanity should be guided to reform itself and to develop the character and behavior that qualify it to be an efficient and effective trustee of God on earth. Humankind, which is weak by nature, has been created to work hard, to struggle in a hostile environment created by its own personal desires, and to be maligned by the jealousy of Satan and the jinn. The possibility of the misuse of human will and the resulting satanic behavior of human beings increases the severity of this hostile environment even more. Because of our weaknesses and the hostile environment of our existence, God explains and provides guidance about the ways that help people to succeed in life. None other than God can guide and help humanity to succeed in its mission as God's trustee on earth. How divine guidance helps reform people is further discussed in the fourth chapter.

The fifth chapter throws light on the weaknesses of human character. Humankind is engendered with numerous physical and emotional shortcomings. Besides, our existence is surrounded by many selfish desires, temptations, and difficulties, leaving a question mark as how we are to survive successfully. Our salvation lies in a passionate and determined belief in our Creator. Under His guidance, we should make efforts to reform our character, overcome our weaknesses, and strive hard with a dedication to accomplish our mission as God's trustee on earth. God commands us to believe and worship Him and to reform ourselves into the best in character and conduct. We should be truthful and just in our dealings with others, and we should patiently fight against discrimination, exploitation, and corruption. We should get involved in the betterment of society, do good deeds, enjoin what is right, and forbid what is wrong. Our specific physical and emotional shortcomings, our attitudes and natural inclinations that negatively impact on our performance, and the ways to overcome these difficulties are discussed in this chapter.

The sixth chapter is a comparative assessment of the believers, hypocrites, and unbelievers. Proper use or misuse of human will and intellect shapes human attitudes that impact behavior during various situations and that transform people into believers, unbelievers, and hypocrites. Why this happens and how to achieve success is discussed in detail in the Qur'an. God loves the believers who seek His pleasure with their words and deeds. He is affectionate to them and those who seek good in this world, as well as in the Hereafter. Such people worship their Lord in fear and in hope and spend out of what He has given them. However, there are some believers who serve God halfheartedly. They are satisfied if good befalls them, but they turn back if a trial afflicts them. There are also some believers who seek the bounties of their Lord only for this world. Such people will have nothing for them in the Hereafter. On the other hand, there are some people who say by their words that they believe in God and the Last Day; but their behavior and deeds show that they are not believers. When they find difficulties in following the way of God, they make excuses, while during times of success they try to be with the believers. Certainly God knows who the believers are and who the hypocrites are. Contrary to the behavior of the believers who are overflowing with their love of God, the unbelievers worship others besides God as His equals. They love them as they should love only God. If the unbelievers could see, they would certainly see their punishment. Among the unbelievers, there are some people who take a frivolous discourse to lead people astray from God's path without knowledge and who ridicule the divine guidance. There are also some people among the unbelievers who dispute about God without knowledge and who follow the rebellious Satan.

Like a solid brick in a house, human individuals have to be strong in character and beautiful in behavior to contribute to the accomplishment of the divine trust of eliminating corruption from human society. As a raw brick of weak mold cannot increase the strength and look of a house, neither can an individual with a raw character full of ugly, selfish desires and undisciplined behavior strengthen society. The logical outcome of believing the truth and of worshipping God is the growth of human moral character and refined behavior, without which it is doubtful that people can fulfill their responsibility of being God's trustee on earth. The contributions of the believers, hypocrites and unbelievers in delivering God's trust are further reviewed in this chapter.

The human personality that God loves is examined in the seventh chapter. Islamic worship, performed with proper attitude and objectives, reforms people. God commanded and motivated humanity when He said: "Say (O Muhammad, to people): If you love Allah, then follow me; Allah will love you and forgive you your faults, and Allah is Forgiving, Merciful."[3] God also said in the Qur'an: "Indeed, there is for you, in the Messenger of Allah, a good example to follow."[4] Why is God again and again commanding us to accept the Messenger as our role model? We find the answer in what the Messenger has himself stated was the foremost purpose of his being sent down to this world and the purpose of his call to the people: "I have been sent only for the purpose of perfecting good morals."[5] The Messenger's achievement as a role model has been confirmed by God Himself in the Qur'an, "Most surely you conform (yourself, O Muhammad) to sublime morality."[6]

Humankind has many physical and moral weaknesses that, if not corrected, hinder its growth and progress. Divine guidance is there to help remove these shortcomings. The divine message has left an indelible impression on the history of humankind, and its purpose is nothing else but to strengthen the moral character of people so that the world can be an abode for humanity and not a jungle inhabited by animals. Islam consists of: (1) faith that embodies correct ideology, (2) the basic principles from which Islamic laws are derived, and (3) actions that implement Islamic law, i.e., the Islamic constitution. This constitution is inseparable from faith and ideology. According to Islam, there can be no split between faith and action, between ideology and law. The one follows the other in the same way that cause produces effect and that a certain premise gives a particular result. What brings the believers nearer to God? God Himself has answered this in the Qur'an. Various verses that specifically describe what God loves and does not love in human personality are further discussed in this chapter.

The development of human character and society is explained in the light of divine discipline in the eighth chapter. God created humanity in a certain way and sent messengers to give guidance so that humans can lead happy lives. The Messenger's role was to highlight what behavior is beneficent and what behavior reprieves problems and misery. What he conveyed is a complete message that outlines an integrated system devised by God, the creator of humankind, Who knows what is appropriate and suitable for implementation in human life that will bring happiness. Thus, whoever obeys God's rules is a beneficiary. The benefit is assured, and the rules are made to spare people affliction, contradiction, and confusion. Our prayers and fasting do not benefit God in any way. However, prayers certainly benefit us by keeping us on our guard against temptation and against falling into sin. Fasting also teaches self-discipline. In contrast, humanity suffers by not implementing God's laws. It does not harm God in any way. The choice is there; we either do what is right and enjoy its benefits in this life, as well as in the Hereafter, or we reject God's guidance and suffer the consequences of this rejection.

God asks humankind to reflect: "We assuredly established you with authority on earth and provided you therein with means for the fulfillment of your life."[7] "Then We appointed you as rulers in the earth after them that We might see how you behave."[8] Therefore, God helps "those who, should We establish them in the land, will keep up prayer and pay Zakah (obligatory charity) and enjoin good and forbid evil, and Allah's is the end of all affairs."[9] Given the above, each one of us should keep up the prayers, pay Zakah, enjoin what is good, and forbid what is evil. This is the only option we have if we want to succeed in life; otherwise, our fate may not be any different from those whose stories we read about in history. One should be beware of, "and guard yourselves against a calamity that cannot fall exclusively on those of you who are wrongdoers, and know that Allah is severe in punishment."[10] What is our ultimate goal in life? This is further discussed in this chapter.

The protection of human character and society is discussed in the ninth chapter. Reviewing and reflecting on the situations that prevailed in different parts of the world during and after the implementation of various socio-political systems devised by people, we determine what they achieved. History tells us that every major social change that took place in the world was achieved at a very high cost in human lives and misery. Humankind has managed very poorly without God's guidance. We continue to face endless misery while resisting acknowledgment of the basic truth that divine guidance is needed. No one can legitimize in the sight of God one's gains or achievements by arrogance, false evidence, exploitation and bribes, or puppet governments installed by the rigging of elections and by the manipulation of voters.

The aim of divine guidance is to serve human interest, to help people build a happy life in a community characterized by justice. Justice must be achieved at all levels, within the family, the local community, the social hierarchy, and the political system. According to a sacred Hadith God says: "My servants, I have forbidden Myself injustice and have made injustice forbidden among you. Therefore, do not act unjustly to one another."[11] Moreover, history proves that whenever people established their system on the basis of true divine guidance and applied God's law, their achievements were really great. God's law suits every community at every level of civilization. Islam lays down certain principles that provide a framework within which human society can operate. Within that framework, we can choose to produce a social system to suit us. Islamic laws are the laws of nature, and there is nothing against nature revealed by God in the Qur'an. That makes it possible to be compatible with diverse traditions and cultures in the world, which is a great characteristic of Islamic law, enabling it to be applicable in all communities. There is, however, a main requirement for Islamic law to be properly applied. It should be applied as a complete whole covering all aspects of human lives and society. Once the Islamic community has been established like what was done at Madinah, it should be properly maintained. What we need to do at all times and continually is discussed in this chapter.

Human moral and social values are evaluated and discussed in the tenth chapter. People should learn to be moral. The purpose of education is to develop personal integrity and professionalism. Both types of education, general as well as religious, are essential for the protection of Islamic values and society. Faith makes people God-conscious and fully human. After developing people's relationship with God, religion builds human character, refines human behavior, and teaches how to deal with others. It is religion, which through its set of beliefs, prayer, fasting, charity, and pilgrimage, makes people conscientious regarding the accountability of their actions and develops patience, a quality of character that is very much needed to succeed in life. Hard work, integrity, and contentment all go together in one's struggle. To such people, God's angels offer assurance: "We are your guardians in this world's life and in the Hereafter, and you shall have therein what you desire, and you shall have therein what you ask for."[12] People should remember what their Lord has proclaimed: "If you give thanks, I would certainly give to you more, and if you are ungrateful for My favors, My chastisement is truly severe."[13] They should also not forget what God said to Moses when he desired to see Him: "O Moses! Surely I have chosen you above the people with My messages and by My speaking (to you); therefore, take hold of what I give to you, and be among the thankful."[14]

Various verses of the Qur'an that motivate and help people to overcome their weaknesses in transforming themselves into individuals of good moral character and behavior, making them worthy of God's love and mercy, are given in the eleventh chapter. Divine knowledge enables us to inculcate those elements of behavior that make people human. It also guides us to manage our desires with patience and to extend forgiveness in dealing with others. God wants people, as His trustees, to conform to these moral and social values.

The twelfth chapter deals with Islamic social behavior. God enquires of people: "Why were there not among the generations before you those possessing sense enough to have forbidden people from making mischief in the earth?"[15] He then states: "However, your Lord never destroys towns unjustly if their people acted well."[16] The coming of the resurrection and the occurrence of the Hereafter is the truth that will inevitably take place. The people of past communities who denied the accountability of their behavior and deeds, and who continued their sinful lives, ultimately were condemned to God's punishment even in this world. Socially, Islam demands unity, brotherhood, mutual help, and cooperation. We are commanded to respect the feelings and emotions of others. There are set rules for social gatherings, social work, and mutual discourse. Believers are commanded to encourage peace by helping quarreling parties to reconcile their differences peacefully. Believers invite people towards good, enforcing what is right and forbidding what is wrong, and they wish for others what they wish for themselves.

NOTES

1. Qur'an 4:1.
2. Qur'an 49:13.
3. Qur'an 3:31.
4. Qur'an 33:21.

5. Malik's Muwatta 47.1.8.

6. Qur'an 68:4.

7. Qur'an 7:10.

8. Qur'an 10:14.

9. Qur'an 22:41.

10. Qur'an 8:25.

11. Sahih Muslim 32.6246.

12. Qur'an 41:31.

13. Qur'an 14:7.

14. Qur'an 7:144.

15. Qur'an 11:116.

16. Qur'an 11:117.

CHAPTER 1

GOD INVITES PEOPLE TO BE HUMAN
(Divine Guidance is for Those Who Desire It)

PEOPLE HAVE BEEN ENDOWED with conscience and free will. Only those people who believe in God, who have respect for Him, and who are sure that they will be held accountable for their deeds desire His guidance. The realization that "All praise is due to Allah, the Lord of the Worlds, the Beneficent, the Merciful, Master of the Day of Judgment" and not blind faith motivates such people to declare, "You alone we worship, and to You alone do we turn for help."[1] These people are genuine candidates for guidance. People's desire for help and guidance, after the realization of their relationship with the Creator, has been fulfilled in the revelations of the Qur'an, with elaboration in the *Sunnah*. This guidance, implemented individually and collectively for the whole society, will "Keep us on the right path. The path of those upon whom You (Allah) have bestowed favors. Not the path of those upon whom Your wrath is brought down, or of those who go astray."[2]

"O PEOPLE! BE CAREFUL OF YOUR DUTY TO YOUR LORD"

The source of all our mutual rights and duties is God, our Creator. His Will is the standard and measure of good, and our duties are measured by our conformity to His Will. Among ourselves, our mutual rights and duties arise out of the divine law and human conscience. God commands us: "O people! Be careful of your duty to your Lord, Who created you from a single being and created its mate of the same kind and spread from these two, many men and women. Be careful of your duty to Allah, by Whom you demand one of another your rights, and to the ties of relationship; surely Allah ever watches over you."[3] Humankind is an embodiment of two equally important facets of its development on earth:

12

its creation and physical development, and the development of its moral character and behavior. God tells us with regard to human creation, "We created man from sounding clay, from mud molded into shape."[4] In Surah Nuh, God describes the stages of creation, death, and resurrection: "Allah has caused you to grow out of the earth so wondrously, and He will later cause you to return to it and will then again bring you out of it."[5] God asks people, "What is the matter with you that you do not look forward to the majesty of Allah, seeing that it is He that has created you in diverse stages?"[6]

To be worthy of God's trust, people need the development of human character and behavior, not just physical development. A complete description of the guidelines for human conduct is given in the Qur'an. About the Qur'an, we are told: "This is the Book; in it is the guidance, without doubt, to those who fear Allah."[7] Humankind needs guidelines and discipline in order to provide a better life on earth for all. The people who do not follow these guidelines create problems. God tells us: "When it is said to them, 'Make not mischief on the earth,' they say, 'Why we only want to make peace!' Surely, they are the ones who make mischief, but they realize it not."[8] The process of learning righteousness can be divided into three distinct stages.

1. Inculcation of proper reasoning to control selfish desires:

The process of learning righteousness can be initiated with belief in and worship of the Creator, along with overcoming our physical and moral weaknesses. This will transform us into a better person of good moral character.

2. Inculcation of fair and just behavior in mutual dealings:

Humankind needs a character that makes it easier for people to be fair and just in their dealings among themselves. Such individuals, motivated by their conscience, fight against injustice and corruption and do righteous deeds for the benefit and welfare of all.

3. Establishment of just communities for mutual welfare:

When living together, many individuals of good moral character and behavior do establish just and peaceful communities by doing and encouraging others to do good deeds and by discouraging deeds that are harmful to society.

1. PRAISE IS DUE TO THE LORD OF THE UNIVERSE

God commands the believers: "when you have finished the prayer, remember Allah standing and sitting and reclining; but when you are secure (from danger) keep up prayer; surely prayer is a timed ordinance for the believers."[9] Remembering God can be by tongue, by heart, and by actions. We should always remember God by not violating any of His commands, no matter the moment, no matter whether standing, sitting, or reclining.

1.1 Worship your Creator to learn Righteousness

Compulsory forms of Islamic worship are designed as exercises and training to enable people to acquire the correct morals and habits to live righteously and to adhere to these virtues till the end, whatever the circumstances. God commands humankind: "O people! Serve your Guardian-Lord, Who created you and those who came before you, that you may have the chance to learn righteousness."[10] Again we are commanded, "Recite that which has been revealed to you of the Book, and keep up prayer; surely prayer keeps one away from shameful and unjust deeds, and certainly the remembrance of Allah is the greatest, and Allah knows what you do."[11]

The purpose of Zakah is to sow the seeds of kindness, sympathy, and benevolence, and to establish the relationship of love and friendliness among various sections of society. The importance of paying Zakah is stated in the Qur'an: "O Prophet! Take charity from their property so that it may clean them and purify them."[12] The wisdom behind the institution of Zakah is to clean individuals from worldly impurities and to raise the standard of the society to new heights of decency and purity. Similarly, fasting is not only keeping away from eating and drinking, but it is keeping away from wicked and obscene things. The purpose of fasting is also stated in the Qur'an: "Fasting has been made compulsory for you, as it was made compulsory for those who preceded you, so that you may become righteous."[13]

Some people may think that Hajj is merely the performance of a ritual or paying homage to the Ka'aba (the cube-shaped building in Makkah that is the focal point of the Hajj pilgrimage) and that it has no relevance to morality and character. This is a misconception. In giving commands about Hajj, God stated: "The months of Hajj are well-known. In these months, whoever intends to perform Hajj should not indulge in any sexual act, wicked act, and fighting during the Hajj. Whatever righteous act you will perform will be known to Allah. Take with you provision for the journey, and the best provision is righteousness. So fear Me, O men of understanding!"[14]

1.2 Following God's Guidance is for Your Own Good

There is a strong relationship between the religion of Islam and people's morality. To keep away from evil and wickedness, and to purify oneself from bad deeds, can only be realized by belief in and worship of God. God commands the Messenger to assure people that what they are being told is the truth: "Say, 'O people! Truth has come to you from your Lord. Whoever then follows the true guidance does so for his own good, and whoever strays, his straying will be to his own loss. I am not a custodian over you. And follow what is revealed to you, and be patient till Allah brings fourth His judgment, and He is the best of those who judge."[15]

Although the modes of various forms of worship are quite different from one another in their spirit and appearance, their purpose and objective is the same. The prayer, fasting, Zakah, Hajj, and all other forms of worships are the stepping-stones for real perfection and are the means of cleanliness and purity that make life secure and prosperous. The high attributes, noble qualities, and the character-transforming consequences of worship make it one of the most important parts of religion.

If these forms of worship do not purify people's hearts, if they do not nourish the best qualities in those who observe them, and if they do not improve and make firm the relationship between God and His servants, then there is nothing left for humanity but destruction and corruption. God says, "Surely, he who appears before his Lord as a criminal, there is Hell for him, in which he will neither die nor live. And he who will appear before Him as a believer who has performed good deeds - for all such people there are high positions, ever green Paradise, beneath which canals will be flowing; they will live in them forever. This is the reward for him who adopts purity."[16]

1.3 People Stand in Need of God and His Guidance

The Qur'an states: "Allah has commanded that we shall not serve but Him (because Allah is He who has created us); this is the right religion, but most people do not know."[17] Life in this world is a test so that we may prove who can utilize one's life to its best purpose and potential. God asks us, "Just think when your Lord said to the angels: 'Lo! I am about to place a trustee on earth.' They said: 'Will You place on it one that will spread mischief and shed blood while we celebrate Your glory and extol Your holiness?' He said: 'Surely I know what you do not know.'"[18] What the angels did not know at that time was that God would provide His trustees with the needed guidance to discharge their duties properly. That is why God reminds us, "O people! You are they who stand in need of Allah, and Allah is He Who is the Self-sufficient, the Praised One. If He pleases, He will take you off and bring a new generation. And this is not hard for Allah."[19]

God has provided humankind with the guidance required for the fulfillment of its duties as His trustee on earth. This guidance has been provided within the human gene in the form of human conscience. Human conscience has further been explained and elaborated by His messengers through His revelations. The teachings of the Qur'an are from God, and it is the very demand of His mercy that He should provide guidance to humanity because it is He Who has created people as rational and intelligent persons. This has been confirmed in Surah Al-Rahman: "The Beneficent Allah has taught the Qur'an, has created man, and has taught him speech (and has given him intelligence)."[20]

1.4 Try to earn Forgiveness and Honorable Provisions

To be forgiven, people have to repent. Every incident of acknowledgment, regret, and the effort not to repeat the mistakes again impacts human character. That is why people's repentance improves their behavior and transforms them into hardworking and honest individuals who when joined together form a just community. By hard work and good deeds, we overcome our weaknesses and earn God's forgiveness. Honest efforts also increase one's productive efficiency, provide people with honorable earnings, and make a community prosperous. God commanded the Messenger to, "Say, O people! I am only a plain warner to you. Then (as for) those who believe and do good, they shall have forgiveness and an honorable sustenance."[21]

God has provided sufficient means for the whole of humanity to live in prosperity. We have to exploit and properly manage these natural resources for our benefit. An Islamic society built on hard work, truth, justice, and charity, and one that is free of corruption, discrimination, exploitation, and oppression, certainly provides all of the proper requirements for this effort. Besides, if He wills, God can increase and decrease the produce. He has promised in Qur'an that if we believe in Him and implement His law, He will increase our provisions: "And if they had kept up the Taurat and the Injeel and that which was revealed to them from their Lord, they would certainly have been nourished from above them and from beneath their feet."[22] God also said in the Qur'an: "If the people of the towns had believed, We would certainly have opened up for them blessings from the heaven and the earth."[23] God encourages people to make efforts to acquire good things, applying lawful means without exceeding limits: "O you who believe! Do not forbid yourselves the good things that Allah has made lawful for you, and do not exceed the limits. Surely, Allah does not love those who exceed the limits."[24]

2. THE BENEFICENT, THE MERCIFUL

God is the Beneficent and the Merciful towards His creation, and He reminds humanity about His mercy in various ways. Citing examples about our life, security, and provisions, He asks us, "Is there any creator besides Allah who gives you sustenance from the heaven and the earth?"[25] Then He tells us that since He is the Beneficent, the Merciful, we should not worry too much about our lives and our provisions because God knows how long one will live, and it is He Who provides: "No one knows what he shall earn on the morrow, and no one knows in what land he shall die."[26]

2.1 Surely God has honored the Children of Adam

God loves humankind, and He wants us to develop a strong relationship with Him. He is the only One Who should be served. He wants us to give the credit where it is due, and He makes us aware of the futility of worshiping false deities, whatever they may be. God tells us in Surah Bani Israel, "(O people)! Your Lord is He Who makes the ship go smoothly for you through the sea that you may seek of His grace; surely He is ever merciful to you. And when distress afflicts you in the sea, away go those whom you call on except He; but when He brings you safe to the land, you turn aside; and man is ever ungrateful," (then He asks us,) "What! Do you then feel secure that He will not cause a tract of land to engulf you or send on you a tornado? Then you shall not find a protector for yourselves. Or, do you feel secure that He will not take you back into it another time, then send on you a fierce gale and thus drown you on account of your ungratefulness? Then you shall not find any helper against Us in the matter."[27] God confirms the honor and excellent qualities with which humankind has been endowed, saying that these qualities of character and behavior should further be developed by following His guidance, "Surely We have honored the children of Adam, and We carry them in the land and the sea, and We have given them of the good things, and We have made them to excel by an appropriate excellence over most of those whom We have created."[28] Reformation of our character and behavior is essential because all our deeds, whether good or bad, have appropriate consequences. Prejudice and self-interest blind some people, and they fail to see the truth. God reminds us that, "One day We shall call together all human beings with their (respective) leaders: those who are given their record in their right hand will read it (with pleasure), and they will not be dealt with unjustly in the least. But those who were blind (to the divine guidance) in this world will be (raised) blind in the Hereafter ..."[29]

2.2 Eat Lawful and Good things and not be Extravagant

Concerning honest living, God commands: "O people! Eat the lawful and good things out of what is in the earth, and do not follow the footsteps of Satan. Surely, he is your open enemy. He only enjoins you evil and indecency and that you may speak against Allah what you do not know."[30] Islam encourages everyone to work hard to earn one's livelihood. It also mandates as the responsibility of the government to help people find jobs or establish a business. In Islam, work is equated with worship. Anas bin Malik narrated: "We were with the Prophet (on a journey), and the only shade one could have was the shade made by one's own garment. Those who fasted did not do any work, and those who did not fast (being exempt from fasting because of journey) served the camels and brought the water to them and treated the sick and wounded. So, the Prophet said, 'Today, those who were not fasting took all the reward.'"[31] Anas bin Malik also narrated: "God's Messenger said, 'There is none amongst the Muslims who plants a tree or sows a seed and then a bird or a person or an animal eats from it, but is regarded as a charitable gift from him.'"[32]

God has called the honest earning as a 'Bounty of your Lord': It is reported in Sahih Bukhari that Ibn 'Abbas narrated: "Ukaz, Majanna, and Dhul-Majaz were market-places in the pre-Islamic period of ignorance. When Islam came, Muslims felt that marketing there might be a sin."[33] So, the divine inspiration came: "There is no harm for you to seek the bounty of your Lord"[34] Striving hard to earn one's livelihood is a form of worshipping God. When one reflects that the purpose of worship is to ensure forgiveness and consequently gain salvation, and that forgiveness can be ensured through hard work, the equation of endeavor with worship becomes clear.

2.3 Remember God's Grace and Mercy toward You

God asks people to reflect on the manifestations of His mercy, "O people! Remember Allah's grace toward you! Is there any creator besides Allah who gives you sustenance from the heaven and the earth? There is no god but He; whence are you then turned away?"[35] Life in this world is a test regarding whether or not individuals fulfill their responsibilities as God's trustee on earth. God Himself has taken the responsibility of providing people with the guidance and wisdom required to overcome inhuman inclinations of pride, arrogance, and greed that compel one to indulge in injustice and miserliness. Prejudice and self-interest generally blind the unbelievers. Such people are so selfish that they do not want to be answerable for their behavior and deeds, not even to God. Therefore, they refuse to believe in the Hereafter. Instead of listening, reasoning, reflecting, and pondering, they resort to name-calling. God confirms that such behavior has also been shown by previous generations, "And if they reject you, so were messengers rejected before you: to Allah are all affairs returned."[36] Such behavior does not suite the dignity and status of humanity as God's trustee on earth.

2.4 Corruption cannot raise one's Standard of Living

God informs us about the basic principle that governs the universe in Surah Al-Rahman and then commands that we should respect that principle: "The sky, He raised it high, and He has set up the balance that you may not be inordinate in respect of the measure. Keep up the balance with justice, and do not make the measure deficient."[37] This is because evil deeds like injustice, corruption, etc. must bear their inevitable fruit. When the wrongdoers suffer, it is not because God is unjust or cruel, nor is it because such suffering serves as a deterrent to others. It is because their evil deeds must bear their inevitable fruit. God's grace is ever ready to offer opportunities for repentance and forgiveness, but some people reject them. Such people are unjust to themselves. While they may escape the consequences of their deeds in the life of this world, their consequences will find them in the Hereafter. God tells us to be aware: "O people! Guard against (the punishment of) your Lord and dread the day when a father shall not make any satisfaction for his son, nor shall the child be the maker of any satisfaction for his father. Surely, the promise of Allah is true. Therefore, let not this world's life deceive you, nor let any deceiver deceive you about Allah."[38] In conclusion, God tells us that the use of unfair means and corruption is not going to increase our standard of living or any of our provisions of life. Our lives do not depend on what is unethical and corrupt. Real knowledge about the Hereafter, this life's provisions, and people's lives is with God, "Surely, Allah is He with Whom is the knowledge of the hour, and He sends down the rain, and He knows what is in the wombs. No one knows what he shall earn on the morrow, and no one knows in what land he shall die. Surely, Allah is Knowing Aware."[39]

3. THE MASTER OF THE DAY OF JUDGMENT

Our concerns about life and life's provisions should not force people to do unethical things or commit any crime. If our earnings fall short of our needs, we should look for honest ways to improve our output in whatever trade or profession we are. One may feel some immediate benefit out of worshipping false deities or following corrupt ways. However, these things are shameful and cause problems in the end. Their worship degrades and humiliates humankind. People should seriously take accountability for their behavior and deeds in this life and should not exploit and oppress their fellow human beings. God warns, "O people! Guard against (the punishment of) your Lord; surely, the violence of the hour is a grievous thing."[40] Salvation can only be assured by believing and living in this world according to God's commands and by doing good deeds.

3.1 Serve only God Who will Cause you to Die

Fear of life or life's provisions should not compel people to do unethical things or commit any crime. They should struggle hard and be honest according to their conscience and fulfill all of God's commands during their everyday activities and dealings with others. In Surah Yunus, God commands the Messenger: "Say O people! If you are in doubt as to my religion, then (know that) I do not serve those whom you serve besides Allah, but I do serve Allah, Who will cause you to die, and I am commanded that I should be of the believers."[41] False deities, may it be Satan, idols, stones, sun, stars, angels, other humans, or even one's own selfish desires, should not be served. Likewise rulers and leaders, be they religious or political, should not be wrongly followed. They neither control people's lives nor their provisions. "Allah is He who causes life and death and provides livelihood to whom He pleases without measure."[42] It is the weakness of faith that makes people afraid of meeting death, of doing one's duties that involve danger, and of losing one's status, honor, or even livelihood. A believer is neither afraid of meeting death nor of any danger, since nothing can happen without the will of God. God tells people: "It is Allah that gives life and death,"[43] and "It is only Satan that causes you to fear from his friends, but do not fear them, and fear Me if you are believers."[44]

3.2 False Deities cannot even Create a Fly

False deities are powerless and have no right to be worshipped and followed. God tells about such deities in Surah Al-Hajj: "O people! A parable is set forth. Therefore, listen to it: surely those whom you call upon besides Allah cannot create a fly, though they should all gather for it, and should the fly snatch away anything from them, they could not take it back from it, and weak are the invoker and the invoked. They have not estimated Allah with the estimation that is due to Him; most surely, Allah is Strong, Mighty."[45] False deities or their intercession will not help those who failed as God's trustees. These gods are nothing but names that some people have devised. Such deities, who never existed or have no authority to intercede, will not be able to help their worshippers on the Day of Judgment. As noted previously, salvation can only be assured by believing and living in this world according to God's commands and by doing good deeds.

3.3 Guard against the Punishment from your Lord

People should seriously take accountability of their behavior and deeds and should not exploit and oppress their fellow human beings. Self-interest, regulated by human conscience and divine guidance, improves people's character and behavior. When guarded by one's conscience and by divine guidance, a person with selfish desires and motives becomes a righteous person. Only such person can truly be human. God tells us: "Certainly We created man in the best make. Then We render him the lowest of the low, except those who believe and do good deeds, so they shall have a reward never to be cut off. Then who can misguide you about the judgment after this? Is not Allah the best of the judges?"[46]

God has provided us with the Qur'an, giving instructions as how to guard against evil in this world. These instructions form the bases by which humankind will be judged and rewarded or punished accordingly. "On that Day shall no intercession avail except of him whom Allah allows and with whose word He is pleased."[47] God commands people in Surah Al-Hajj, "O people! Guard against (the punishment of) your Lord; surely the violence of the Hour is a grievous thing. On the day when you shall see it, every woman giving suck shall quit in confusion what she suckled, and every pregnant woman shall lay down her burden. You shall see men (acting) intoxicated, but they shall not be intoxicated; but the chastisement of Allah will be severe. Yet, among men there is he who disputes about Allah without knowledge and follows every rebellious Satan. Against him it is written down that whoever takes him for a friend, he shall lead him astray and guide him to the chastisement of the burning fire."[48]

3.4 Consider Your own Birth if you doubt the Hereafter

The belief in One God, prayers, fasting, Zakah and Hajj all tend to build human character and should improve one's behavior as an individual and as a member of the society. If the people fulfill all their moral, financial, and socio-political obligations, they are successful in this life, and their community will be prosperous, peaceful, and secure. They will also be successful on the Day of Judgment. On the other hand, if most of the people follow their personal desires with a disregard for any moral and socio-political laws of nature, that community is bound to fail and eventually be destroyed. God commands: "And guard yourselves against a chastisement that cannot fall exclusively on those of you who are wrongdoers (it may afflict both the bad as well as the good people), and know that Allah is severe in punishment."[49] Then He informs us: "And certainly We did destroy generations before you when they were unjust, and their messengers had come to them with clear arguments, but they would not believe. Thus do We recompense the guilty people. Then We made you successors in the land after them so that We may see how you behave."[50] God tells us in Surah Al-Anbiya: "I am your Lord; therefore, serve Me only…Whoever shall do good deeds and he is a believer, there shall be no denying of his exertion, and surely We will write it down for him."[51] Therefore, only those who follow the right way will come out successfully in the final judgment of God, and those who discard the right way shall meet with the worst consequences in the Hereafter.

To remove any doubt whatsoever about the Hereafter, God asks us to reflect on our own birth and on the growth of vegetation after rain. "O people! If you are in doubt about the Hereafter, then surely We created you from dust, then from a small seed, then from a clot, then from a lump of flesh, complete in make and incomplete, that We may make clear to you; and We cause what We please to stay in the wombs till an appointed time. Then We bring you forth as babies, then that you may attain your maturity; and of you is he who is caused to die, and of you is he who is brought back to the worst part of life, so that after having knowledge he does not know anything; and you see the earth sterile land, but when We send down on it the water, it stirs and swells and brings forth every kind a beautiful vegetation. This is because Allah is the Truth and because He gives life to the dead and because He has power over all things."[52] The resurrection of people will be like the growth of vegetation after rain, and the dead will come out of their graves after God's command.

4. YOU DO WE SERVE AND ASK FOR HELP

We have to remind ourselves as frequently as required that we are human. God gave us the responsibility to guard ourselves against any behavior that falls below the dignity of humanity. We are hardworking, honest, truthful and just. That is how we worship God, and in the time of difficulty we ask for His help and guidance. We seek His forgiveness if we fall below our dignity, and we keep trying to improve ourselves. It is our overall conduct that makes us honorable. God confirms this in the Qur'an: "O people! Lo! We created you all from a male and a female and made you into nations and tribes that you may know one another. Lo! The noblest of you in the sight of Allah is the best in conduct. Lo! Allah knows and is aware."[53]

4.1 Satan is People's Enemy, so take him as Such

Satans are the unbelievers among jinn and humans who became people's enemies due to their jealousy and arrogance. "Certainly We raised in every nation a messenger, saying: 'Serve Allah and shun Satan.' So there were some of them whom Allah guided, and there were others against whom error was due. Therefore, travel in the land, and see the nature of the consequence for those who denied the truth!"[54] The denial of the truth is an evil deed, and evil deeds have evil consequences.

Only those people among humankind can benefit from the guidance of the Qur'an and become worthy of God's bounties who accept the physical, moral, and socio-political realities presented in the Book as the basic laws of nature that God has put in place and then follow up their belief with obedience and submission in their practical lives. The people who deny the Hereafter and accountability for their selfish behavior do not follow the guidance of the Qur'an. This makes them irresponsible and selfish and compels them to commit unlawful activities during their worldly lives. For such people, it is impossible to accept the moral restrictions put on them in pursuing their selfish interests and desires. God tells us in Surah Fatir: "O people! Surely, the promise of Allah is true. Therefore, let not the life of this world deceive you, and let not Satan deceive you about Allah. Surely, Satan is your enemy, so take him for an enemy; he only invites his party that they may be inmates of the burning. (As for) those who disbelieve, they shall have a severe punishment, and (as for) those who believe and do good, they shall have forgiveness and a great reward."[55]

4.2 O People! Your Rebellion is only Against Yourselves

God tells us in Surah Al-Hajj: "Among people there is one who disputes about Allah without knowledge and follows every rebellious Satan...and among people there is one who disputes about Allah without knowledge and without guidance and without an illuminating book, turning away haughtily that he may lead others away from the way of Allah; for him is disgrace in this world and on the Day of Resurrection. We will make him taste the punishment of burning."[56]

The implementation of divine law will, no doubt, result in a just society that is prosperous and in peace and security. Then why do people ignore the implementation of the divine law? God tells us: "And they did not become divided until after knowledge had come to them out of envy (rivalry) among themselves."[57] They also wanted to benefit from the injustice done to others. Many of them are guilty of corruption and try to take advantage of others, paying no attention to other people's rights. According to the Qur'an, such people are identified as those:

(1) Who are unjustly proud in the earth and
(2) who do not believe in the Hereafter;[58]
(3) Who missed prayers and
(4) who followed after their selfish desires.[59]

God reminds us: "He it is Who makes you travel by land and sea until when you are in the ships, and they sail on with them in a pleasant breeze, and they rejoice, a violent wind overtakes them, and the billows surge in on them from all sides, and they become certain that they are encompassed about. They (then) pray to Allah, being sincere to Him in obedience: 'If You deliver us from this, we will most certainly be of the grateful ones.' Yet, when He has delivered them, behold! They rebel in the earth wrongfully. O people! Your rebellion is only against yourselves. (You have) enjoyment of the life of the world; then to Us is your return, and We will inform you of what you did."[60] Illustrating the story of Adam, the unbelievers could be told: 'The way you are following is the way of Satan, whereas the right way for humanity is to follow its father Adam. He was misguided by Satan, but when he realized his mistake, he plainly confessed it and repented and again turned back to the servitude of God and won His favor. On the other hand, if a person follows Satan and arrogantly sticks to his error in spite of admonition, he does harm to himself alone, just like Satan did.

4.3 Believers do not make Mischief in the Earth

The Qur'an inculcates: "(O people!) Call upon your Lord humbly and in secret. Lo! He loves not aggressors. And do not make mischief in the earth after its reformation, and call on Him fearing and hoping; surely, the mercy of Allah is near to those who do good to others."[61] One may ask: "What is the mischief-making that people should not do to assure their safety and success?" Citing examples from history, this has been elaborated at various places in the Qur'an. We should try our best not to follow the behavior of the people of 'Ad, Thamud, Lut, and Aykah (Midian). These nations were destroyed because of their mischievous behavior, as is highlighted below:

(1) Tyranny and Corruption Destroyed Peoples of 'Ad: Their behavior could be characterized by the cruelty of its leaders, who were more interested in building monuments and fortresses for themselves than in fulfilling their duties to God and to their fellow humans. Their messenger asked, "'Do you ('Ad) build on every height a monument? Vain is it that you do. And you make strong fortresses that perhaps you will live therein forever. And when you lay hands on someone, you lay hands like tyrants'...So they rejected him, and We destroyed them."[62]

(2) Arrogance and Extravagance Destroyed Thamud: People are warned that they will surely be tested in their prosperity and wealth.

Salih, the messenger of God to the Thamud, warned his people, who used to "carve houses out of the mountains with great skill…do not obey the bidding of the extravagant, who make mischief in the land and reform not."[63] They did not obey their messenger, and punishment ultimately overtook them.

(3) Perversion and Unnatural Behavior Destroyed Lut's People: Lut said to his people: "'Surely, I am of those who hate your conduct…What! Of all creatures do you come unto the males and leave what your Lord has created for you of your wives? Nay, you are a people exceeding limits.' (Instead of listening to their messenger, they threatened) 'If you desist not, O Lut, you shall surely be of those who are expelled.'"[64] Thus, the perverted people of Lut were destroyed.

(4) Fraud and Corruption Destroyed the People of Aykah (Midian): Because of cheating and corruption that were prevalent in their society, Shu'aib asked his people to: (1) give full measure and be not of those who shortchange, (2) weigh things with a right balance, (3) not defraud people by reducing their goods, and (4) refrain from making evil, corruption, and mischief in land.[65]

Instead of listening to their messenger, the unbelievers among Shu'aib's people said: "You are only one of those bewitched! And you are nothing but a mortal like ourselves, and we know you to be certainly of the liars. Therefore, cause a portion of the heaven to come down upon us, if you are one of the truthful."[66] (At the end), "The punishment of the day of covering overtook them; surely, it was the punishment of a grievous day."[67]

4.4 The Best in Conduct is the Noblest among People

In God's creation, there are the angels who can do only what is good. Angels cannot do something evil or disobey God. On the other hand, satans, either from the jinn or humankind, are the opposite. They can do only evil. Humankind and jinn are given the power of choice, and they determine for themselves whether to follow the guidance provided by God through His messengers or to indulge in satisfying their own wanton desires as they wish. This option is clear to people right from their early years, and the choice to rectify their attitude and choose what is good is offered at every juncture. In fact, if one errs, one can at any moment correct the error, repent, and turn to God for forgiveness. If one does so, then one is forgiven. When people abandon God's guidance, their lives on earth are nothing more than eating, drinking, and self-indulgence. God says in the Qur'an: "Allah will admit those who believe and perform good deeds into gardens through which rivers flow, while those who disbelieve will enjoy themselves (in this world) and eat just as cattle do, and the fire will be their lodging place."[68]

Humanity is born with a mission to contribute its efforts in the implementation of God's commands in managing its affairs to build a just human society in the world. In this assignment, we are being tested and evaluated in our attitude and in our efforts, in order to prove who among us can utilize one's life to the best purpose. God states in the Qur'an: "He is the One Who created the heavens and the earth in six days and – His throne was over the Waters – that He may try you, which of you is best in conduct."[69] God tells people in Surah Al-Hujurat that the one who is best in conduct is the noblest among you: "O people! Lo! We created you all from a male and a female and made you into nations and tribes that you may know one another. Lo! The noblest of you in the sight of Allah is the best in conduct. Lo! Allah knows and is aware."[70]

5. SHOW US THE RIGHT PATH

In response to people's prayer and to the need for guidance when they pray, "Show us the straight path, the path of those upon whom You have bestowed favors—not the path of those upon whom Your wrath is brought down, nor of those who go astray,"[71] God informs people about the Qur'an in Surah Yunus, "O people! There has come to you, indeed, an admonition from your Lord and a healing for what is in the breasts and guidance and a mercy for the believers."[72] In Surah Al-Anbiya, God tells people that He has revealed the Qur'an and that it is up to us to understand and implement it: "We have bestowed upon you a Book that mentions you. Don't you then understand?"[73]

5.1 There has come a Clear Proof from your Lord

Divine guidance like a clear bright light has come to us in the Qur'an: "O people! Surely there has come to you manifest proof from your Lord, and We have sent to you clear light."[74] The verses of the Qur'an are God's commands, full of wisdom: "These are the verses of the Wise Book[75]...A Book, with verses basic or fundamental (of established meaning), further explained in detail, from One Who is Wise and Well-acquainted (with all things)[76]...The verses of the Book that make things clear[77]...These are the verses of the Book that are the truth."[78] The Qur'an is, "A guide and good news for the believers, who keep up prayer and pay the poor-rate, and they are sure of the Hereafter."[79] It is, "A Book, the verses of which are explained in detail: an Arabic Qur'an for a people who know."[80] God tells us in Surah Al-Kahf: "Indeed, We have put forth every kind of example in this Qur'an for humankind. But man is more quarrelsome than anything."[81]

God has, "Revealed the best announcement, a Book, its various parts resemble each other, oft-repeating, whereat do shiver the skins of those who fear their Lord, then their skins and their hearts soften to the remembrance of Allah; this is Allah's guidance. He guides with it whom He pleases, and as for him whom Allah makes err, there is no guide for him."[82] God has, "Set forth to humankind, in this Qur'an, every kind of similitude in order that they may remember."[83] It is, "the Book that makes things clear; We have made it an Arabic Qur'an that you may be able to understand (and learn wisdom)."[84] Again, it is the Qur'an in Arabic, "Without any crookedness, so that people may avoid all evil."[85] It is, "the

Book that makes the truth manifest...Therein every wise affair is made distinct...a command from Us... a mercy from your Lord...easy in your tongue that you may remember."[86] "It is the Word brought by an honored messenger...and it is not the word of a poet...or the word of a soothsayer."[87] The Qur'an is, "a revelation from the Lord of the worlds...It is a reminder for those who guard against evil...a great grief to the unbelievers, and most surely it is truth of absolute certainty."[88] "Verily, this is no less than a message to (all) the worlds: (With profit) to whoever among you wills to go straight."[89]

5.2 The Messenger has come with the Truth

God tells people that he has sent a messenger for their guidance, "O people! Surely the Messenger has come to you with the truth from your Lord. Therefore, believe; (it shall be) good for you, and if you disbelieve, then surely whatever is in the heavens and the earth is Allah's."[90] The Messenger showed humanity how to live and establish justice according to the divine law. God commanded the Messenger: "Surely, We have revealed the Book to you with the truth that you may judge between people by means of that which Allah has taught you, and be not an advocate on behalf of the treacherous."[91] "A Book revealed to you - so let there be no qualm in your heart about it—that you may warn thereby and that it may serve as a reminder to the believers."[92] "It is a Qur'an that We have revealed in portions so that you may read it to the people by slow degrees."[93] "We did not reveal the Qur'an to you to cause you distress."[94] "Blessed is He Who sent down the criterion on His servant, to be a warner to all creatures."[95] "And most surely this is a revelation from the Lord of the worlds. The trustworthy Spirit has brought it down upon your heart that you may be one of the warners, in plain Arabic language."[96] "I swear by the Qur'an full of wisdom – it is a revelation of the Mighty, the Merciful -- most surely you are one of the messengers -- on a right way."[97] "We have revealed to you the Book with the truth; therefore, serve Allah, being sincere to Him in obedience."[98]

5.3 Believers Believe in God and His Messenger

God commands the Messenger: "Say: 'O people! I am sent unto you all as the Messenger of Allah, to Whom belongs the dominion of the heavens and the earth. There is no god but He; it is He that gives both life and death. So believe in Allah and His Messenger, the Unlettered Prophet, who believes in Allah and His words. Follow him that you may be guided."[99] Islam is not a matter of birth or of belonging to a family or a nation. We cannot describe a person as Muslim simply on the basis that he was born to Muslim parents or that he belongs to a Muslim tribe or community. Being a Muslim is a matter of conscientious and free choice. A person is a Muslim because he chooses to believe in Islam and accepts its tenets, ideology, and beliefs. If someone asks what brings a person into the fold of Islam, the answer is the declaration that God is the only deity in the universe. He makes a conscientious choice to believe in his religion. If he accepts Islam only because he is brought up as a Muslim, his faith remains deficient. There should be a practical interpretation of beliefs. Otherwise, it will remain theoretical. Hence, faith can be defined as something that is well established in people's minds and hearts and to which credence is given by practice. Therefore, faith is not an academic theory or an abstract idea. Its practical effect has to be seen so that the claim of being a believer is seen to be true. Hence, Islam is an embodiment of statements and practices. According to the Messenger, "Islam is built on five pillars: the declaration that there is no deity save Allah and that Muhammad is His Messenger, regular attendance to prayer, the payment of Zakah, fasting during Ramadan, and pilgrimage to the Sacred House when a person is able to do so."[100] Although Islam is built on five pillars, it needs a lot of good deeds to complete its structure.

People who claim to be Muslims only because they have been born into Muslim families do not provide a practical proof of their claim. Yet, if they genuinely believe in the Oneness of God and the message of Islam, they are considered Muslims. If they do not go beyond that declaration, they are doing badly because of their negligence. Their faith is not complete unless they attend to their Islamic duties. On the other hand, we must not pass judgment on people, claiming that certain people are true Muslims while others are not. If a person tells us that he is a Muslim, we take his statement at its face value. However, if he does not confirm his statement by doing the duties that God has imposed on Muslims, we advise him that he is exposing himself to the risk of God's punishment. Some of these people say that God is too merciful to punish them, that they are not doing anything bad, and that they are simply not attending to their duties. This is a false argument. A person who does not fulfill the duty that God has imposed is certainly doing something bad. What is worse than the deliberate negligence of a duty that God has imposed? Besides, a believer cannot say that God will certainly forgive him. One certainly hopes for God's forgiveness, but it cannot be taken as though it were a certainty. One must always balance that hope with the fear that one might not be forgiven. This balance should provide a motivation to people to attend to their Islamic duties: both worship of God and good deeds.

5.4 Qur'an is Guidance and a Mercy for the People

"O people! There has come to you indeed an admonition from your Lord and a healing for what is in the breasts and a guidance and a mercy for the believers."[101] The only people who can benefit from this guidance are those who: (1) turn to Allah in repentance, (2) worship and praise Him, (3) go about in the world to serve His cause, (4) bow down and prostrate themselves, (5) enjoin doing what is right and forbid doing what is wrong, and (6) keep within the limits set by Allah.[102]

(1) *The People who turn to God in Repentance*: One of the qualities that enable people to benefit from divine guidance and God's mercy is that they turn to God in repentance. They appeal to Him for forgiveness,

regretting any slip they may have made and resolving to turn to Him and follow His guidance in the future. They will not revert to sin, and they do good deeds in order to make their repentance a reality. Repentance is a means of purging themselves of the effects of temptation and of improving one's character and behavior so that they can earn God's acceptance.

(2) *The People who Worship and Praise Only God*: They submit and dedicate their worship to God alone, acknowledging that He is the only Lord. They dedicate all their actions to the pursuit of God's pleasure. Their worship provides a practical confirmation of their belief in God's Oneness. They praise Him, acknowledging His grace, which He bestows upon them. They praise Him in times of happiness and in times of adversity. When they are happy, they praise God to thank Him for His blessings, and when they go through difficult times, they praise Him because they know that the difficulty is a test that they need to pass. They realize that God will show them His mercy when they prove themselves by going through the test with unshaken faith. True praise is not that expressed only in times of ease and happiness. It is the praise genuinely expressed in times of adversity, recognizing that God, the Just and Merciful, will not put a believer through a trial unless it is eventually for his own good. A believer may not know that at the time, but God certainly knows it.

(3) *The People who go about the World to serve His Cause*: It is in reference to such quality that God says in Surah Al-Imran, "In the creation of the heavens and the earth and in the succession of night and day, there are signs for men endowed with insight, who remember Allah when they stand, sit, and lie down and reflect on the creation of the heavens and the earth: 'Our Lord, You have not created all this in vain. Limitless are You in Your glory. Guard us, then, against the torment of the fire.'"[103] With repentance to, worship of, and praising of God comes the quality of reflecting on God and His dominion, which inevitably leads to turning to Him and acknowledging that His wisdom is manifested in all His creation.

This investigation and reflection are not meant for their own sake or for gaining more knowledge of the world around us, but they should be made the foundation on which human society is built.

(4) *The People who Bow Down and Prostrate Themselves*: People who believe attend to their prayers, which become an essential part of their life. Praying is thus made one of the distinctive characteristics of the believers. During prayer, as they stand up to address God, they feel closeness to God that is associated with prayer, and their hearts are thus filled with gratitude and submission to the will of God. It is in the prayer that we renew the pledge of our servitude with our Lord: "You do we serve, and You do we ask for help." Nearness to God gives us the strength and resolve to fight in God's way and to follow His divine guidance. Our minds and hearts are purged of even the slightest alien thought or feeling. In such a situation, a lonely individual is reunited with its source, a wandering spirit finds its way, and a heart that has been long in isolation finds its company. Thus, all values, concerns, and considerations diminish, except for the ones related in some way to God.

(5) *The People who Enjoin what is Right and Forbid what is Wrong*: When a Muslim community conducts its life in accordance with God's law, making clear that it submits to God only, then the institution of enjoining the doing of what is right and forbidding what is wrong is seen to be fully operative within this community. It points towards any shortcomings in implementation of or deviation from the divine law. In the case of an un-Islamic community that does not give supremacy to the implementation of divine law, then the enjoining of what is right should be addressed totally to the most important thing, which is acceptance of God's Oneness, submission to His authority, and the establishment of a truly Islamic community. Similarly, the forbidding of what is wrong should also address the greatest wrong, namely, submission to authorities other than God, e.g., through enforcing laws that are at variance with His law.

(6) *The People who keep within the Limits set out by God*: Believers make sure of the implementation of God's law in their own lives and in the community, and they resist anyone who tries to forestall it. Like enjoining what is right and forbidding what is wrong, this quality can only work in an Islamic community that is governed by God's law in all its affairs. By definition, such a community acknowledges God's sovereignty as the only God, the Lord, and the Legislator. Efforts must concentrate initially on the establishment of such a community. Only when it comes into being will those who keep within the limits set out by God have their rightful place in it, as happened in the first Islamic community at Madinah.

NOTES

1. Qur'an 1:2-5.
2. Qur'an 1:6-7.
3. Qur'an 4:1.
4. Qur'an 15:26.
5. Qur'an 71:17-18.
6. Qur'an 71:13-14.
7. Qur'an 2:2.
8. Qur'an 2:11-12.
9. Qur'an 4:103.
10. Qur'an 2:21.
11. Qur'an 29:45.
12. Qur'an 9:103.
13. Qur'an 2:183.
14. Qur'an 2:197.
15. Qur'an 10:108-109.

16. Qur'an 20:74-76.

17. Qur'an 12:40.

18. Qur'an 2:30.

19. Qur'an 35:15-17.

20. Qur'an 55:1-4.

21. Qur'an 22:49-50.

22. Qur'an 5:66.

23. Qur'an 7:96.

24. Qur'an 5:87.

25. Qur'an 35:3.

26. Qur'an 31:34.

27. Qur'an 17:66-69.

28. Qur'an 17:70.

29. Qur'an 17:71-72.

30. Qur'an 2:168-169.

31. Sahih Bukhari 4.52.140.

32. Sahih Bukhari 3.39.513.

33. Sahih Bukhari 2.26.822.

34. Qur'an 2:198.

35. Qur'an 35:3.

36. Qur'an 35:4.

37. Qur'an 55:7-9.

38. Qur'an 31:33.

39. Qur'an 31:34.

40. Qur'an 22:1.

41. Qur'an 10:104.

42. Qur'an 3:27.

43. Qur'an 3:156.

44. Qur'an 3:175.

45. Qur'an 22:73-74.

46. Qur'an 95:4-8.

47. Qur'an 20:109.

48. Qur'an 22:1-4.

49. Qur'an 8:25.

50. Qur'an 10:13-14.

51. Qur'an 21:92 & 94.

52. Qur'an 22:5-6.

53. Qur'an 49:13.

54. Qur'an 16:36.

55. Qur'an 35:5-7.

56. Qur'an 22:3 & 8-9.

57. Qur'an 42:14 & 45:17.

58. Qur'an 7:146-147.

59. Qur'an 19:59.

60. Qur'an 10:22-23.

61. Qur'an 7:55-56.

62. Qur'an 26:128-130 & 139.

63. Qur'an 26:149 & 151-152.

64. Qur'an 26:168 & 165-167.

65. Qur'an 26:181-183.

66. Qur'an 26:185-187.

67. Qur'an 26:189.

68. Qur'an 47:12.

69. Qur'an 11:7.

70. Qur'an 49:13.

71. Qur'an 1:6-7.

72. Qur'an 10:57.

73. Qur'an 21:10.

74. Qur'an 4:174.

75. Qur'an 10:1.

76. Qur'an 11:1.

77. Qur'an 12:1.

78. Qur'an 13:1.

79. Qur'an 27:2-3.

80. Qur'an 41:3.

81. Qur'an 18:54.

82. Qur'an 39:23.

83. Qur'an 39:27.

84. Qur'an 43:2-3.

85. Qur'an 39:28.

86. Qur'an 44:2, 4-6 & 58.

87. Qur'an 69:40-42.

88. Qur'an 69:43, 48 &50-51.

89. Qur'an 81:27-28.

90. Qur'an 4:170.

91. Qur'an 4:105.

92. Qur'an 7:2.

93. Qur'an 17:106.

94. Qur'an 20:2.

95. Qur'an 25:1.

96. Qur'an 26:192-195.

97. Qur'an 36:2,5 & 3-4.

98. Qur'an 39:2.

99. Qur'an 7:158.

100.Sahih Bukhari 1.2.7.

101.Qur'an 10:57.

102.Qur'an 9:112.

103.Qur'an 3:190-191.

CHAPTER 2

EFFORTS SHAPE THE HUMAN PERSONALITY
(Only Good Deeds Make People Honorable)

GOD TELLS US IN Surah Al-Hujurat (Qur'an, chapter 49), verse 13, that only good deeds make people noble and honorable. Doing good deeds requires good intentions and human efforts in the right direction. Generally people think that a believer is simply the one who is correct in the observance of religious rituals. Indeed, this is not true. If the ritual observances of a believer do not help the person to be humble, virtuous, and truly God-fearing, then he or she is not a real believer. Similarly if a person, no matter what is his religion, is not good and just in dealing with others, and does not take special care to keep away from all shameful and sinful things, he is not very human. To be a human is to believe in all human values and to be an embodiment of all that is good. Furthermore, since people are social beings, they have to have a specific social behavior.

1. THE RIGHTEOUS WILL SURELY BE SUCCESSFUL

To be human is an attitude that leads to continual improvements in individual character and behavior. Human physical and emotional needs, coupled with free will, make the perfection of human character and actions virtually impossible. Everyone is liable to make mistakes, and every one does. But when people seek God's forgiveness, it is always granted if the request is genuine. Human character is improved with every incident of acknowledgment, regret, and effort not to repeat the mistakes again. Various aspects of human personality and attitudes that impact their development are highlighted below.

1.1 The Corruption of Racial and National Arrogance:
The racial and national distinctions that cause universal corruption in

the world have been condemned in Islam. Nationalism, tribalism, family pride, pride of ancestry, looking down upon others as inferior, and pulling down others only for the sake of establishing one's own superiority are factors that have filled the world with injustice and tyranny. Those who engage in such behavior may have human physiology, but have nothing of human morality.

What does it mean to be human? In Surah Al-Hujurat, verse 13, God answered this question by stating that all men are descendants of the same one pair and that their division into tribes and communities is only for the sake of recognition, not for boasting and pride. He further stated that there is no lawful basis for one individual's superiority over another except on the basis of moral excellence: "O people! Lo! We created you all from a male and a female and made you into nations and tribes that you may know one another. Lo! The noblest of you in the sight of Allah is the best in conduct. Lo! Allah knows and is aware."[1] In various translations of the Qur'an, the Arabic word 'al-muttaqeen' has been translated differently, either as "the God-fearing" or "careful of their duty" or "most righteous" or "best in conduct." Reflecting on these various translations, it becomes clear that the God-fearing people, are most careful of their duty, are most righteous, and are best in conduct, all at the same time.

1.2 A Believer is known by his Behavior and Conduct:

A mere verbal profession of faith is not sufficient. To believe truly in God and His Messenger is to obey them in practical life and to strive sincerely with one's self and wealth in the cause of God. Only those who adopt this attitude are true believers. A person who is best in conduct does good deeds. God commands such people in Surah Al-Baqarah: "Everyone has a direction to which he should turn. Therefore, hasten to do good deeds wherever you are..."[2] In Surah Al-Maidah, God reassures such people: "Whoever believe in God, the Last Day, and do good deeds, they shall have no fear, nor shall they grieve."[3]

As for those who profess Islam merely orally and without affirmation by the heart, and then adopt an attitude as if they had done someone a favor by accepting Islam, they may be counted among the Muslims in the world and even treated as Muslims in society, but they cannot be counted as believers in the sight of God and in the Hereafter. Racial and national arrogance is clearly a mean, satanic behavior. It is the same behavior that Satan displayed before God at the time of Adam's prostration: "(Allah) said: 'What prevented you from prostrating when I commanded you?' He said: 'I am better than he. You did create me from fire and him from clay.' (Allah) said: 'Get you down from this. It is not for you to be arrogant here. Get out, for you are of the meanest of creatures.'"[4]

2. IMPACT OF PEOPLE'S BEHAVIOR ON SOCIETY

God completely destroyed some past communities by natural disasters or by some other form of punishment because they arrogantly refused to follow the prophets and messengers sent to them. The people of Nuh, for example, were destroyed with the flood, while the people of A'ad were destroyed by winds and the people of Thamud by an earthquake accompanied by a heart-piercing sound. The fact that God mentions these punishments to people serves as a reminder that He is able to inflict similar punishments on them if they do not admit their mistakes and reform. Continual improvement in individual character and behavior is what God demands from people. We should always be conscious of this divine requirement and try our best to behave like humans as much as possible. Exerting such effort is certain to spare us the collective punishment in this world.

2.1 God's Punishment or Consequence of Bad Behavior?

Volcanoes, cyclones, floods, and other forms of natural disaster take place as a result of natural laws, which God has set in operation. They may be caused when the balance set by God in the universe as a whole is upset. However, when a cyclone hits certain areas, we cannot say that the people of that area have earned such a punishment by God. How can we tell? After all, cyclones also regularly hit in certain parts of the world when the people there may be better than those who live in another part of the world. God is the most just of all judges. If He punishes some people, His punishment is just. It does not follow that those were the only people who deserved punishment. God may choose to delay the punishment of others until the Day of Judgment. No one who disobeys God may escape punishment, unless God chooses to forgive him. Therefore, we should always be in fear of incurring God's anger, lest His punishment takes us unaware. The Messenger used to appeal to God for protection against natural disasters. In short, we should always maintain a balance between the realization that God controls all natural laws and that He can easily inflict on us any type of punishment He may choose. His punishment is always just and the consequence of our collective bad behavior.

2.2 Why Resurrection? Is it to benefit People or God?

Some people may ask, "What is the purpose of punishing people here in this world or after the resurrection?" They may say that the creation of Hell is meant to pressurize humankind to do what either they don't want to do or what is not in their self-interest. They might also ask, "Why doesn't God motivate us by His love?" Such people forget that God created them in various types; some are motivated by love, while others by fear. His system of total life caters to the needs of the people of all generations and the needs of all individuals of the same generation. On the other hand, God will not resurrect animals because He did not give them free will, nor are they endowed with intellect and wisdom. Armed with free will and reasoning, humankind has a tremendous power to act either in the best interest of the community or selfishly and in a corrupt manner. Hell is meant for the corrupt because: "If Allah had destroyed people for their wrongdoing immediately, He would not have left on the earth a single creature, but He respites them till an appointed time. So when their time expires, they shall not be able to delay it a single moment, nor can they bring it on before its time."[5] Since their term expired, some former communities were destroyed during their life on earth. Resurrection is required for ultimate accountability for an individual's character, behavior, and deeds.

2.3 God did not do Injustice; They were Unjust to Themselves

God is forgiving and merciful. He is just, and His punishment is the direct outcome of our behavior and deeds. Let us be honest and reflect: "What can Allah gain by your punishment if you are grateful and you believe? Allah is always responsive to gratitude, All-Knowing."[6] After mentioning the fate of the unbelieving communities of the past, God tells people: "We did not do them injustice, but they were unjust to themselves, so their gods whom they called upon besides Allah did avail them nothing when the decree of your Lord came to pass, and they added but to their ruin. Such is the punishment of your Lord when He punishes the towns while they are unjust; surely, His punishment is painful, severe."[7] The coming of the resurrection and the occurrence of the Hereafter is a truth that inevitably has to take place. The people of past communities who denied their accountability in the Hereafter for their behavior and deeds, and who continued their sinful lives, ultimately became worthy of God's punishment even in this world.

3. THE DOCTRINE OF EFFORTS AND REWARD

It is often said that the prosperity of nations cannot come without an attitude that encourages hard work, honesty, and justice. No doctrine that has managed to raise certain people to the state of nationhood has ever failed to emphasize the need for hard work on the part of individuals and the community. However, emphasis must be placed in the first instance on the individual because the work of the community is the total sum of the contribution of its members. Since Islam is the system that God has devised for human life, it is natural, therefore, to expect that Islam stresses the importance of hard work. Additionally, Islam places particular emphasis on hard work because it is only through good deeds that a person attains salvation in the Hereafter. Even when people go about earning their livelihoods, they can hope to be rewarded for their efforts in this life as well as in the Hereafter. What believers have to do is to steer away from what is forbidden and to link their immediate purpose to their wider one of earning God's pleasure. People generally think that efforts to earn honest provisions are of a lower value than worshipping God. However, such efforts are actually one form of worshipping God. For example, 'Abdullah bin Masud reported that the Messenger of Allah said: "To search after lawful earnings is compulsory after the compulsory things."[8] Al-Miqdam narrated that the Messenger of God said: "Nobody has ever eaten a better meal than that one has earned by working with one's own hands. David, the Prophet of Allah, used to eat from the earnings of his manual labor."[9]

3.1 Righteous Deeds Help People Live Honestly

The idea of effort and reward is central to Islamic thinking. Every action can earn rewards from God if it is intended for the right purpose. The Messenger was always keen to point out what action or attitude could earn rewards in order to encourage his companions to do it. He often emphasized the importance of certain types of work by pointing out that they were bound to earn reward. This could very well be illustrated by a Hadith narrated by Abu Huraira that God's Messenger said: "If one gives in charity what equals one date-fruit from honestly earned money—and Allah accepts only honestly earned money, Allah takes it in His right (hand) and then enlarges its reward for that person (who has given it), as anyone of you brings up his baby horse, so much so that it becomes as big as a mountain."[10] The fruit of our efforts will always be there, both in this life and in the Hereafter. Besides, all efforts in which we do not violate any of God's commands are worship of Him.

How terrible will be the results of dishonest earnings can best be learnt from a Hadith reported by Abu Bakr, in which the Messenger said: "A body that has been nourished by unlawful things shall not enter Paradise."[11] On the other hand, striving for lawful earnings makes people honorable, both in this world and the Hereafter. Abu Huraira reported that the Messenger of God said: "Whoever seeks the world in a lawful manner, abstaining from begging and striving for his family and being sympathetic to his neighbor, will meet the Almighty Allah on the Resurrection Day while his face will be like the moon in a full, moon-lit night."[12]

3.2 Every Deed has its Inevitable Consequences:

In Surah Al-Rahman, God informs us about the basic principle that governs the universe and then commands that we should respect that principle: "The sky, He raised it high, and He set up the balance that you may not be inordinate with respect to the measure, keep up the balance with justice and do not make the measure deficient."[13] This is because good, as well as evil, deeds (injustice, corruption, etc.) must bear their inevitable fruit. Wrongdoers suffer neither because of divine injustice or cruelty nor as a deterrent to others. Rather, it is on account of their own evil deeds that they must bear the inevitable recompense. For good deeds the reward will be: "...the Garden of which you are made heirs for your good deeds (in life). You shall have therein abundance of fruit, from which you shall have satisfaction. The sinners will be in the punishment of Hell, to dwell therein. It is not relaxed for them, and they despair therein. We wronged them not, but they it was who did the wrong."[14] God's grace has always been there and is ever ready to offer opportunities for repentance and forgiveness, but unbelievers rejected them. They were and are unjust to themselves.

3.3 God Rewards Good Behavior and Deeds

The real object for which God has destined a second life for humanity after the present worldly life is to reward people for their good behavior and deeds. We are told that upon resurrection, all people will appear in the court of their Lord, where none of their secrets will remain hidden and where each person's record will be given to him. Those who spent their lives in the world with the realization that one day they would have to give an account of their deeds before their Lord, and who worked righteously in the world, will rejoice when they see that they have been acquitted and blessed with the eternal bliss of Paradise. With excitement, such people will say, "'Lo! Read my book. Surely, I knew that I shall meet my account.' So he shall be in a life of pleasure, in a lofty garden, the fruits of which are near at hand. Eat and drink pleasantly for what you did in the days gone by."[15] In contrast, those who neither recognized the rights of God nor discharged the rights of the people will have no one to save them from God's punishment, and they will be thrown into Hell.

4. EFFORTS SHAPE THE HUMAN PERSONALITY

The Messenger described as his main objective that he was sent for the purpose of perfecting good morals. How did he achieve this? God tells him in Surah Al-Anam: "Say: 'I do not say to you, 'I have with me the treasures of Allah,' nor do I know the unseen, nor do I say to you that I am an angel. I follow only that which is revealed to me.' Say: 'Are the blind and the seeing one alike? Do you not then reflect?'"[16] On reflection, one will realize that it is one's belief and individual efforts by which one's personality is developed and shaped. The Messenger did it, as will those who follow him and what is revealed to him. God testified to the Messenger's efforts in Surah Al-Qalam, "By your Lord's grace, you are not afflicted with madness, and yours shall be a never-ending reward, and you are certainly on the most exalted standard of moral excellence."[17]

4.1 Same People but Different in Personalities

People start their journey from the same point at birth, but their belief and efforts lead them to different destinies. There are many factors that impact the development of individual potential and personalities. God tells in Surah Ta Ha: "And whoever turns away from My message, his shall be a straitened life, and We will raise him on the Day of Resurrection blind."[18] On the other hand, God guides those who desire His guidance: "And (as for) those who strive hard for Us, We will most certainly guide them in Our ways, and Allah is most surely with the doers of good."[19] Therefore, those who are interested in their success and salvation should: (1) seek knowledge and learn wisdom, (2) know that believers are not like unbelievers, (3) believe in God alone, the Creator of the universe, (4) believe and do righteous deeds, (5) be careful of one's duty as God's trustee, and (6) strive hard with one's wealth and self. These six points, which if followed, lead people to their success and salvation, as further discussed below.

(1) *Seek Knowledge and Learn Wisdom*: Acquiring knowledge and learning is one of most productive activity in which people can engage to elevate themselves. "Allah will exalt those of you who believe and those who are given knowledge in high degrees, and Allah is aware of what you do."[20] Both types of education, religious as well as professional and scientific, are essential for the development of a prosperous and peaceful society that is based on the integrity and professionalism of its members. Religion makes an individual conscious of one's accountability for one's actions, reminds him of what is lawful and unlawful, and guards against corruption and dishonesty. A truly religious person is honest, trustworthy, and hardworking. At the same time, he is not corrupt, dishonest, and lazy. Islam is open to all horizons of knowledge and demands from its followers that they excel in them, be they men or women. This, of course, includes knowledge of the Qur'an and the Ahadith. In our pursuit of

other horizons of knowledge, we must not neglect our basic obligation towards knowledge of the Qur'an and the Ahadith, through which we realize the need for knowledge in other fields of learning. We, indeed, need experts in all disciplines, and only qualified persons should work in their respective trades and occupations. We, indeed, need experts in all disciplines, and only qualified persons should work in their respective area of excellence.

(2) *Know that Believers are not like Unbelievers*: Believers are not like the unbelievers, and the learned are not like those who are ignorant. God asks: "What! Is he whose heart Allah has opened for Islam so that he is in a light from his Lord (like the hard-hearted)? Nay, woe to those whose hearts are hard against the remembrance of Allah; those are in clear error."[21] Again God asks people: "Is he who is obedient during hours of the night, prostrating himself and standing, takes care of the Hereafter, and hopes for the mercy of his Lord (to be equal to an unbeliever)? Say: 'Are those who know and those who do not know alike?' Only the men of understanding are those who receive adminition."[22]

(3) *Believe in God alone, the Creator of the Universe*: Humankind is innately inclined to worship and is impelled to worship something. If they do not worship one God, a power above them, they will worship something else, idols of their own creation, an ideology, a personality, or whatever impresses them. God commands His Messenger to ask people: "'Who is the Lord of the heavens and the earth?' (People will) say: 'Allah.' Say: 'Do you take then besides Him guardians who do not control any profit or harm for themselves?' Say: 'Are the blind and the seeing alike, or can the darkness and the light be equal?' Or have they set up with Allah associates who have created creation like His, so that the question of creation has become dubious to them? Say: 'Allah is the Creator of all things, and He is the One, the Supreme.'"[23]

(4) *Believe and Do Righteous Deeds*: Divine treatment of the people

who believe and do good deeds will certainly be better than for those who are wicked and corrupt. God asks: "Shall We treat those who believe and do good works as those who spread corruption in the earth, or shall We treat the pious as the wicked?"[24] These two kinds of people may be compared to the blind and deaf, and those who can see and hear well. God asks: "Are they equal when compared? Will you not then take heed?"[25] "The blind and the seeing are not alike, nor are those who believe and do good and the evildoer; little is it that you are mindful."[26] "Not alike are the inmates of the fire and the dwellers of the garden; the dwellers of the garden are they that are the successful."[27]

(5) *Be Careful of your Duty as God's Trustee*: People are certainly rewarded for their good deeds in this life, but their best reward will be Paradise. God commands His Messenger: "Say: 'O my servants who believe! Be careful of your duty to your Lord; for those who do good in this world is good, and Allah's earth is spacious; only the patient will be paid back their reward in full without measure.'"[28] In Surah Yunus, we are told: "For those who do good is a good (reward) and even more than that...Those who have earned evil will have a reward of like evil"[29] The purpose of Islam is to establish a just and peaceful society in which all people are at liberty to contribute by their good deeds, which will be rewarded in this world, as well as in the Hereafter. "Allah invites people to the abode of peace and guides whom He pleases into the right path."[30]

(6) *Strive Hard with Wealth and Person*: The divine rule is that people are rewarded according to the extent of their efforts. People who are active in the way of God are much better than those who are inactive and lazy: "Not equal are those believers who sit (at home) and receive no hurt and those who strive and fight in the cause of Allah with their goods and their persons. Allah has granted a grade higher to those who strive and fight with their goods and persons than to those who sit (at home). Unto all (in faith) has Allah promised good: But those who strive and

fight has He distinguished above those who sit (at home) by a special reward. Ranks specially bestowed by Him, and forgiveness and mercy. "[31]

4.2 Same People but Different in Destinies

Each individual and society can benefit from divine guidance in this world to the extent of its implementation of that guidance, irrespective of whether one believes in God and the Hereafter or not. However, those who believe in God and their accountability for their deeds and are motivated by their faith will surely be successful in the Hereafter. God tells us about unbelievers: "How woeful is the plight of him who has nothing except his face to shield him from the severe chastisement on the Day of Resurrection? Such evildoers will be told: 'Taste now the consequences of your deeds.'"[32] The unbeliever is a person who is unable to do anything for the good of the people and, therefore, cannot be equal to an individual who enjoins what is just and follows the right path: "Allah sets forth a parable of two men. One of them is dumb, not able to do anything, and he is a burden to his master. Wherever he sends him, he brings no good. Can he be held equal with him who enjoins what is just and he who is on the right path."[33] People should know that: (1) the good and the bad are not equal, (2) unlike people earn unlike rewards, (3) unbelievers worship their own low desires, and 4) unbelievers are those who break their contracts.

(1) *The Good and the Bad are not Equal*: People's fate very much depends on their knowledge and understanding. Learned people are not blinded by prejudice. God asks us to reflect: "Is he then who knows that what has been revealed to you from your Lord is the truth like him who is blind? Only those possessed of understanding will receive admonition."[34] God commands His Messenger: "Say: 'The bad and the good are not equal, though the abundance of the bad may please you; so be careful of your duty to Allah, O men of understanding, that you may be successful.'"[35] In Surah Fatir, after comparing good and bad and the

learned and the blind with the living and the dead, God tells the Messenger that it is not possible for the dead to listen to you: "Neither are the living and the dead alike. Surely Allah makes whom He pleases hear, and you cannot make those hear who are in the graves."[36]

(2) *Unlike People Earn unlike Rewards*: God has established the entire universe on justice, precisely and equitably. The nature of this system requires that those who dwell in it should also adhere to justice within the bounds of their authority and should not disturb the balance. Humankind is warned of the dire consequences of disobeying God and made aware of the best results of obeying Him, both in this world and the Hereafter. God asks the people: "What! Shall We then treat those who submit as the guilty? What has happened to you? How do you judge?"[37] "The blind and the seeing are not alike, nor those who believe and do good and the evildoer; little do you learn by admonition."[38]

(3) *Unbelievers Worship their Own Low Desires*: Unbelievers, since they do not believe in the resurrection and accountability for their behavior and deeds, keep on following their personal, low desires and refuse to follow the divine guidance. Consequently, their exploitations, injustice, and tyranny eventually destroy their societies. With God, such people are like nothing but animals. He asks: "Have you seen him who takes his low desires for his god? Will you then be a protector over him? Or do you think that most of them do hear or understand? They are nothing but as cattle; nay, they are straying farther off from the path."[39]

(4) *Unbelievers are Those who Break their Contracts*: Implementation of the divine laws in the individual and social lives of the people is essential to establish a just society. Part of the covenant with which God has bound people through their conscience and their religions requires that they should deal among themselves on the basis of absolute justice. A covenant, in its most general sense, is a solemn promise to engage in or refrain from a specified action. It is a type of contract in which the

covenanter makes a promise to a covenanted to do or not do some action. It is justice that is based on the duty to remain steadfast in devotion to God alone. No influence is ever allowed to tilt the balance of justice, especially when believers are mindful that God watches over them and knows what is in the bottom of their hearts. The unbelievers are like those who are habitual in breaking their contracts. God reminds us: "For the worst of beasts in the sight of Allah are those who reject Him. They will not believe. They are those with whom you did make a covenant, but they break their covenant every time, and they have not the fear of Allah."[40]

5. HOW TO BE A BETTER PERSON?

Discrimination, social exclusion, economic injustice, military ambitions, lack of good governance, and geopolitical rivalries play a decisive role in shattering the peace and tranquility of human societies. Even in the case of culturally and religiously rooted conflicts, violence and extremism generally stem from the exploitation of religion for political and ideological goals. Human dignity and freedom come from God. Belief in One God frees humanity from any bondage that results in discrimination, exploitation, and corruption. On the other hand, worship of false gods, idol worship, and worship of selfish desires or of any human being degrade humanity to physical, mental, and spiritual slavery.

5.1 Conscience is to Regulate Human Desires

The self-reproaching part of an individual is the conscience because conscience reproaches a person whenever he commits evil deeds. The very existence of conscience bears testimony that each and every individual is born with the capability to know what is good and what is bad and what their effects are on human performance. God tells us in the Qur'an: "He taught Adam all the names (wisdom, all what is right and what is wrong), then presented them to the angels."[41] "He inspired to understand what is right for it and what is wrong for it; he will indeed be successful who purifies it, and he will indeed fail who corrupts it."[42] God also commands us: "Read, and your Lord is Most Honorable, Who taught with the pen—taught man what he knew not."[43] God has sent His messengers to tell us what is evil, what is good, and the consequences of being good or evil. Therefore, listening to one's conscience makes people better persons.

5.2 Conscience and Guidance make People Righteous

People should take accountability for their behavior and deeds and not exploit and oppress their fellow human beings. It is through divine guidance and our own consciences that we can reform our character and behavior. It is through our conscience and faith that we learn what is right and wrong, what is legal and illegal. Conscience and faith also motivate us to do good deeds and avoid things that are evil. God tells us: "Certainly, We created man in the best make. Then We render him the lowest of the low, except those who believe and do good deeds, so they shall have a reward never to be cut off. Then who can misguide you after this, about the judgment?...Is not Allah the best of the judges?"[44]

A contented self is an individual who has not committed evil to satisfy his self-interest. It is a person who has used honest ways to satisfy his physical needs. On the Day of Judgment, it will be said to the people with good conscience: "O you, in complete rest and satisfaction! Return to your Lord well-pleased about yourself and well-pleasing unto Him; so enter among My servants and enter into My Paradise."[45] Behaving as our conscience tells us and satisfying our desires by moral and ethical ways make us human and honorable even in our own eyes.

5.3 Learning and Following the Divine Guidance

We are commanded to learn and implement divine guidance in our lives and in our communities. God promises us in Surah Al-Ankabut: "And (as for) those who strive hard for Us, We will most certainly guide them in Our ways, and Allah is most surely with the doers of good."[46]

Then God reassures us in Surah Muhammad: "And (as for) those who were led to the guidance, Allah increases them in their guidance and causes them to grow in piety."[47] God commands people to learn and relearn to reform their character and behavior by: (1) acquiring knowledge of the Qur'an and Ahadith; and (2) repenting, reforming, and propagating the divine guidance.

(1) *Reading and Understanding the Qur'an and Ahadith*: God commands in Surah Al-Alaq: "Read in the name of your Lord Who created—created man from a clot. Read, and your Lord is Most Honorable, Who taught (man to write) with the pen—taught man what he knew not."[48] It is through the knowledge of religion that we learn to act righteously and ask for forgiveness. After Adam and Eve committed their first mistake, they were regretful. God taught them how to ask for forgiveness, "Then Adam received words from his Lord, so He turned to him mercifully; surely He is Oft-returning, the Merciful."[49]

(2) *Repent, Reform, and help Propagate Guidance*: Each individual should continuously evaluate his character and behavior. This should then be followed by repentance, self-reformation, and the implementation of improved behavior in society. Remember that God commanded Adam and Eve at the time of their leaving Paradise: "We said: 'Get you down from here, all of you, and guidance will come to you from Me. Then whoever follow (act upon, implement) My guidance, need have no fear, nor shall they grieve."[50]

5.4 Unguided People, their Works are Fruitless

Generally self-interest leads people to corruption, exploitation, and oppression. "Surely one's self commands to do evil, except such as my Lord has had mercy on. Surely, my Lord is Forgiving, Merciful."[51] Self-interest and a secular life style take away all human values from humankind. About corrupt people, God tells us in the Qur'an: "Certainly We created man in the best make. Then We render him the lowest of the low."[52] Such people have been described in Surah Al-Araf: "Those who behave arrogantly on the earth in defiance of right – them will I turn away from My signs: Even if they see all the signs, they will not believe in them, and if they see the way of right conduct, they will not adopt it as the way, but if they see the way of error, that is the way they will adopt. For they have rejected our signs and failed to take warning from them. Those who deny Our revelations and the meeting of the Hereafter, their works are fruitless. Shall they be rewarded except for what they have done?"[53]

NOTES

1. Qur'an 49:13.

2. Qur'an 2:148.

3. Qur'an 5:69.

4.\ Qur'an 7:12-13.

5. Qur'an 16:61.

6. Qur'an 4:147.

7. Qur'an 11:101-102.

8. Al-Hadith: vol. I, no. 129w, p. 407.

9. Sahih Bukhari 3.34.286.

10. Sahih Bukhari 2.24.491.

11. Al-Hadith: vol. II, no 304, p. 260.

12. Al-Hadith: vol. II, no. 308w, p. 261.

13. Qur'an 55:7-9.

14. Qur'an 43:72-76.

15. Qur'an 69:19-24.

16. Qur'an 6:50.

17. Qur'an 68:2-4.

18. Qur'an 20:124.

19. Qur'an 29:69.

20. Qur'an 58:11.

21. Qur'an 39:22.

22. Qur'an 39:9.

23. Qur'an 13:16.

24. Qur'an 38:28.

25. Qur'an 11:24.

26. Qur'an 40:58.

27. Qur'an 59:20.

28. Qur'an 39:10.

29. Qur'an 10:26-27.

30. Qur'an 10:25.

31. Qur'an 4:95-96.

32. Qur'an 39:24.

33. Qur'an 16:76.

34. Qur'an 13:19.

35. Qur'an 5:100.

36. Qur'an 35:22.

37. Qur'an 68:35-36.

38. Qur'an 4:78.

39. Qur'an 25:43-44.

40. Qur'an 8:55-56.

41. Qur'an 2:31.

42. Qur'an 91:8-10.

43. Qur'an 96:3-5.

44. Qur'an 95:4-8.

45. Qur'an 89:27-30.

46. Qur'an 29:69.

47. Qur'an 47:17.

48. Qur'an 96:1-5.

49. Qur'an 2:37.

50. Qur'an 2:38.

51. Qur'an 12:53.

52. Qur'an 95:4-5.

53. Qur'an 7:146-147.

CHAPTER 3

HUMAN VULNERABILITIES AND DEVELOPMENT
(Living a Moral Life is Worshipping God)

THE ISLAMIC FAITH HAS, perhaps, a stronger hold on the lives of its followers than has any other religion of the world. Whatever a believer does, he or she must first make sure that it is not contrary to the teachings of Islam. If a contradiction exists, then the believer must abandon whatever it was that he wanted to do that was against the teachings of Islam. This applies to matters that are universally recognized to be within the religious sphere, as well as to issues that most people believe to be of no concern to religion. This is due to the fact that Islam is not merely a relationship between an individual and God. It is also a code of living that organizes human life in such a way as to make the pleasure of God their goal, and the pleasure of God is achieved only by living one's life by following God's commands. The Qur'an consists of the true moral and socio-political code that has to be followed by believers to achieve their status as God's trustee, which is a much higher status than achieved by those who live their lives only to fulfill their selfish needs and desires. Again, the people who adopt obedience to divine guidance and lead a life of piety and righteousness certainly become worthy of God's mercy and friendship.

1. ALL RIGHTEOUS ACTIVITIES ARE WORSHIP OF GOD

Islam is the religion revealed by God, the Creator of the universe. Islam consists of faith, which embodies the ideology and the basic principles from which Islamic laws are derived, and actions, which implement the Islamic law or the Islamic constitution. This constitution is inseparable from faith and ideology. It is extremely important to understand that, according to Islam, there can be no split between faith and action, between ideology and law. One follows the other in the same way as cause produces effect and as a certain premise gives a particular result. For this reason, action is firmly linked with faith in many verses of the Qur'an: "Man is a certain loser, save those who have faith and do righteous deeds;"[1] and "Give good tidings to those who believe and do good deeds that they shall reside in gardens beneath which rivers flow."[2] "Be they men or women, those who embrace the faith and do what is right, We shall surely grant a happier life (in this world), and We shall reward them according to their noblest actions (in the Hereafter)."[3] Islam very strongly impacts the welfare of the people of this world and encourages all those activities that are beneficial to individuals and society. A believer is hardworking, honest, trustworthy, and just—qualities that free human society from discrimination, exploitation, and corruption. Islamic values produce results that are beneficial to society, even if they are followed by those who do not believe.

1.1 Islamic Reformation of Human Character

How does Islam achieve the reformation of the character and behavior of people, and how does it relate faith in God and the observance of religious teachings to matters that are purely materialistic? In Islam, if human moral values and human rights are not violated, all individual activities are acts of worshipping God. God commands in Surah Al-Ahzab: "O you who believe! Be careful of your duty to Allah, and speak the truth. He will put your deeds into a right state for you and forgive you your faults, and whoever obeys Allah and His Messenger, he indeed achieves a mighty success."[4]

1.2 In Reality, there is only One Religion for Humankind

The Islamic faith is not different from the faith preached by all the other prophets whom God entrusted with messages through revelation. Starting with Adam and including Nuh (Noah), Ibrahim (Abraham), Ismail, Ishaq (Isaac), Yaqub (Jacob), Musa (Moses), Dawud (David),

Zakaria, John, and Jesus, the line of prophethood reached its final destination with Muhammad, the last of God's messengers. The faith preached by all these messengers is the same. There can be no variation in what God considers acceptable to Him as a faith. All nations and all generations need to have the same basic principles. In Surah Al-Shura, God tells us: "In matters of faith, He has ordained for you that which He had enjoined upon Nuh — and into which We gave you, Muhammad, insight through revelations — as well as that which We had enjoined upon Ibrahim, and Musa, and Jesus. Steadfastly uphold the true faith, and do not break up your unity therein."⁵

1.3 Human Mission, Its Prerequisites and Implications

God created humankind, gave it wisdom, free will, and guidance, and appointed each one of us, male or female, rich or poor, as His trustee on earth to serve Him through implementing His commands in managing our affairs to build a just human society on earth. God tells people in Surah Al-Ahzab: "Surely, We offered the trust to the heavens and the earth and the mountains, but they refused to undertake it, being afraid thereof, but man undertook it; surely he was unjust, ignorant; (with the result) that Allah has to punish the hypocrites, men and women, and the unbelievers, men and women, and Allah turns in mercy to the believers, men and women: for Allah is forgiving, merciful."⁶ The Qur'an has been revealed for the guidance of all humanity. It contains the instructions that, if followed, will help us in our growth as human beings by developing our human character and behavior, which is a prerequisite for establishing a prosperous and peaceful human society based on justice and mutual respect.

1.4 Mobilization to Succeed as God's Trustee on Earth

Life in this world is a test so that we may prove who can utilize one's life to its best purpose and potential. This requires that we know our duties and live our lives according to the divine law. God has provided the required guidance for the fulfillment of one's duties as His trustee on earth. This guidance has been given within the human gene in the form of human conscience and has been taught and implemented by all of His messengers. The commands given in the Qur'an encompass the entire moral, economic, and socio-political areas of human activity that are required to develop and protect human character and society. Before implementation, we have to know what is required from us. This can be learned from the Qur'an and from the lives of the prophets and messengers.

2. PATH OF HUMAN JOURNEY UNDER THE GUIDANCE

One of the main objectives of Islam is to guide and help people to achieve an excellent moral character and behavior, which are reflected in truth, honesty, and sincerity of action, and to provide people with ideals that constantly elevate them to a higher standard of morality. The Islamic ideal is that humans observe the noble values that Islam tries so hard to inculcate within human behavior. To help people to achieve this high standard of nobility and perfection, God has sent messengers as role models to different nations throughout the ages, to preach His message and to guide people to the way of life that ensures their happiness in both this life and in the life to come. Some people say, "Why does God force us to be good by bribing us with Paradise or threatening us with Hell? Why can't He love us as we are?" This argument seems like a child telling his/her parent: "Why do I have to go to school? I am good enough! Just love me as I am." Although success or failure depends on our efforts, divine guidance motivates and helps us to excel in life, in learning, in character, and in our worth to society. God, like our parents, is interested in our success as humanity, and He wants trustworthy people to be His trustees.

2.1 Why Develop Human Character and Behavior

All divine religions stress the importance of reforming people's character and behavior. Due to their very nature, all divine religions profess the righteous self as the pivot of their program of reform and consider a firm and strong moral character as a permanent guarantee for the establishment and upkeep of civilization. The development of human character and behavior is the first item of importance after achieving belief in the religion's program of reforms. As such, the development of human personality based on Islamic teaching is of extremely high importance in Islam. Real understanding of Islamic teaching makes the process of worshipping God and individual character development inseparable. This was the teaching of all of the messengers of God as consolidated into Islam, and it is to continue till the Day of Judgment.

Humanity, as God's trustee, needs its true personality to deliver the divine trust. These teachings are not like something externally pasted onto the rituals of worship, so that they can be separated from people during the movements of their daily life. These principles and teachings go to the very core of human personality, save people from the wickedness of their selfish desires, and serve as a basis for their decisions.

Corrupt people can only spread disruption and disorder in society and in a system of government. Such people use the community law enforcement system for the fulfillment of their mean and wicked objectives. On the other hand, righteous people consider it their responsibility to bring in regularity and fairness in the use of power and to enhance good governance. If no attention was paid to reforming the individual character, this world would become the dominion of tyranny and would be ruled by corruption. God says in the Qur'an: "Verily, Allah will never change the condition of a people until they change it themselves. But when Allah wills a people's punishment, there can be no turning it back, nor will they find beside Him any to protect."[7] Why were some of corrupt communities of the past destroyed? Answering this God says: "Like (the deeds of) the people of Pharaoh and of those before them, they rejected the communications of Allah, and Allah punished them for their crimes; for Allah is strong and strict in punishment. This happened because Allah will never change the grace that He has bestowed on a people until they have changed their attitudes."[8]

2.2 Emotions and Moral Growth of Human Personality

Islam considers two aspects of human personality for development and reform. The first aspect represents a decent and pure human nature inclined towards righteousness, which feels happiness in doing good and hates wickedness and evil. It feels remorse and sorrow on committing sin. It considers that the future of its existence is in truth and justice. The second aspect of human personality is an embodiment of exciting emotions and satanic inclinations, which turn it away from righteousness. They present injurious human inclinations that lead to mean and arrogant human behavior, often in a very glamorous way.

It is irrelevant to ascertain whether these emotions or desires enter the human nature from outside or whether they are ingrained in the human himself. We do know for a fact that both these conditions are found in people and that they are in mutual struggle for achieving the leading role in human existence. Conscientious choice and individual free will decide the final outcome of this inner struggle. In Surah Al-Shams, God says: "By the human self and by Him Who made it perfect, then He inspired it to understand what is right and wrong for it; he will indeed be successful who purifies it, and he will indeed fail who corrupts it."[9]

2.3 If Our Worship Fails to Improve Our Character

Describing the main objective of his mission, the Messenger of Islam informed people that he was sent only for the purpose of perfecting good morals. The transformation of people's character is initiated by belief in God and continues with worshipping God. Although different forms of Islamic worship may vary in their spirit and appearance, their aim and purpose is the same, which is to help people build their character and refine their behavior. Our prayers, fasting, Zakah, and Hajj are the stepping stones for real perfection and are the means of cleanliness and purity of character and behavior. It is through these steppingstones that one develops the proper character and behavior of one who is God's trustee, who is in the world to help establish just communities in which life is peaceful, secure, and prosperous, which is desired by God.

When these forms of worship do not purify the hearts of people, when they do not nourish the best qualities in those who observe them, and when they do not improve and make firm the relationship between God and His servants, then one should revisit the intentions and purpose of one's worship. If the purpose is not the perfection of good moral character and behavior in the worshipper himself, then there is nothing left for people but corruption and destruction, both in this life and in the Hereafter. God tells us in Surah Al-Nisa: "Whoever acts hostilely to the Messenger after that guidance has become manifest to him and follows other than the way of the believers, We will turn him to that to which he has (himself) turned and make him enter Hell, and it is an evil resort."[10] Also, in Surah Ta Ha, we are told, "And whoever turns away from My message, his shall be a straitened life, and We will raise him on the Day of Resurrection blind."[11]

2.4 Success or Failure is Proportionate to Effort

God says: "(As for) those who strive hard for Us, We will most certainly guide them in Our ways, and Allah is most surely with the doers of good."[12] Selfish intensions and behaviors, which will not help people in their pursuit of success and which should be changed, are highlighted in the Qur'an. God tells us in Surah Al-Baqarah: "There are some people who say: 'We believe in Allah and the Last Day,' and they are not at all believers."[13] Such people are those who: "Among men is he who says: 'We believe in Allah,' but when he is persecuted in the way of Allah, he thinks the persecution of men to be as the chastisement of Allah."[14] "And among men is he whose speech about the life of this world causes you to wonder, and he calls on Allah to witness as to what is in his heart. Yet, he is the most violent of adversaries, and when he turns back, he runs along in the land that he may cause mischief in it and destroy crops and the stock. Allah does not love mischiefmaking."[15]

2.5 God Wants the Trustworthy to be His Trustee

The human individual in society is like a brick in a building. Only an honest, hardworking person can help make a just and prosperous society. Lazy, dishonest, and corrupt people can only help to evolve a corrupt society. For this reason, Islam, after correcting people's beliefs, focuses on reforming the character and behavior of the believers. God's trustee works hard to overcome his weaknesses and strives hard to improve his character and behavior. Therefore, God's trustee is hardworking, honest, truthful, trustworthy, and just. It is easy for such a person to learn the religion of Islam and to serve God by implementing His commands in managing everyday affairs, in order to build a just human society on earth. Furthermore, God reassures such people of His help: "As for those who were led to the guidance, Allah increases them in their guidance and causes them to grow in their piety...So know that there is no god but Allah and ask forgiveness for your fault and for the believing men and the believing women, and Allah knows how you move about and how you dwell in your homes."[16]

3. DIMENSIONS OF THE HUMAN MISSION

We are not only the smartest animal on the planet, but we are also human. We are the trustee of what is in the world, and we are responsible for managing the world's resources, those things of the earth that we use and upon which we depend. Our physical needs are the same as every other animal. This makes it an important part of our mission to secure the basic requirements to stay alive, e.g., food, shelter, and whatever other modern conveniences we consider as necessities. To do this, we need general and technical know-how and efforts. Besides being animal, we are also human due to our conscience and rationality. Being endowed with free choice, human behavior can either be driven by one's own personal desires without any regard for others, or it can be need-based and well-organized by human conscience and rationality. Know-how for this purpose has been provided by God, the Creator of the universe, in the form of revealed religions.

Due to our freedom of choice, it becomes necessary that we be made accountable for our behavior and deeds. This life is also made a test for us so that we can prove what we deserve of reward or punishment, which determines whether we will be happy in the Hereafter or not. God states in the Qur'an, addressing the believers: "This is Paradise; you have inherited it by virtue of your past (good) deeds."[17] This is a clear statement confirming that there is no pre-judgment as to the final destination of any member of humanity. The destination is determined by one's actions in life, made on the basis of his or her free choice. Hence, God commands us to do what we can to secure a happy ending in the Hereafter. People have to answer for their good and bad behavior and deeds directly to God on the Day of Judgment. Since human behavior carries with it an eternal reward, everyone should be motivated to learn what duties Islam expects people to fulfill. Those who do not inquire about these duties put themselves into a very difficult position, because ignorance of the law is not an acceptable justification for breaking it. God has made our duties known to us through His messengers. He has revealed the Qur'an and guaranteed that it will be preserved intact so that people can have easy access to it and learn their duties properly.

3.1 Guidance is to save Humankind from Evil

Complete description of the guidelines for the development of human character and conduct is given in the Qur'an. These guidelines educate, and their implementation makes us disciplined. In referring to the Qur'an, God tells people: "This is the Book; in it is the guidance, without doubt, to those who fear Allah...O humankind! Worship your Lord, Who created you and those who came before you that you may have chance to learn righteousness."[18] What is righteousness? As highlighted in the Qur'an: "It is not righteousness that you turn your faces towards east or west, but righteousness is to believe in Allah and the Last Day and the angels and the Book and the messengers, to spend of your substance out of love for Him for your kin, for orphans, for the needy, for the wayfarer, for those who ask, and for the ransom of slaves, to be steadfast in prayer and practice regular charity; to fulfill the contracts that you have made, and to be firm and patient in pain (or suffering) and adversity and throughout all periods of panic. Such are the people of truth, the God-fearing."[19]

Belief and worshipping God make people helpful to the needy and honor one's promises and contracts. They help save people from harm both individually and socially. Humanity needs guidelines and discipline in order to provide a better life on earth for all. The people who do not follow the guidelines create problems. "When it is said to them, 'Make not mischief on the earth,' they say, 'Why we only want to make peace!' Surely, they are the ones who make mischief, but they realize it not."[20]

3.2 Belief Motivates People to Excel in Life

God tells the believers: "In matters of faith, He has ordained for you that which He had enjoined upon Noah — and into which We gave you, Muhammad, insight through revelations — as well as that which We had enjoined upon Abraham and Moses and Jesus. Steadfastly uphold the true faith, and do not break up your unity therein."[21] Therefore, the basic requirements of the divine faith, as preached by all of God's messengers, and the faith of Islam are the recognition of the Creator; the worlds of seen and unseen; God's messengers and His books; resurrection and accountability, and God's power of foreordination and predestination as highlighted below.

1. Recognition of God, His names and attributes, and to believe in Him as Creator of the universe. Such recognition helps generate noble motives within an individual and keeps one conscious of God in whatever situation he happens to be and whatever action he is doing.

2. Recognition of another world, which exists along with our world—a world of good forces represented by the angels and that of evil forces represented by Satan and his soldiers.

3. Recognition of the books and scriptures God has revealed to the prophets over time, to define what is right, good, and permissible, on the one hand, and what is false, evil, and forbidden, on the other. This helps us understand the way of life God has prescribed for humanity to achieve a standard of moral and material wellbeing that can't be achieved without it.

4. Recognition of God's prophets and messengers whom He has chosen to be the leaders, guides and role models for humanity along the path of truth. This is to help people follow in their footsteps and to establish good and noble values and traditions for human life.

5. Recognition of the Day of Resurrection, when each and every person will have to be accountable for his or her good and bad actions in life, and be rewarded accordingly. The reward is represented in admission to Heaven for those who have won God's pleasure or commitment to Hell for those who have incurred His displeasure. This is, perhaps, the strongest motive for people to do what is good and to abandon what is evil.

6. Recognition of God's power of foreordination and predestination, which determines the system of the whole universe. This recognition imparts to the believer the strength to face up to any difficulty and hardship that he or she may have to endure.

3.3 Worship Helps People to Develop their Strengths

Humanity is God's trustee on earth to serve Him by implementing His commands in managing its affairs to build a just human society on earth. One may ask what type of character and behavior is required of humanity in order to establish a just and welfare-oriented society on earth. Only people of good moral character and behavior can help to establish such a society. Therefore, the purpose of religion is nothing else but to strengthen the moral character of the people so that a peaceful and prosperous world may be illuminated before their eyes and so they may try to achieve it conscientiously and with knowledge. About such people God says: "(As for) those who say: 'Our Lord is Allah,' then continue in the right way, the angels descend upon them, saying: 'Fear not, nor be grieved, and receive good news of the garden that you were promised. We are your guardians in this world's life and in the Hereafter, and you shall have therein what you desire, and you shall have therein what you ask for, a provision from the Forgiving, the Merciful.'"[22]

Worshipping God is obligatory in Islam. Worship in Islam is not some mystical exercises that link people with some unknown, mysterious being and that compel people to perform useless acts and meaningless movements. All Islamic compulsory forms of worship are designed as exercises and training to enable people to acquire correct morals and habits, to live righteously, and to adhere to these virtues throughout life under all and every circumstances.

1. *Truth, Prayer, and Giving Alms create Mutual Love*: Truth, prayer, and giving alms create trust among people and an atmosphere of mutual love in society. God tells us in Surah Maryam about Ismail: "He was a messenger, a prophet. He was truthful in his promise. He enjoined on his family prayer and giving alms, and was one in whom his Lord was well-pleased."[23] These three qualities of believers result in mutual respect and create a state of perpetual love among the members of society: "Surely Allah will soon create enduring love for those who believe and do good deeds."[24] Prayer precludes indecency and wrongdoing, as God states in Surah al-Ankabut that people who perform prayer are kept away from indecency and evil. God inspires the avoidance of wrongdoing by prayer:

"Recite what has been revealed to you of the Book and establish prayer. Prayer precludes indecency and wrongdoing, and remembrance of Allah is greater still. Allah knows what you do."[25] Acceptance of prayers by God is reflected in the behavior of the worshipper who keeps away from evil, wickedness, and bad deeds.

2. *Zakah is for Self-purification and Social Welfare*: The primary purpose of Zakah is to encourage kindness, sympathy, and benevolence among people. It also provides a vehicle of interaction among various sections of society and establishes a relationship of love and friendliness. The purpose of paying Zakah is stated in Surah Al-Tawbah: "Of their goods, take alms, so that you might purify and sanctify them, and pray on their behalf. Verily, your prayers are a source of security for them, and Allah is One Who Hears and Knows."[26] Individual self-cleaning from worldly impurities and the uplifting of social decency by providing help to the weak segment of the society are the logical interpretations of the obligation of Zakah.

Along with Zakah, comes charity, which has many aspects. It was narrated by Abu Huraira that the Messenger said, "Charity is obligatory everyday on every joint of a human being. If one helps a person in matters concerning his riding animal by helping him to ride it or by lifting his luggage on to it, all this will be regarded charity. A good word and every step one takes to offer the prayer at the mosque are regarded as charity, and guiding somebody on the road is regarded as charity."[27] Similarly, to smile in the company of another person is charity. To command to do good deeds and to prevent others from doing evil are charity. To guide a person in a place where he can go astray is charity. To remove troublesome things like thorns and bones from the road is charity.

3. *Fasting is a Steppingstone to Righteousness*: The Qur'an informs us of the purpose of fasting: "Fasting is prescribed for you as it was

prescribed for those before you so that you may learn self-restraint."[28] Fasting is not merely keeping away from eating and drinking during daylight hours, but it is also keeping away from all wicked and obscene things throughout the day and night. It is an exercise to teach us how to keep away from various illegal temptations, not only during fasting, but throughout life.

4. *Hajj is to Weaken the Passionate Love of the World*: One may think that Hajj is a form of worship with no impact on the development of morality and character, which would be a clear misunderstanding. Giving commands about Hajj, God states in Surah Al-Baqarah: "The months of Hajj are well-known. In these months, whoever intends to perform Hajj should not indulge in sexual acts, wicked acts, and fighting during the Hajj. Whatever righteous act you will perform will be known to Allah. Take with you provision for the journey (for Hajj), and the best provision is righteousness. So fear me, O men of understanding!"[29]

3.4 Divine Guidance is to Eradicate Social Injustice

There is simply no man-made system that has been able to eradicate social injustice. Injustice is the result of people turning their backs on God's guidance. True justice can only be achieved through the system that God has revealed, because He has tailored it for the benefit of humanity, and there is no one who knows what suits people better than God does. History tells us that humankind has managed very poorly when it turned its back on God's guidance. We continue to achieve endless misery while resisting acknowledging the basic truth that divine guidance is needed.

In Islam, justice is the basis of all human interaction. The aim of divine guidance is to serve human interests, to help people build a happy life in a community characterized by justice. Justice must be achieved at all levels, within the family, the local community, the social hierarchy, and the political system. God says in a sacred Hadith: "My servants, I have forbidden Myself injustice and made injustice forbidden to you.

Therefore, do not act unjustly to one another."[30] Besides, history proves that whenever people established their system on the basis of true divine guidance and applied God's law, their achievements were really great.

3.5 Learning to Manage Our Affairs on Earth

Learning to manage our affairs on earth is the first obligation of humankind after being appointed as God's trustee on earth or after being born. With knowledge comes understanding and then obedience. God commands in Surah Al-Alaq: "Read in the name of your Lord Who created—created man from a clot. Read, and your Lord is Most Honorable, Who taught (man to write) with the pen—taught man what he knew not."[31] An Islamic community cannot neglect the education of its children—both types of education, general as well as religious.

1. *Religious Education and Practice*: The first thing God did after the creation was to teach Adam the "names of things," i.e., He gave Adam knowledge of good and bad and the willpower to implement his choice. This was his orientation for his assignment as God's trustee on earth. Similarly, children need education to provide guidelines as to what is expected from them. They need to be taught how they have to live on earth and why they have to excel in character and behavior. All this is needed to develop a most humane society on earth. To achieve this, it is mandatory that men and women should be given two types of education. Religious education is needed to inculcate the purpose of life and to develop the character, leadership traits, and wisdom required to set up a just society on earth. At the same time, general and professional education is required to explore the universe for the prosperity of society and to earn an honest livelihood.

2. *Professional Education and Practice*: The Qur'an invites people to look around them in the universe and to try to discover its secrets. How can this be done unless we acquire appropriate knowledge? Besides, God has made everything in the universe subservient to us, and He wants us

to use these things to build human society. This is an assignment for humankind to complete, and education in all fields of knowledge is required to complete this assignment successfully. If the community is composed of ignorant people, then they have no hope of a good future. The task of an Islamic community is to provide a model of everything good in life. That can only be achieved through excellence in all fields of knowledge. This was how the early Muslims understood their task. They were able, as a result, to build a civilization that was unique in the history of humankind.

3. *Both Types of Education are Essential*: As noted previously in chapter two, both religious and general-technical types of education are needed to build a truly successful society. The latter type of knowledge is crucial for developing a society that provides the highest standards in the social sciences, natural sciences, etc. The former type of knowledge is a prerequisite for developing human character and a moral and ethical society. God commands us that we should not be the: "One who disputes about Allah without knowledge and without guidance and without an illuminating book, turning away haughtily that he may lead others away from the way of Allah; for him is disgrace in this world and on the Day of Resurrection. We will make him taste the punishment of burning."[32]

3.6 Inculcation of Core Human Values

A review and analysis of the early history of Islam reveals how the Messenger managed the implementation of God's commands by developing a group of people with integrity of character who then succeeded in the development of a just human society. The efforts of the Messenger and the believers in Makkah and Madinah have been described in the Qur'an. About Makkah, God tells us in Surah Al-Jumuah: "It is He Who has sent amongst the unlettered ones a messenger from among themselves, to rehearse to them His communications, to sanctify them, and to instruct them in scripture and wisdom, although they had been, before, in manifest error."³³ This effort could have been wasted if not utilized to establish a just human society at Madinah. Since this was done by the Messenger and his companions, a just human society is a necessary objective of humanity, without which the assignment of being God's trustee may remain incomplete. Therefore, it is incumbent on the believers to work hard collectively to achieve this ultimate divine aim. In short, the continual improvement of individual moral character, the inculcation of core human values, and the establishment of a just community should proceed simultaneously.

3.7 Establishment of the Best Community

The core human values that were developed among the early followers of Islam were a prerequisite to the establishment of a just community at Madinah. The end result of these efforts was seen in God's declaration: "You are the best community ever raised for mankind. You enjoin what is right, forbid what is wrong, and you believe in Allah."³⁴ For the protection of such a community, God commands: "Fight in the way of Allah with those who fight you."³⁵ In present day Islamic communities, efforts are required to improve the character and behavior of the people, as well as the character and working of the state. It is an individual's responsibility to elect honest and trustworthy people to the government, and these people should be ready to account for their behavior, both to the people and to God. Muslims cannot and should not be ruled by corrupt people or corrupt governments.

Individually and collectively, it is obligatory that we improve our moral values and ethical behavior. We all are responsible, in our own sphere of influence, for the improvement of individual moral character, the inculcation of core human values, and the establishment of a just community. That is what the Messenger of God and his companions did at Madinah. Our efforts should be continuous and compatible with what God commands, in order to ensure that progress is made in meeting the needs of the people and society in all spheres of life. For example, the basic necessities of life should be readily available to all people. Education should be provided to develop personal integrity and professionalism. Moral and social values should be inculcated in each individual and throughout society. Individual rights and dignity should be insured, and society and its institutions should be protected.

NOTES

1. Qur'an 103:2-3.

2. Qur'an 2:25.

3. Qur'an 16:97.

4. Qur'an 33:70-71.

5. Qur'an 42:13.

6. Qur'an 33:72-73.

7. Qur'an 13:11.

8. Qur'an 8:52-53.

9. Qur'an 91:7-10.

10. Qur'an 4:115.

11. Qur'an 20:124.

12. Qur'an 29:69.

13. Qur'an 2:8.

14. Qur'an 29:10.

15. Qur'an 2:204-205.

16. Qur'an 47:17 & 19.

17. Qur'an 43:72.

18. Qur'an 2:2 & 21.

19. Qur'an 2:177.

20. Qur'an 2:11-12.

21. Qur'an 42:13.

22. Qur'an 41:30-32.

23. Qur'an 19:54-55.

24. Qur'an 19:96.

25. Qur'an 29:45.

26. Qur'an 9:103.

27. Sahih Bukhari 4.52.141.

28. Qur'an 2:183.

29. Qur'an 2:197.

30. Sahih Muslim 32.6246.

31. Qur'an 96:1-5.

32. Qur'an 22:8-9.

33. Qur'an 62:2.

34. Qur'an 3:110.

35. Qur'an 2:190.

CHAPTER 4

GUIDANCE IS TO REFORM HUMANKIND
(God Ordained the Trustworthy as His Trustee)

LIFE ON EARTH IS A challenge and an opportunity for the people to prove who among them can live a life to their best purpose and potential. We are told in the Qur'an that God is He: "Who created death and life that He may try you— which of you is best in deeds."[1] Humankind, which is weak by nature, has been created to work hard and struggle in a hostile environment created by its own personal desires and by the jealousy of Satan, as manifest in the satanic temptations experienced by humanity. The possibility of individuals misusing their freedom of choice increases the severity of this hostile environment even more. Addressing humanity, God describes the situation like this: "Allah wishes to turn to you, but the wish of those who follow their lusts is that you should turn away (from Him)—far, far away. Allah wishes to lighten your (difficulties), for man was created weak."[2] Because of our weaknesses and the hostile environment of our existence, God provides guidance regarding the ways that help people succeed in life. None other than God can guide and help humankind to succeed in its mission as God's trustee on earth.

1. HUMAN WEAKNESSES AND DIFFICULTIES

God has brought people to the present stage of their existence by passing through various earlier stages in the creation process. The physical creation of Adam from dust and water was united with the spiritual one consisting of the human soul and human conscience. This was then followed by the creation of the human race from birth to adulthood and death. At a certain time in the future, human existence will be continued into an eternal life, which will occur after the general resurrection and the accountability for our behavior and deeds during our lives on earth. Since

God created humankind for developing life on earth, Iblis (Satan), who belongs to another of God's creation, did not like this honor being bestowed on humankind and became its enemy. Further, people have freedom of choice and personal needs, which make them prone to mistakes, especially if divine guidance is not followed.

At the time of the Adam's creation, God made the human soul, its nature, proportion, and relative perfection, in order to adopt it for the particular circumstances in which it has to live its life. He breathed into it an understanding of what is sin, impiety, and wrongdoing and what is piety and right conduct. This faculty of distinguishing between right and wrong is the most precious gift of all given to humanity.

1.1 Humankind's Creation in Stages

God brought man to the present stage of his existence after passing through various earlier stages in the creation process. In Surah Nuh, a simile is drawn between man's creation out of different elements taken from the earth and the growth of vegetation. There was a time when there was no vegetation on earth, and then God caused vegetation to appear. In like manner, there was a time when man did not exist on earth, and then God planted him on it. With regard to creation, God tells us: "We created man of clay that gives forth sound, of black mud fashioned in shape."[3]

God asks people: "What is the matter with you that you do not look forward to the majesty of Allah when He has created you in stages? Do you not see how Allah has created the seven heavens, one above another, and made the moon therein a light and made the sun a lamp? And Allah has caused you to grow out of the earth so wondrously, and He will later cause you to return to it and will then again bring you out of it."[4] Humankind's coming out of the earth again will be yet another stage in human development. This will be based on the human's efforts and accomplishments during the previous stage.

1.2 Iblis (Satan) did not like God's Choice

Iblis did not like God's choice that humankind would be God's trustee on earth: "When your Lord said to the angels, 'I am going to create a mortal of the essence of black mud fashioned in shape, so when I have made him complete and breathed into him My spirit, fall down making prostration to him.' The angels made prostration, all of them together, but Iblis did not; he refused."[5] When asked about the reason, Iblis replied that since Adam had been created out of clay, he (Iblis) was not going to prostrate to him. Without reason, Satan considered himself to be better than Adam and arrogantly rejected God's command.

Jealousy made Iblis humankind's enemy. After refusing to prostrate, Iblis told God that because his life has been made evil, he would make evil fair seeming to humankind on earth. He said that he would cause all of humanity to deviate from God's guidance, except for God's devoted servants. God told Iblis that he would have no influence on God's people, except for those who chose to follow Iblis. The details of the conversation between God and Iblis, as described in Surah Al-Hijr, are given below:

1. "(Allah) said: 'O Iblis! What is your reason for not being among those who prostrated themselves?' (Iblis) replied: 'I am not one to prostrate myself to man, whom You did create from sounding clay, from mud molded into shape.'"[6]

2. "(Allah) said: 'Then get you out from here, for you are rejected accursed. And the curse shall be on you till the Day of Judgment.' (Iblis) replied: 'O my Lord! Give me then respite till the day the dead are raised.'"[7]

3. "(Allah) said: 'Respite is granted you till the Day of the Time Appointed.' (Iblis) replied: 'My Lord! Since You have made life evil to me, I will certainly make (wrong) fair-seeming to them on earth, and I will deviate all of them, except Your sincere servants among them.'"[8]

4. "(Allah) said: 'This is, indeed, a way that leads straight to Me. For

over My servants no authority shall you have, except such as put themselves in the wrong and follow you.'"⁹

1.3 The Angels Highlighted the Human Weaknesses

When God told the angels about His intention to appoint humanity as His trustee on earth, they questioned its suitability due to the numerous weaknesses of character with which humanity is born. It seems that the angels were unaware that humankind would be capable of overcoming its weaknesses with the help of divine guidance and the teachings of messengers whom God would later send to humanity. This also stresses the importance of developing the requisite human character and behavior with God's help and His guidance if we want to succeed. The dialogue between God and His angels is reported in Surah Al-Baqarah: "Behold, your Lord said to the angels: 'I will create a trustee on earth.' They (the angels) said: 'Will You place therein one who will make mischief therein and shed blood, while we do celebrate Your praises and glorify Your holy (name)?' Allah said: 'I know what you know not.'"¹⁰

1.4 Life on Earth is a Test and a Trial

God tells people that he created them to test them: "Has there not been over man a long period of time when he was nothing—(not even) mentioned? Verily, We created man from a drop of mingled sperm, in order to try him: so We made him hearing, seeing."¹¹ God first outlines the nature of the trial and then tells who will succeed: "We will most certainly try you with somewhat of fear and hunger and loss of property and lives and fruits, and give good news to the patient."¹² "If Allah had so willed, He would have made you a single people, but (His plan is) to test you in what He has given you. So strive as in a race in all virtues."¹³ It is God: "Who made you successors in the land and raised some of you above others by various grades that He might try you by what He has given you."¹⁴ Other relevant verses of the Qur'an telling us that life on the earth is a test and a trial are as follows.

1. In Surah Al-Anfal, people are told: "…know that your possessions

and your children are but a trial and that it is Allah with Whom lies your highest reward."[15]

2. In Surah Hud, God tells people: "He is the One Who created the heavens and the earth in six days and – His throne was over the Waters – that He may try you, which of you is best in conduct."[16]

3. In Surah Al-Kahf, God tells people: "That which is on earth we have made but as a glittering show for the earth, in order that We may test them as to which of them are best in conduct."[17]

4. In Surah Ta Ha, God commands people: "Do not stretch your eyes after that with which We have provided different classes of them, the splendor of this world's life, that We may thereby try them, and the sustenance (given) by your Lord is better and more abiding."[18]

5. In Surah Al-Anbiya, God reminds people: "Every soul must taste of death, and We shall subject to ill and good by the way of trial; and to Us you shall be brought back."[19]

6. In Surah Al-Ankabut, God asks people: "Do men think that they will be left alone on saying, 'We believe,' and not be tried? And certainly We tried those before them, so Allah will certainly know those who are true, and He will certainly know the liars."[20]

7. In Surah Muhammad, God informs people: "We shall try you until We test those among you who strive their utmost and persevere in patience, and We shall make your case manifest."[21]

8. In Surah Al-Jinn, God's message to people is: "If they (people) had remained on the (right) way, We should certainly have bestowed on them rain in abundance so that We might try them by that (means). If any turns away from the remembrance of his Lord, He will thrust him into ever-growing torment."[22]

2. HUMAN CONSCIENCE AND DIVINE GUIDANCE

Each one of us has been given an assignment in life. To complete the assignment successfully, we have been given conscience, free will, and guidance. God has told us the requirements of our assignments and what are His expectations. We have also been instructed about our developmental needs and how we should train ourselves to complete the assignment. We also know how the outcome of our work will be evaluated and rewarded. God states in the Qur'an that it is He: "Who made you successors in the land and raised some of you above others by various grades that He might try you by what He has given you."[23] In Surah Ash-Shams, after mentioning six of His external evidences of creation (the sun and the moon, the day and night, and the sky and earth), God describes the human soul as an internal evidence of His goodness. By these various pointers, humanity is to learn that their success, prosperity, and salvation depend on themselves—on keeping their soul pure as God made it; and their failure, their decline, and their destruction depend on soiling their souls by choosing evil behavior and deeds.

2.1 Guidance is to Overcome Human Weaknesses

Angels were right in their evaluation of humanity. Not every person can be included among the best of God's creation. God says in the Qur'an: "We have, indeed, created humankind in the best of molds, and then We brought him down to the lowest of the low, except for those who believe and do righteous deeds."[24] These verses make it clear that among humankind there are those who can attain the highest level of the creation and those who can sink to the lowest depth. What determines this elevation or fall is one's efforts to overcome one's weaknesses. Without this effort, people cannot attain their individual potential to achieve the highest level of humanity. The messengers relayed divine guidance to humankind and provided a practical code of living that has been perfected in the message of Islam. Therefore, when people implement Islam, they reach their highest level. When they abandon God's guidance, they sink into the depth of ignorance in which Satan tries hard to keep them.

God's help and guidance are always there for those who strive hard. God tells people that: "(As for) those who strive hard for Us, We will most certainly guide them in Our ways, and Allah is most surely with the doers of good."[25] Furthermore, He assures them: "And (as for) those who were led to the guidance, Allah increases them in their guidance and causes them to grow in piety."[26] Now, it is up to people to take benefit from their own conscience and from God's guidance or to ignore them. God says in Surah Al-Dahr: "Surely, We have shown him the way; he may be thankful or unthankful."[27] Whether he is thankful or unthankful is a product of his own free will and choice.

2.2 God's Trustee has to Follow His Commands

What sort of life should we lead? Whether we realize it or not, we have and we make a choice at every moment in our lives. We must decide if our lives should be lived according to the divine laws and for what benefit our lives should be lived. Our efforts in obeying certain rules in this world do not mean that we will be saved from suffering only in the Hereafter. Who benefits here on this earth? Does the benefit of our compliance accrue to someone else or to God? God does not benefit by our obedience to or compliance with His rules; we do. The Messenger quotes God in a sacred Hadith as saying: "My servants, it is but your deeds that I reckon up for you and then recompense you for (in this world). Therefore, let him who finds good praise Allah, and let him who finds other than good blame no one but himself."[28]

2.3 Divine Laws Help Improve Life on Earth

God created humankind in a certain way and sent messengers for guidance to lead a happy human life. The role of the messengers was to highlight what behavior is beneficent and reprieves problems and misery. What the messengers conveyed was a complete message that outlines an integrated system that was devised by God, the Creator of humankind, Who knows what is appropriate and suitable for implementation in human life and what will bring happiness. Thus, whoever obeys God's rules is a beneficiary. The benefit is assured, as the rules are made to spare people affliction, contradiction, and confusion.

Our prayers and fasting do not benefit God in any way, but prayers certainly benefit us by keeping us on guard against temptation and against falling into sin. Fasting also teaches self-discipline. In contrast, humankind suffers by not implementing God's laws, a failing that does not harm God in any way. The choice is there: do we do what is right and enjoy its benefits in this life, as well as in the Hereafter, or do we reject divine guidance and suffer the consequences of this rejection.

3. DELIVERING THE DIVINE TRUST

Islam is a constitution that regulates all aspects of human life. A person who accepts Islam in full and follows all its commandments is a believer, while a person who follows some other method, even though this may be in a single question or issue, is one who rejects faith and transgresses against God's authority. As such, he is not a believer, although he may profess to respect faith and claim to be a Muslim. When he follows some other law in preference to God's law, he falsifies all his claims and takes himself out of the realm of faith altogether. This is so because false religion gives rise to false values and to a society in which the weak are scorned and oppressed and in which power is held securely in the hands of a few. And among these few who hold power, the very worst of men are the most powerful and respected.

Am I a believer? One can find the answer by asking and truthfully answering the following questions. Do I listen to my conscience? Do I believe and worship God and try to live according to His commands? Am I truthful, honest, trustworthy, and hardworking? Do I wish for others what I wish for myself? A person who answers all these questions in the affirmative should continue being a believer by helping others and doing good deeds.

3.1 People should listen to their Conscience

The perfection of character and behavior without divine guidance is not humanly possible, due to the existence of people's needs, desires and free will. Each of us is prone to making mistakes. This is why God equipped each individual with a conscience, an automatic and self-correcting device. By listening to our conscience, we self-evaluate ourselves at each moment in life, admit our mistakes, and try to correct them. In this way, we develop an attitude that leads us to a continual improvement of our character, behavior, and eventually society. God forgives everyone who turns to Him in genuine repentance, even the most wicked of humankind. Human character is improved with every incidence in which we acknowledge and regret our shortcomings and make the effort not to make these mistakes again. Swearing by the human self and Himself, God tells people in Surah Al-Shams who among them will be successful and who will fail, "By the soul, and the proportion and order given to it, and its enlightenment as to its wrong and its right, truly he succeeds that purifies it, and he fails that corrupts it!"[29]

3.2 People Should Believe and Do Good Deeds

In Islam, those who believe worship God and do good deeds. As explained in the Qur'an, worship and good deeds are two completely separate, different, and equally important parts of the believers' efforts, efforts in which God commands us to engage. That is why these are mentioned individually and together in several places in the Qur'an. In Surah Al-Baqarah, God tells us: "Those who believe and do good deeds, establish Salah, pay Zakah, they will most surely have their reward with their Lord, and they will have nothing to fear or to grieve."[30] Although in general, to do or refrain from, as God commands, are both good deeds, the good deeds mentioned in the above verse are those actions that are taken for the care of His creation, including humankind. Worship motivates and leads us to do good deeds. If worship does not make us do good deeds, then our worship needs to be improved. In conclusion God tells people: "We have indeed created man in the best of molds. Then We render him the lowest of the low, except those who believe and do good deeds, so they shall have a reward never to be cut off."[31]

3.3 People's Morality makes their Belief Grow

In Surah Al-Asr, swearing by time itself, God tells us: "Most surely man is in loss, except those who believe and do good deeds, and enjoin on each other truth, and enjoin on each other patience."[32] Comparing morality and good deeds with immorality and evil, God asks us: "Have you not considered how Allah sets forth a parable of a good word (being) like a good tree, whose root is firm and whose branches are in Heaven, yielding its fruit in every season by the permission of its Lord? And Allah sets forth parables for men that they may reflect. (In contrast), the parable of an evil word is as an evil tree pulled up from the earth's surface; it has no stability."[33] God's Messenger nicely explained this by saying that when faith is firm and belief is strong, then strong and lasting morals will be developed, and if the moral character is low, then faith will be proportionally weak. The Messenger said, "Faith (belief) consists of more than sixty branches. And Haya (the term "Haya" covers a large number of concepts that are to be taken together; among them are self-respect, modesty, bashfulness, scruples, etc.) is a part of faith."[34] How then can an individual who is immodest and ill-mannered, and who adopts bad habits without caring for others, be a believer?

3.4 Enjoin what is Good and Forbid what is Evil

In an Islamic community, there should be some people assigned to the task of inviting to all that is good, enjoining the doing of what is right, and forbidding what is wrong. An Islamic community does not come into existence unless it has this essential quality by which it is distinguished from the rest of humanity. Its invitation to all that is good, enjoining what is right, and forbidding what is wrong, in addition to believing in God, gives credence to its Islamic existence. God says about believers in Surah Al-Imran: "They believe in Allah and the Last Day, and they enjoin what is right and forbid the wrong, and they strive with one another in hastening to do good deeds, and those are among the good."[35] Then He commands the believers: "From among you there should be a party who invite to good and enjoin what is right and forbid the wrong, and these it is that shall be successful."[36] However, all believers have been assigned this responsibility to them by God within their own sphere of influence.

In Surah Al-Tawbah, God describes the believers: "The believers, men and women, are protectors one of another. They enjoin what is just and forbid what is evil. They observe regular prayers, practice regular charity, and they obey Allah and His Messenger. On them will Allah pour His mercy, for Allah is Exalted in Power, Wise."[37] In Surah Luqman, we find Luqman advising his son: "My son! Keep up prayer, and enjoin the good and forbid the evil. Bear patiently that which befalls you; surely, these acts require courage."[38] All these verses highlight the importance of promoting good and forbidding evil in the protection of human character and society.

4. PHYSICAL AND PSYCHOLOGICAL LIMITATIONS

Humankind is by nature weak, both physically and psychologically. Addressing humanity, God describes this situation of human weakness: "Allah wishes to turn to you, but the wish of those who follow their lusts is that you should turn away (from Him)—far, far away. Allah wishes to lighten your (difficulties), for man was created weak."[39] For this reason, God offers guidance to humanity, for it is only God who can truly guide us to success in life.

4.1 People are Created Weak, Physically and Morally

Islam is a very tolerant religion and easy to implement. These qualities support its appeal to people's sense of nobility, purity, cleanliness, and willingness to obey God. Its commandments, as well as its legal provisions and punishments, work for the same aim, i.e., refining people's characters and establishing a pure and healthy society. Islam does not ignore human weakness and does not charge people with what is beyond their ability. Islam is not unaware of the complexity of factors working on people's minds, and it does not ignore human nature and motivation. It strikes the right balance between duty and ability, motives and restraints, ideals and necessities, orders and prohibitions, and forgiveness of sins and fear of being punished for them.

No doubt, people are so weak that sometimes they cannot even comprehend what is good and bad for them. They have no say whatsoever in how they are going to live or die. They have no control over the result of their efforts and the environment that surrounds them. Even a small germ can cause them sickness and pain. Humans are so weak that like a drowning person clutching at a straw, we start calling upon those entities that cannot help us. God elaborated on this when He said: "O people! A parable is set forth. Therefore, listen to it: surely those whom you call upon besides Allah cannot create a fly, though they should all gather for it, and should the fly snatch away anything from them, they could not take it back from it, and weak are the invoker and the invoked!"[40]

4.2 People are Created into Struggle and Hard Work

God commands us: "O people! Surely you must strive to attain to your Lord, a hard striving until you meet Him."[41] "Verily, We created man into toil and struggle. Does he think that no one has power over him? He may say (boastfully): 'Wealth (natural resources) have I squandered in abundance!'"[42] God then warns us: "And whoever turns away from My message, his shall be a straitened life, and We will raise him on the Day of Resurrection blind. He will say: 'My Lord! Why have You raised me up blind, while I had sight (before)?' Allah will say: 'Even so, Our signs came to you, but you neglected them; even thus shall you be forsaken this day.' And thus do We recompense him who is extravagant and does not believe in the signs of his Lord. Certainly the chastisement of the Hereafter is severer and more lasting."[43]

In the face of all this struggle, toil, and hard work, which we are called upon to bear, we are comforted by God's promise to bestow His mercy on people and to forgive their sins if they avoid cardinal sins: "If you (but) eschew the most heinous of the things that you are forbidden to do, We shall remit out of you your evil (minor) deeds in you, and admit you to a gate of great honor."[44] God, thus, takes into account the weaknesses of people and reassures them about their destiny once they repent and refrain from the gravest of sins.

4.3 People need Shelter from the Evil Suggestions of Satan

Jealousy made Iblis (Satan) humankind's enemy, but usually only the unbelievers and the people who do not remember God become the victims of Satan. After refusing to prostrate, "(Iblis) said: 'My Lord! Since, You have made life evil to me, I will certainly make (wrong) fair-seeming to them on earth, and I will deviate all of them, except Your sincere servants among them'…(God said): 'Surely, as regards to My servants, you have no authority over them, except those who put themselves in the wrong and follow you.'"[45] God tells people: "It was We Who created man, and We know what dark suggestions his soul makes to him, for We are nearer to him than his jugular vein."[46] Just for our sake, God commands us: "Say: 'I seek refuge with the Lord of mankind, the king (or ruler) of mankind, the god (or judge) of mankind, from the mischief of the whisperer (Satan), who withdraws (after his whisper), who whispers into the hearts of mankind, from among the jinn and the men."[47] In Surah Al-Araf, we are told how the enmity of Satan compelled Adam to disobey God: "And (We said): 'O Adam! Dwell you and your wife in the garden;

so eat from where you desire, but do not go near this tree, for then you will be of the unjust.' But Satan made an evil suggestion to them that he might make manifest to them what had been hidden from them of their evil inclinations. He said: 'Your Lord has not forbidden you this tree except that you may not both become two angels or that you may not become of the immortals.'"[48]

Humankind tends to receive evil suggestions from Satan, as well as from other humans and even from its own self, due to its weaknesses of character and selfish desires. About this, God informs us: "Most surely the satans suggests to their friends that they should contend with you; and if you obey them, you shall most surely be polytheists."[49] Satan himself admits: "I will certainly come to them from before them and from behind them, and from their right-hand side and from their left-hand side; and You shall not find most of them thankful."[50] God tells us that only unbelievers are influenced by Satan: "Surely, he has no authority over those who believe and rely on their Lord. His authority is only over those who befriend him and those who associate others with Him."[51] Satan can also influence those people who fail to remember God. God warns us: "If anyone withdraws himself from remembrance of (Allah) Most Gracious, We appoint for him an evil one (Satan), to be an intimate companion to him. And most surely they turn them away from the path, and they think that they are rightly guided."[52]

NOTES

1. Qur'an 67.2.
2. Qur'an 4:27-28.
3. Qur'an 15:26.
4. Qur'an 7:13-18.

5. Qur'an 15:28-31.

6. Qur'an 15:32-33.

7. Qur'an 15:34-36.

8. Qur'an 15:37-40.

9. Qur'an 15:41-42.

10. Qur'an 2:30.

11. Qur'an 76:1-2.

12. Qur'an 2:155.

13. Qur'an 5:48.

14. Qur'an 6:165.

15. Qur'an 8:28.

16. Qur'an 11:7.

17. Qur'an 18:7.

18. Qur'an 20:131.

19. Qur'an 21:35.

20. Qur'an 29:2-3.

21. Qur'an 47:31.

22. Qur'an 72:16-17.

23. Qur'an 6:165.

24. Qur'an 95:4-6.

25. Qur'an 29:69.

26. Qur'an 47:17.

27. Qur'an 76:3.

28. Sahih Muslim 32.6246.

29. Qur'an 91:7-10.

30. Qur'an 2:277.

31. Qur'an 95:4-6.

32. Qur'an 103:2-3.

33. Qur'an 14:24-26.

34. Sahih Bukhari 1.2.8.

35. Qur'an 3:114.

36. Qur'an 3:104.

37. Qur'an 9:71.

38. Qur'an 31:17.

39. Qur'an 4:27-28.

40. Qur'an 22:73.

41. Qur'an 84:6.

42. Qur'an 90:4-6.

43. Qur'an 20:124-127.

44. Qur'an 4:31.

45. Qur'an 15:39-42.

46. Qur'an 50:16.

47. Qur'an 114:1-6.

48. Qur'an 7:19-20.

49. Qur'an 6:121.

50. Qur'an 7:17.

51. Qur'an 16:99-100.

52. Qur'an 43:36-37.

CHAPTER 5

WEAKNESSES OF HUMAN CHARACTER
(People's Attitudes and Habits)

HUMANKIND IS BORN WITH numerous physical and emotional weaknesses. In addition, our existence is surrounded by many selfish desires, temptations, and difficulties. How should we survive and still be successful? Our salvation lies in our belief in our Creator. With His guidance, we should make efforts to reform our character, overcome our weaknesses, and strive hard with a dedication to our mission as God's trustee on earth.

God commands us to believe in and worship Him and reform ourselves to be the best in character and conduct. We should be truthful and just in our dealings with others, and we should patiently fight against discrimination, exploitation, and corruption. We should get involved in the betterment of society, do good deeds, enjoin what is right, and forbid what is wrong.

1. PEOPLE ARE EXTREMELY EMOTIONAL

One of the human weaknesses is that during hard times people despair and start complaining and cursing, while in good times these same people are very proud and arrogant. Since no evil befalls on the earth or in people's lives except with God's will, so one should not grieve for what is lost or be exultant at what one achieves. One should be patient, show gratitude, be humble, and try to keep one's emotions in balance

1.1 People are Either Boasting or Despairing

Generally, people spend their lives between two extreme conditions of poverty and prosperity. They seldom think that God Who has given them all the comforts of life can take them back at any time. In Surah

Hud, God tells us that people are extremely emotional; in difficulty they are despairing and ungrateful, while in prosperity they are exulting and boasting. "If We make man taste mercy from Us, then take it off from him, most surely he is despairing, ungrateful. And if We make him taste a favor after distress has afflicted him, he will certainly say: 'The evils are gone away from me.' Most surely he is exulting, boasting."[1] In Surah Bani Israil, God says: "When We bestow favor on man, he turns aside and behaves proudly, and when evil afflicts him, he is despairing. Say: 'Each acts according to his manner, but your Lord best knows who is best guided in the path.'"[2] In Surah Al-Rum, we are told that when evil befalls people due to their own behavior, they despair and loose hope: "And when We make people taste of mercy they rejoice in it, and if an evil befalls them for what their hands have already wrought, lo, they are in despair."[3]

1.2 Behavior of Boasting and Despairing People

The behavior of boasting and despairing people does not allow them to develop a permanent relationship with their Creator. As described in Surah Hud, they approach Him only when in need: "And when affliction touches a man, he calls on Us, whether lying on his side or sitting or standing, but when We remove his affliction from him, he passes on as though he had never called on Us on account of an affliction that touched him. Thus, that which they do is made fair-seeming to the extravagant."[4] Being selfish by nature, people are also ungrateful and easily forget the help they have received from God. Since they are not serious in their relationship with God, or perhaps they cannot recognize God's mercy, at least some of them start looking for alternatives. God tells us about such people in Surah Al-Rum: "And when harm afflicts men, they call upon their Lord, turning to Him (in repentance); then when He makes them taste of mercy from Him, lo, some of them begin to associate others with their Lord."[5]

1.3 Boasting and Despairing People Should Reform

God commands people who are boasting or despairing to reform themselves by telling them in Surah Al-Hadid that, although it is their duty to make their best efforts, their success or failure is not the outcome of their efforts only: "No evil befalls on the earth or in your own selves, but it is in a book before We bring it into existence. Surely, that is easy for Allah: So that you may not grieve for what has escaped you or be exultant at what He has given you, and Allah does not love any arrogant boaster, those who are miserly and enjoin miserliness on men, and whoever turns back. Then surely Allah is He Who is the Self-sufficient, the Praised."[6] Since it is not only people's own efforts that cause success or failure, they have no reason to be boastful or despairing. Instead, people should be patient, show gratitude, be humble, and try to keep their emotions in balance. This will increase their strength and their capacity to survive.

2. PEOPLE ARE IMPATIENT, GRIEVING, AND MISERLY

People react differently to the motivations and the incidents that generate feelings of sorrow and pain. Some people are provoked by ordinary things, and they become unmindful of everything and in haste take a very unwise step. However, there are also people who go through various hardships and adversities and yet do not forget to behave wisely, with tolerance and good manners. People should condition themselves to face hardships and difficulties and should not be complaining or grieving all the time. Neither misgivings and doubts nor hardships should prompt one's intellect to indulge in what is unlawful and immoral.

2.1 People are Hasty in Nature and Impatient

Sometimes in haste and ignorance, people do things to satisfy their selfish desires that are very harmful to their eventual welfare. God tells us in Surah Bani Israel: "The prayer that man should make for good, he makes for evil, for the man is ever hasty."[7] In Surah Al-Anbiya we are told: "Man is a creature of haste. Soon will I show you My Signs; then you will not ask Me to hasten them!"[8]

2.2 Behavior of Hasty and Impatient People

People in their haste and impatience forget that God is the Provider and Sustainer. Their behavior during life's difficulties and prosperity is described in Surah Al-Maarij, where God tells us: "Truly man was created very impatient—fretful when evil touches him and miserly when good reaches him."[9] When difficulties and hardships confront people, and suffering becomes long, it is impatience that compels people to act in strange ways. They become extremely grieved, desperate, or frustrated at some disappointment. Patience is a basic quality that people need to shape their lives. They should attend to their work with patience and make it a guiding-light throughout the journey of life, or else they will fail.

2.3 Believers do not Grieve and are Patient

One should have plenty of self-confidence and not be frightened by the dark clouds appearing on the horizon of life, even if they appear continually. One should be fully assured that these clouds of adversities and hardships will disappear and that the clear and bright atmosphere of success and glory will reappear. Therefore, wisdom and far-sightedness suggest that coming success should be awaited with patience and not with grieving. Being confident of God's help throughout one's entire life, one should also not become miserly during good times. Various traits and behaviors of the believers essential to the development of contentment and patience during the trials of life, as given in Surah Al-Maarij, are:

1. Those who pray and remain steadfast in their prayers.

2. Those whose wealth is a recognized right for the (needy) who ask and for (the needy) who are prevented (from asking for some reason).

3. Those who accept the truth of the Judgment Day.

4. Those who fear the displeasure of their Lord, for their Lord's displeasure is that before which none can feel secure.

5. Those who guard their chastity, except with their wives and the (captives) whom their right hands possess, for (with lawful mates) they are not to be blamed. But those who trespass beyond this are transgressors.

6. Those who respect their trusts and covenants, and those who stand firm in their testimonies.

7. Those who guard their worship. Such will be the honored ones in the gardens (of bliss).[10]

3. PEOPLE ARE UNJUST AND UNGRATEFUL

Being God's trustee, humankind carries the burden of responsibilities that has been placed on it after having been endowed with reason, as well as power and authority in the earth. Even though humankind is the bearer of a great trust from God, it does not show the requisite sense of responsibility and is inclined to wrong itself by committing a breach of trust. People should remember their trust and try to behave accordingly. They should not be unjust to others. People as God's trustee are responsible individuals and accountable for their actions. Anything short of this makes people unjust and ungrateful to their Creator.

3.1 People are Unjust and Ignorant

God reminds humankind: "Surely, We offered the trust to the heavens and the earth and the mountains, but they refused to undertake it, being afraid thereof, but man undertook it; surely he was unjust, ignorant."[11] People should know that the consequence of man's carrying the burden of responsibilities associated with the trust is that: "Allah may chastise the hypocritical men and the hypocritical women, and the polytheistic men and the polytheistic women, and accept the repentance of believing men and believing women, and Allah is Forgiving, Merciful."[12] Therefore, God tells the believers among people that in order to succeed they should: "O you who believe! Be careful of your duty to Allah, and speak the truth. He will put your deeds into a right state for you and forgive you your faults, and whoever obeys Allah and His Messenger, he indeed achieves a mighty success."[13]

3.2 People should not be Rebellious and Ungrateful

As God's trustees, people should not be rebellious and ungrateful to Him by their actions and behavior. God reminds people: "He gives you of all that you ask Him, and if you count Allah's favors, you will not be able to number them. Most surely, man is very unjust, very ungrateful."[14] In spite of man's humble creation and God's favors to humanity, some among humanity are so ungrateful that: "They give a share of (Him) to some of His servants. Surely man is clearly ungrateful."[15] Therefore, God declares: "Cursed be man! How ungrateful is he! Of what thing did He create him? Of a small seed; He created him; then He made him according to a measure."[16] God warned the believers: "If you obey most of those in the earth, they will lead you astray from Allah's way; they follow but conjecture, and they only lie,"[17] and "Most men will not believe though you desire it eagerly."[18] Why is this so? God tells us in Surah Al-Aliq: "Nay, but verily man is rebellious, in that he looks upon himself as independent."[19] Additionally, God says in Surah Al-Adiyat: "Most surely, man is ungrateful to his Lord, and to that fact he bears witness (by his behavior and deeds)."[20]

4. PEOPLE'S WEAKNESSES AND THE TRUTH

Selfish desires, satanic inclinations, and weaknesses of character incite people to argue and dispute about the truth without knowledge and reason. God granted reason to humankind for use in regulating its emotions from extremes. However, Satan taught people to use their intellect to justify the fulfillment of their selfish desires at the expense of other people's rights. That is why people are forgetful, heedless, and negligent.

They are jealous and do not help others in their times of need. Rather, they arrogantly prefer self-deception and ignore their duties and responsibilities as God's trustee.

4.1 People Argue and Dispute without Knowledge

Although God has provided guidance to humankind through so many channels, first through human conscience, then through his messengers and books, some people still dispute about the Creator of the universe even without reflecting on the universe that engulfs them. God reminds people in Surah Al-Nahl: "He created the heavens and the earth with the truth, highly exalted is He above what they associate with Him. He has created man from a sperm-drop, and behold this same (man) becomes an open disputer!"[21] This is so even though God has: "...explained in detail in the Qur'an, for the benefit of mankind, every kind of similitude: but man is, in most things, contentious."[22] Such people quote theories, trying to negate facts, only to misguide themselves and others by justifying their corruption and injustices. To counter such arguments, the believers are asked in Surah Al-Nahl to, "Invite (all) to the way of your Lord with wisdom and beautiful preaching, and reason with them in ways that are best. Your Lord knows best who is straying from His path and who is being guided."[23]

4.2 People are Forgetful and lack Resolve

A deficient memory and lack of resolve are two weaknesses that interfere with people performing their duties. People who are overwhelmed by hardships, various difficulties, and different pressing problems even forget open and clear realities. To them, clear things appear blurred, and realities that are as striking as the light of the sun disappear from their sight. God tells us in Surah Al-Zumar: "When distress afflicts a man, he calls upon his Lord, turning to Him frequently; then when He makes him possess a favor from Him, he forgets that for which he called upon Him before and sets up rivals to Allah that he may cause people to stray off from His path. Say: 'Enjoy yourself in your ungratefulness a little; surely, you are of the inmates of the fire.'"[24] Human nature is such that: "When harm afflicts a man he calls upon Us; then when We give him a favor from Us, he says: 'I have been given it only by means of knowledge.' Nay, it is a trial, but most of them do not know. Those before them boasted (in this way), but what they earned availed them not."[25]

God took a promise from Adam that he would not go near the forbidden tree while living in Paradise, but Adam forgot his promise within a short time. He became a prey to his weakness and broke his promise: "We had already beforehand taken the covenant of Adam, but he forgot, and We found on his part no firm resolve."[26] Memory and determination are two of the essential qualities of humankind that are required for fulfilling God's commands. If a person has a strong memory, it is also necessary that he should have a determination to overcome difficulties and his own rebellious desires. He should be determined to set an example of selfless sacrifice for others. At times, this requires sacrificing one's wealth, property, and even one's self. However, these difficulties, sacrifices, and trials of determination prove in the end to be the steps for achieving greatness and honor.

Since life in this world is a trial, in Surah Al-Baqarah, God severely criticizes people who seek to achieve success and glory in the shadow of comfortable living: "Do you think that you will enter Paradise without such trials as came to those who passed away before you? They experienced suffering and adversity and were so shaken in spirit that even the prophet and the faithful who were with him cried: 'When will Allah's help come?' Ah! Verily, Allah's help is near."[27] When a person develops a conscientious and wakeful mind and a heart full of determination, only then can he be considered to be among the faithful people. This can be achieved by following what God commanded Adam: "He said: 'Both of you go down and away from here, enemy one to another: If there ever comes to you any guidance from Me, then whoever follows My guidance, will not go astray or be unhappy."[28]

4.3 People are Negligent and Heedless

Lack of seriousness and indifference to God's commands are common weaknesses of humanity. Maybe this is because people lack the imagination to visualize the consequences of their mistakes in this world and because they do not believe in the accountability for their deeds in the Hereafter. God warns people in Surah Al-Anbiya: "Their reckoning has drawn near to men, and in heedlessness are they turning aside."[29] In Surah Bani Israel, people are reminded: "When We bestow favor on man, he turns aside and behaves proudly, and when evil afflicts him, he is despairing."[30] In Surah Yunus, God says, "And most surely the majority of the people are heedless to Our signs."[31] No doubt, there are many people, even among the believers, who do not know why God created them, what their mission in life is, and how they should live their lives. They are ignorant of God's commands because they have never tried to understand what God has revealed in the Qur'an. Such people enjoy the good things God has created but fail even to know how to thank God for all these bounties from Him.

We are commanded to remind ourselves and others about the accountability for our deeds in the Hereafter: "And warn them of the day of intense regret when the matter shall have been decided, and they are now in negligence, and they do not believe."[32] God commands us to behave as His trustees by following His guidance sincerely and with dedication, in order to spare us cursing ourselves later: "Lest a person should say: 'O woe to me! I fell short in my duty to Allah, and I was of those who laughed in scorn.'"[33]

4.4 People are Miserly and Greedy

The inordinate desire for wealth and possessions, even if they belong to someone else, is one of those human weaknesses that has a very adverse effect on people's character. It is this desire that leads people to commit all types of injustice. God tells us in Surah Bani Israel: "Say: 'If you control the treasures of the mercy of my Lord, then you would withhold (them) from fear of spending, and man is miserly.'"[34]

Greediness and the fear of losing wealth make people stingy. God tells people that their greediness and withholding from giving charity will not save them from the difficulties of life. In Surah Al-Hadid, it is confirmed: "No evil befalls on the earth or in your own selves, but it is in a book before We bring it into existence. Surely, that is easy for Allah: So that you may not grieve for what has escaped you or be exultant at what He has given you, and Allah does not love any arrogant boaster, those who are miserly and enjoin miserliness on men, and whoever turns back. Then surely Allah is He Who is the Self-sufficient, the Praised."[35]

God commands people to be generous and charitable, and He loves those who trust Him instead of their wealth and possessions. In Surah Al-Imran, God tells people: "Surely, Allah loves those who trust Him."[36] In Surah Al-Baqarah, He commands people: "Spend in the way of Allah, and make not your own hands contribute to your destruction, and do good to others. Surely, Allah loves the doers of good."[37] In Surah Al-Imran, we are told to spend in charity, restrain anger, and forgive people: "They spent, whether in prosperity or in adversity, restrained their anger, and pardoned people. Allah loves those who do good deeds."[38] All these commands are there to help people treat their disease of greed and miserliness.

4.5 People are Deceived and Arrogant

God asks: "O people! What has made you careless of your Lord, the Gracious One, Who created you, made you complete, imbued you with a sense of justice, and made you into whatever form He pleased."[39] God answers His Own question by saying: "That is because you took the revelations of Allah for a jest, and the life of this world deceived you[40]...and you caused yourselves to fall into temptation, and you waited and doubted, and vain desires deceived you till the threatened punishment of Allah came. Satan deceived you about Allah."[41] One may well ask, "Who is there to help under such circumstances other than God?" Nonetheless, "Verily, the unbelievers are deceived."[42] Such deception can only exist because of boasting and arrogance. The most villainous beings in history were filled with arrogance and false pride: Satan, Pharaoh, the opponents of the God's messengers, and extremely wicked tyrants since then. God says: "I will divert from My signs those who show arrogance without right."[43] God also says: "He sets the seal upon the heart of every arrogant tyrant."[44] "He does not love those who are steeped in arrogance."[45]

Arrogance is present if a person thinks that he is superior to others, resulting in behavior that shows contempt and scorns people. This arrogance could be due to lineage, race, nationality, beauty, personal strength, wealth, power and authority, or even knowledge. Ironically, the factors that cause arrogance in people also cause them to forget that every blessing we have is a gift from God that has been given to us as a trust and for which we are responsible and answerable before Him. In Surah Al-Mulk, people are told that it is God, "Who has created life and death that He may try which of you is best in conduct."[46] We are told in Surah Al-Hadid: "Know that this world's life is only sport and play and gaiety and boasting among yourselves, and a vying in the multiplication of wealth and children...and what is the life of this world, but goods and chattels of deception."[47] This ailment can only be removed by acknowledging our weak nature, humble birth, and ultimate return to God. Honor is entirely based on one's servitude to God and individual usefulness as a person. God reminds us of our ultimate accountability in Surah Luqman: "O people! Guard against (the punishment of) your Lord, and dread the day when a father shall not make any satisfaction for his son, nor shall the child be the maker of any satisfaction for his father. Surely, the promise of Allah is true. Therefore, let not this world's life deceive you, nor let any deceiver deceive you about Allah."[48]

5. THE ARROGANT VS. THE SUCCESSFUL PEOPLE

Although an embodiment of numerous physical and emotional shortcomings, the most corrupt people in history were filled with arrogance and false pride. Satan, Pharaoh, the opponents of the divine messengers, and many tyrants since then—all were slaves of their selfish desires and temptations. Arrogance makes people think that everyone else is beneath them in honor and status. It is the arrogance of the learned that gives them a feeling of superiority. It is arrogance by which people shows contempt and scorn others. Another type of arrogance is related to lineage, nationality, or even looks. In some cultures, people of so-called high birth behave arrogantly.

It is very difficult to make such people realize that everyone among us has the same humble, organic origin and that honor comes not from individual looks, but only from noble character and behavior. All people have to struggle to improve themselves and to work hard to earn honor by their usefulness to society. To be successful, they have to serve God and reform their conduct. That is why successful people are those who believe and are truthful, honest, and patient. The honored among people are those role models who encourage themselves and others to do good deeds and who discourage people from doing what is injurious to society.

5.1 The Successful are Those who Worship God and are Best in Conduct

God commands us to believe and worship Him and to reform ourselves into the best character and conduct. After reminding us of His bounties, God asks in Surah Luqman why some people disbelieve in Him without any reason and knowledge. "O humankind, do you not see that

Allah has subjected to your use all things in the heavens and on earth and has made His bounties flow to you in exceeding measure, seen and unseen? Yet, there are among people those who dispute about Allah without knowledge and without guidance and without a Book to enlighten them!"⁴⁹ God again reminds in Surah Al-Araf that He has given people power and authority on earth: "We assuredly established you with authority on earth and provided you therein with means for the fulfillment of your life."⁵⁰

He has appointed us His trustees to see how we behave in the use of our power and authority: "Then We appointed you as rulers in the earth after them that We might see how you behave."⁵¹ What does God expects from people? We are told in Surah Al-Hajj that: "...those who, should We establish them in the land, will keep up prayer and pay the poor-rate and enjoin good and forbid evil, and Allah's is the end of all affairs."⁵²

This demand of the faith that we should believe and reform our behavior is very well summarized in Surah Luqman in Luqman's advice to his son: "My son! Keep up prayer, and enjoin the good and forbid the evil. Bear patiently that which befalls you; surely, these acts require courage. Do not turn your face away from people in contempt, nor go about in the land exulting overmuch. Surely, Allah does not love any self-conceited boaster. Walk moderately, and speak softly, for the most hateful of voices is the braying of a donkey."⁵³

5.2 Other Traits of the Successful

The demand of Islam that people should believe and reform their behavior is well summarized in Surah Al-Asr: "I swear by the time. Most surely man is in loss, except those who believe and do good deeds, and enjoin on each other truth, and enjoin on each other patience."⁵⁴ A parable in Surah Ibrahim helps us reflect on truth and falsehood: "Have you not considered how Allah sets forth a parable of a good word (being) like a good tree, whose root is firm and whose branches are in Heaven, yielding its fruit in every season by the permission of its Lord? And Allah sets forth parables for men that they may reflect. (In contrast), the parable of an evil word is as an evil tree pulled up from the earth's surface; it has no stability."[55] Since there is only one God, the likeness of a person: "...who assigns partners to Allah is as if he had fallen from Heaven and been snatched up by birds, or the wind had swooped (like a bird on its prey) and thrown him into a far-distant place."[56]

It is belief in God that gives people strength and stability. Those who believe in God stand firmly in this world, and they will stand firmly in the Hereafter. God confirms this in Surah Ibrahim: "Allah will establish in strength those who believe, with the word that stands firm, in this world and in the Hereafter; but Allah will leave to stray those who do wrong. Allah does what He wills."[57]

The demand of the faith that we should believe and reform our behavior is also very well summarized in Surah Yusuf where God asks the Messenger to tell people: "This is my way: I call you to Allah on the basis of clear perception, both I and those who follow, and glory be to Allah, and I am not one of the polytheists."[58] History confirms that the core human values that were developed among the early followers of Islam were implemented in Madinah. The end result of these efforts was what God told them: "You are the best of the nations raised up for (the benefit of) men; you enjoin what is right, forbid what is wrong, and believe in Allah."[59]

This makes it an obligation of contemporary believers that they should believe as early Muslims believed, inculcate Islamic values in their character and behavior, and enjoin what is right and forbid what is wrong in their circle of influence and communities. Only then can they claim to be the best of nations; otherwise, they will be the losers and the unsuccessful.

NOTES

1. Qur'an 11:9-10.

2. Qur'an 17:83-84.

3. Qur'an 30:36.

4. Qur'an 10:12.

5. Qur'an 30:33.

6. Qur'an 57:22-24.

7. Qur'an 17:11.

8. Qur'an 21:37.

9. Qur'an 70:19-21.

10. Qur'an 70:22-35.

11. Qur'an 33:72.

12. Qur'an 33:73.

13. Qur'an 33:70-71.

14. Qur'an 14:34.

15. Qur'an 43:15.

16. Qur'an 80:17-19.

17. Qur'an 6:116.

18. Qur'an 12:103.

19. Qur'an 96:6-7.

20. Qur'an 100:6-7.

21. Qur'an 16:3-4.

22. Qur'an 18:54.

23. Qur'an 16:125.

24. Qur'an 39:8.

25. Qur'an 39:49-50.

26. Qur'an 20:115.

27. Qur'an 2:214.

28. Qur'an 20:123.

29. Qur'an 21:1.

30. Qur'an 17:83.

31. Qur'an 10:92.

32. Qur'an 19:39.

33. Qur'an 39:56.

34. Qur'an 17:100.

35. Qur'an 57:22-24.

36. Qur'an 3:159.

37. Qur'an 2:195.

38. Qur'an 31:17.

39. Qur'an 82:6-8.

40. Qur'an 45:35.

41. Qur'an 57:14.

42. Qur'an 67:20.

43. Qur'an 7:146.

44. Qur'an 40:35.

45. Qur'an 16:23.

46. Qur'an 67:2.

47. Qur'an 57:20.

48. Qur'an 31:33.

49. Qur'an 31:20.

50. Qur'an 7:10.

51. Qur'an 10:14.

52. Qur'an 22:41.

53. Qur'an 31:17-19.

54. Qur'an 103:1-3.

55. Qur'an 14:24-26.

56. Qur'an 22:31.

57. Qur'an 14:27.

58. Qur'an 12:108.

59. Qur'an 3:110.

CHAPTER 6
Believers, Hypocrites, and Unbelievers
(Various Types of People)

SPECIFICALLY ADDRESSING THE BELIEVERS, God commands in Surah Al-Baqarah: "O you who believe, enter into Islam wholeheartedly; and do not follow the footsteps of Satan. Surely, he is your open enemy."[1] God loves the believers who seek His pleasure with their words as well as their deeds. He is affectionate to those who seek good in this world and good in the Hereafter, who worship their Lord in fear and in hope, and who spend out of what He has given them. However, there are some believers who serve God halfheartedly. They are satisfied if good befalls them but turn back if misery afflicts them. There are also some believers who seek the bounties of their Lord only for this world! Such people will find nothing for them in the Hereafter.

God knows the hypocrites, people who say by their words that they believe in God and the Last Day, but their behavior and deeds show that they are not really believers. When they find it difficult to follow the way of God, they make excuses and backslide. Certainly God knows who is a believer and who is a hypocrite. Hypocrites try to prove with their speech and by swearing that they are the best among the believers; yet, at heart, they are the most violent troublemakers and cause mischief in the land. God does not love the mischief-makers.

In contrast to the behavior of the believers who are overflowing with their love for God, unbelievers follow Satan. Unbelievers worship others besides God as His equals. They love others as they should love only God. If such people could see, they would certainly see their punishment. A humiliating punishment awaits those ignorant unbelievers who try to lead people astray from God's path through frivolous discourse and by ridiculing the divine guidance. There are some people among the unbelievers who dispute about God without knowledge and follow every rebellious Satan. Thus: "Allah did make for every prophet an enemy, evil ones from among men and jinn, inspiring each other with varnished falsehood to deceive. Had your Lord pleased, they would not have done it. Therefore, leave them and that which they forge. Let the hearts of those who do not believe in the Hereafter indulge in (their falsehoods); let them feel pleased about it, and let them earn what they are going to earn of evil."[2]

1. BELIEVER'S CHARACTER AND BEHAVIOR

Like bricks joined together in a house, human individuals have to be strong in character and beautiful in behavior in order to contribute in the accomplishment of the divine trust of eliminating corruption from the human society. As raw bricks of ugly mold cannot increase the strength and looks of a house, neither can an individual with a raw character full of ugly, selfish desires and undisciplined behavior strengthen society. The logical outcome of believing in God and of worshipping Him is the growth of people's moral character and the refinement of their behavior, without which they cannot fulfill their responsibility of being God's trustee.

1.1 Believers Do What They Believe

God tells people in Surah Al-Baqarah: "Among men is he who sells himself to seek the pleasure of Allah, and Allah is full of kindness to (His) servants."[3] Humankind, being God's trustee, is constantly being supervised and evaluated. Human efforts, behavior, and deeds, whether good or bad, are a reflection of people's intentions and beliefs. There are only two possibilities: either they are directed towards the completion of the divine assignment, or they follow an aimless existence. God states in the Qur'an: "He it is Who created the heavens and the earth…that He might try you, which of you is best in conduct."[4] The description of the believers, their character and behavior, is given in Surah Al-Fath: "Muhammad is the Messenger of Allah, and those with him are firm of heart against the unbelievers but compassionate among themselves. You will see them bowing down and prostrating themselves (in prayer), seeking the grace of Allah and His good pleasure. On their faces are the marks of their prostration. That is their description in the Taurat and their description in the Injeel. (The believers are) like a seed that sends forth its blade and makes itself strong. Then it becomes thick and stands on its own stem, filling the sowers with wonder and delight. As a result, it fills the unbelievers with rage at them. Allah has promised those among them who believe and do righteous deeds forgiveness and a great reward."[5] The ways people can transform themselves into believers by enhancing their faith with good intention and continual efforts are listed below:

1. *Believers Claim their Belief with Intention and Struggle*: Belief is not a mere word that people proclaim; it is a reality that imposes duties, a trust that carries requirements, and a struggle that demands patience and perseverance. It is not enough that people claim to believe. When they make this claim, they are not left alone. They are subjected to tests of their character and behavior to prove their sincerity and truth, just as gold is tested with fire to separate it from any cheap elements. Such testing of people's belief is a general and long-established, divine rule. God tells believers in Surah Al-Ankabut: "We did test those before them, and Allah will certainly know those who are true from those who are false."[6] One has to make a conscientious choice to believe in one's religion. A person is a believer because he chooses to believe and accepts the tenets, ideology, and beliefs of his religion. If he accepts Islam only because he is brought up as a Muslim, his faith remains deficient.

2. *Faith is a Trust that is Given to the Trustworthy*: Faith is a trust that is borne only by those who are worthy of it, have the strength to bear it, and are totally devoted to it. They must prefer it to their own comfort,

safety, security, and all temptations. This trust entails the implementation of God's commands in one's life and leading other people along the way, and it needs people who can patiently endure adversity. Believers often realize that they have no support or someone to defend them and that they lack the power with which to face tyranny. Another test is seeing corrupt people enjoying success, appreciated by the masses, and free of any hurdles in their way. Glory comes easily to them, and everything in life is theirs to enjoy. In contrast, the believer may find himself ignored, unnoticed, and undefended.

3. *People are not born but Struggle to become Trustworthy:* Why did God put believers to such hard tests or cause them so much suffering? People should realize that this is part of their development to overcome their weaknesses of character. This is required before they can take up the trust and fulfill its requirements. They must go through special preparations that can only be achieved through enduring real difficulties, withstanding pain, and overcoming desires, while being truly certain of God's support and His reward. The nature of testing and training depends on one's circumstances and the part one has to play. Therefore one should face the hardships with courage and patience, knowing well that these are for one's eventual good. God assigns people only those responsibilities for which they are suitable. God tells people in Surah Al-Araf: "As for those who believe and do good deeds, We do not impose on any person a duty except to the extent of his ability. They are the dwellers of Paradise; in it they shall abide."[7]

1.2 Believers' Behavior Confirms their Belief

Believers are described in Surah Al-Sajdah: "Their sides draw away from beds, they call upon their Lord in fear and in hope, and they spend out of what We have given them."[8] Believers are hardworking; they are not lazy, and they diligently attend to their duties towards God and their duties towards His creation. They are honest in their dealings and do not fulfill their needs and desires in wrong ways. Being human, people are likely to commit mistakes. In such situations, they call upon their Lord in fear and hope, repent, reform their behavior, and do good deeds.

Believers' character and behavior is fully described in Surah Al-Furqan: "The servants of (Allah) the Compassionate are those who walk on the earth in humility, and when the ignorant address them, they say, 'Peace.' (Allah's servants are) those who pass their night in worship, prostrating and standing. They are the ones who say: 'Our Lord! Avert from us the wrath of Hell, for its wrath is indeed an affliction grievous. Evil, indeed, is it as an abode and as a place in which to rest.' When they spend, they are not extravagant and not miserly, but (they) hold a just (balance) between those (extremes). They invoke not, with Allah, any other god, nor do they slay such life as Allah made sacred, except for just cause, nor do they commit fornication. Any who does this (not only) meets punishment, (but) the penalty on the Day of Judgment will be doubled for him. He will dwell therein in ignominy unless he repents, believes, and works righteous deeds, for Allah will change the evil of such persons into good, and Allah is forgiving, merciful. Whoever repents and does good has truly turned to Allah with an (acceptable) turning. (Allah's servants) do not bear witness to what is false, and when they pass by what is vain, they pass by nobly. When (Allah's servants) are reminded of the communications of their Lord, they do not fall down thereat deaf and blind. They are the ones who pray: 'O our Lord! Grant unto us wives and offspring who will be the comfort of our eyes, and give us (the grace) to lead the righteous.'"[9]

2 . GOD REWARDS PEOPLE'S EFFORTS

Life on earth is the most important part of peoples' existence according to Islam. Three of the most important objectives of a believer's life are to (1) live a good life in this world, (2) arrange for a good life in the

Hereafter and (3) secure safety from the torment of Hell. One's belief, worship of God, and good deeds are there for help. People have to reform themselves and work hard to achieve their objectives. God reminds people that it judgment depends on their efforts and that they shall have their portion of what they have earned. Efforts, however, should be proportionate to the relative importance of one's objectives. People have a life in this world and a life in the Hereafter. The life in this world is short, and in it people have to survive, overcome their weaknesses of character, and learn to adopt human behavior as required by God. They have to develop and establish just societies on earth for the welfare of its people. In doing so, they have to meet the expectations of their assignments as God's trustee. If people work hard honestly and to the best of their abilities, and if they behave like humans, following the divine model of humankind, then they will have good life in both worlds and be free from Hell.

However, if we go about in this world fulfilling our selfish needs and desires with a disregard for the legal and ethical ways in our efforts to achieve our needs and desires, it will not land us in a good eternal life, and it will not earn us freedom from Hell. God warns people: "But there are some people who say (by their behavior and deeds): 'Our Lord! Give us (Your bounties) in this world!' However, they will have no portion in the Hereafter."[10] God commands: "Be not like those who forgot Allah, so He made them forget their own selves!"[11] Such people ignore their mission of being God's trustee, and their efforts are only for the satisfaction of their desires, without any regard for what is right and permissible or unlawful according to the divine guidance. God's commands either motivate people to be honest and just or highlight the consequences of ignoring the divine guidance.

2.1 Islam consists of Honest Efforts and Just Dealings

God tells people in Surah Al-Baqarah that there are men who say (by their behavior and deeds): "Our Lord! Give us good in this world and good in the Hereafter and defend us from the torment of the Fire!' They shall have (in this world and in the Hereafter), their portion of what they have earned, and Allah is swift in reckoning."[12] For a Muslim, both the life in this world and life in the Hereafter are important. However, life in this world is the most important part of life because our lives in the Hereafter depend on our lives in this world and how we spend them. If they are spent according to God's commands, then they assure our salvation in the Hereafter. Both life in the world and life in the Hereafter are parts of Islam.

God has sent us to the earth with a mission as His trustee to develop earth as a habitat for humanity. How can He expect Muslims to ignore this world and to make only mosques as their living quarters? Islam does not expect humankind to take shelter in caves or to spend all life there worshipping God. However, Islam commands Muslims to own excellent character completely and to build a society on the Islamic principles of piety, hard work, justice, and charity and to be free of corruption, discrimination, exploitation, and oppression. Islam commands that we should excel all other societies in prosperity, learning, and wisdom, in order to make us the best nation. Islam also stresses the fact that happiness in the Hereafter greatly depends on the honest efforts of the believers to improve the life in this world. In this, we are being tested. This test requires that we follow God's commands during all facets of our lives on earth.

2.2 Life on Earth is the Most Important part of Islam

Our lives in the Hereafter depend on our lives on earth, and how we live them will determine our destiny. God tells us: "It is We Who have placed you (O humankind) with authority on earth and provided you therein with means for the fulfillment of your life: small are the thanks that you give!"[13] God has provided sufficient means for the whole of humanity to live in prosperity. We have to exploit and properly manage these natural resources for our benefit. An Islamic society that is built on hard work, truth, justice, and charity and that is free of corruption, discrimination, exploitation, and oppression would certainly provide all of the genuine requirements for this effort. Besides, if He wills, God can increase and decrease the produce. He has promised in the Qur'an that if we believe in Him and implement His law, He will increase our provisions: "And if they had kept up the Taurat and the Injeel and that which was revealed to them from their Lord, they would certainly have been nourished from above them and from beneath their feet."[14] "If the people of the towns had but believed and feared Allah, We should indeed have opened out to them (all kinds of) blessings from heaven and earth."[15] God also encourages us to make efforts to acquire good things, applying lawful means without exceeding limits: "O you who believe! Do not forbid yourselves the good things that Allah has made lawful for you, and do not exceed the limits. Surely, Allah does not love those who exceed the limits."[16]

2.3 Ignorance Breeds Weak and Marginal Believers

At the present time, the world is full of weak and marginal believers. Most of us are born in families of the believers, whether we are Muslims or the followers of other religions. Since religion is not taught in most contemporary secular schools, our knowledge of religion is marginal at best. We do not know much about the purpose of our creation, the responsibilities of our mission, the testing of our abilities, and our accountability for our behavior and deeds. That is why, "There are among men some who serve Allah, as it were, on the verge. If good befalls them, they are, therewith, well content, but if a trial comes to them, they turn on their faces,"[17] and start looking for alternatives, due to lack of trust in the Creator and His guidance. In desperation, such people generally look for support from false deities and corrupt people, adopting corrupt ways to survive: "He calls besides Allah upon that which does not harm him and that which does not profit him; that is the great straying. He calls upon him whose harm is nearer than his profit; evil certainly is the guardian, and evil certainly is the associate."[18]

Being God's trustee on earth, learning to manage our affairs is the very first obligation of humankind. With knowledge comes understanding, then obedience. One should know the guidelines before attempting to implement them. This makes it obligatory that believers should understand what is mentioned in Qur'an. To achieve this purpose, we have to study, understand, and implement the Qur'an in our lives. We are told in the Qur'an that those who will receive the highest places in Heaven are: "Those who, when reminded of the revelations of their Lord, do not behave like they were deaf and blind (but try to understand and act upon them)."[19] "We have made it a Qur'an in Arabic that you may be able to understand (and learn wisdom)."[20] Why was the Qur'an revealed? God reminds us: "(Here is) a book, which We have sent down to you, full of blessing, so the people may try to understand and take guidance."[21] "Those who listen to the advice and follow the best thereof; such are those whom Allah has guided, and such are the people of understanding."[22] God commands the believers, "And follow the best of the guidance revealed to you from your Lord, before the doom comes on you suddenly without your knowledge."[23] Believers are assured of God's help if they increase their knowledge of the Qur'an and follow it to the best of their abilities. God says in Surah Fatir: "Those who read the Qur'an, establish worship, and spend of what we have provided for them, secretly and openly, they look forward to a perpetual gain."[24]

3. HYPOCRITE'S CHARACTER AND BEHAVIOR

God has appointed people His trustees on earth to test their behavior and deeds. However, there are some people whose efforts, behavior, and deeds are directed towards the achievement of their own selfish desires and worldly gains without any regard for others. Since the objective of such people is to acquire all the comforts of this world in any way possible, whether legal or illegal, they will have nothing left for them in the Hereafter.

In Islam, the importance of one's obligations towards other people is of no less value than one's obligation towards God Himself. In many sayings of the Messenger, we have been told that God may forgive any shortcomings in the fulfillment of our duties towards Him, but He may not forgive our mistreatment of each other. An unjust oppressor will have to pay back the price of his misdeeds. Since the duties towards other human beings are the part of God's commands, these obligations towards God and His creation are equally important. Forgetting divine guidance during one's daily efforts is like forgetting God Himself. God warns: "And be not like those who forgot Allah, so He made them forget their own selves (that they are Allah's trustees). Such are the rebellious transgressors!"[25] Arrogance and envy blind such people's intellect and wisdom.

3.1 The Hypocrite's Behavior Negates Their Belief

In Surah Al-Baqarah, God highlights one of the worst weaknesses of human character and behavior. It is when people want to achieve their goals not by hard work, not by honesty, but by conceit, "And there are some people who say: 'We believe in Allah and the Last Day; and they are not at all believers. They desire to deceive Allah and those who believe, and they deceive only themselves, and they do not perceive. There is a disease in their hearts, so Allah added to their disease, and they shall have a painful chastisement because they lie."[26] Such people initiate conflicts in the guise of being a peacemaker, and they think that the believers are fools. God describes them in Surah Al-Baqarah: "When it is said to them, 'Make not mischief on the earth,' they say, 'Why we only want to make peace!' Surely, they are the ones who make mischief, but they realize it not. And when it is said to them, 'Believe as the people believe,' they say, 'Shall we believe as the fools believe?' Now surely they themselves are the fools, but they do not know. And when they meet those who believe, they say, 'We believe,' and when they are alone with their Satan, they say, 'Surely we are with you, we were only mocking.' Allah shall pay them back their mockery, and He leaves them alone in their inordinacy, blindly wandering on. These are they who buy error for the right direction, so their bargain shall bring no gain, nor are they the followers of the right direction."[27]

There is nothing more hateful in Islam than hypocrisy. This is due to the fact that hypocrites are not only perpetual liars, but also think that they can easily fool people without being noticed. They see themselves perfectly shielded by their intellect. The hypocrites claim to be believers when they truly do not believe. Thus, they try to deceive God and make fun of His knowledge and power. It was narrated by 'Abdullah bin 'Amr that the Prophet said: "Whoever has the following four (characteristics) will be a pure hypocrite, and whoever has one of the following four characteristics will have one characteristic of hypocrisy unless and until he gives it up. (1) Whenever he is entrusted, he betrays. (2) Whenever he speaks, he tells a lie. (3) Whenever he makes a covenant, he proves treacherous. (4) Whenever he quarrels, he behaves in a very imprudent, evil, and insulting manner."[28] All four of these character traits of hypocrites, as defined by the Prophet, involve lying in one form or another. They represent falsehood in intention, words, and action. Hence, when a person portrays all four, his case is that of complete hypocrisy. Anyone of these four traits represents a quarter of full hypocrisy. The first is being untrue to one's trust. A hypocrite thinks nothing of violating his trust if there is anything to be gained by such violation. Secondly, a hypocrite is a habitual liar. He thinks that he can get away with anything by assuring his listener that whatever he says is true, even though he is fully aware that it is not. The third trait is being untrue to one's promises. When he gives a promise, a hypocrite knows that he will be violating it at the first opportunity. He has no intention of remaining true to his promises unless there is nothing to be gained by breaking them. The last trait is being too hard when involved in a dispute. He goes far beyond good manners. He resorts to exaggeration as well as name-calling, paying no respect to Islamic values. By contrast, a believer is a person whose actions give credence to his beliefs. Whatever he claims is certainly true.

3.2 Cowardice and Lack of Courage lead People to Hypocrisy

Why are some people hypocrites by nature? On a superficial level, it could be lack of courage or cowardice, but in reality it is lack of faith because it is faith that makes people physically and morally strong. God tells us in Surah Al-Ankabut: "And among men is he who says: 'We believe in Allah,' but when he is persecuted in (the way of) Allah, he thinks the persecution of men to be as the chastisement of Allah. And if there was assistance from your Lord, they would most certainly say: 'Surely, we were with you.' What! Is not Allah the best knower of what is in the breasts of mankind? And most certainly Allah will know those who believe, and most certainly He will know the hypocrites."[29] These verses describe a type of people who may be found in every community, just as they were found at the time of the Prophet. They are those who do not have the courage of their convictions, who cannot stand in defense of what they profess to believe. They are not prepared to fulfill the duties imposed by faith, and instead they stand behind, taking no share in the struggle for faith. If those who fight and struggle for their faith suffer a defeat, these hypocrites raise their heads and boast about their wisdom and realism. If the fighters come back victorious, the hypocrites waste no time in pretending to have given them their full support, claiming that they were part of their victory. In this way, they seek praise for something that they have not done. This is a type of people who thrives on cowardice and false pretenses.

Hypocrites are those people who do not honor even their self-imposed commitments and promises. In Surah Al-Tawbah, people are told of those whose cowardice induced stinginess and forced them to dishonor their promises, even with God: "And some of them made a covenant with Allah: 'If He gave us out of His grace, we will certainly give alms and act righteously.' But when He gave them out of His grace, they became miserly, and they turned their backs (upon their covenant). So He caused hypocrisy to take root in their hearts and to remain therein till the day when they shall meet Him because they failed to perform towards Allah what they had promised to Him and because they told lies."[30]

3.3 Hypocrisy forces People to be Unjust, even to their Ownselves

How can a good believer turn into a hypocrite? This could be the natural outcome of a certain type of individual behavior as described in Surah Al-Araf: "And recite to them the narrative of him to whom We give Our communications, but he withdraws himself from them, so Satan overtakes him, so he is of those who go astray. If We had pleased, We would certainly have exalted him thereby, but he clung to the earth and followed his low desire. So his parable is as the parable of the dog: if you attack him he lolls out his tongue, and if you leave him alone he lolls out his tongue. This is the parable of the people who reject Our commands. Therefore, relate the narrative that they may reflect. Evil is the likeness of the people who reject Our commands and are unjust to their own-selves."[31] God warns that such people cannot escape His punishment. They cannot spare themselves the grievous suffering that awaits them, and they may have no support in trying to evade it. Such people have been advised to reflect and reform or be ready for sufferings: "Do not think that they will escape punishment. A grievous suffering awaits them."[32] If such people do not reform their character and behavior, how can they escape from God's punishment? "(Consider) a town safe and secure to which its means of subsistence come in abundance from every quarter, but its people became ungrateful to Allah's favors, so Allah afflicted them with hunger and fear in punishment for their evil deeds."[33] Such is the punishment of your Lord when He punishes the towns (people) while they are unjust; surely, His punishment is painful, severe."[34]

The coming of the resurrection and the occurrence of the Hereafter are a truth that inevitably has to take place. The people of past communities who denied the accountability for their behavior and deeds in the Hereafter and continued their sinful lives ultimately became worthy of God's punishment even in this world. God asks people, "What can Allah gain by your punishment, if you are grateful and you believe? Allah is always responsive to gratitude, All-Knowing."[35] After mentioning the fate of corrupt communities of the past, God tells the people: "We did not do them injustice, but they were unjust to themselves. So their gods whom they called upon besides Allah did avail them nothing when the decree of your Lord came to pass, and they added but to their ruin."[36] God assures prosperity for people who behave properly. Remember when your Lord proclaimed: "If you give thanks, I would certainly give to you more, and if you are ungrateful for My favors, My chastisement is truly severe."[37] Greedy people who always desire more should not forget what God said to Moses when he desired to see Him: "O Moses! Surely I have chosen you above the people with My messages and by My speaking (to you); therefore, take hold of what I give to you, and be among the thankful."[38] God enquires from people: "Why were there not among the generations before you those possessing sense enough to have forbidden people from making mischief in the earth, except a few of those whom We delivered from among them? The wrongdoers followed after nothing more than what pleased them, and they were truly wicked. However, your Lord never destroys towns unjustly if their people acted well."[39]

3.4 Hypocrites are Pleasingly Humble and Arrogantly Corrupt

One of the worst characteristics that Islam dislikes is hypocrisy. The Messenger spoke about it several times, and every time he used some graphic description that showed how ugly and unbecoming all types of hypocrisy are. In one Hadith narrated by Abu Huraira, the Messenger, who wanted his audience to fully understand his purpose, said: "One of the worst people is a double-faced man who comes to one group with one face and to another group with a totally different face."[40] A similar Hadith is reported by Ammar ibn Yasir, who quotes the Messenger as saying: "Whoever is double-faced in this life will have two tongues of fire in the Hereafter."[41] In this latter Hadith, the Messenger gave a graphic description of hypocrites. The description concentrates on the hypocrite's tongue because it is with his words that he tries to cheat people. His speech is always pleasing to his audience. It is immaterial to him if what he says is untrue because all that he cares about is his own interest. In this way, he appears to be pleasingly humble, even though he is arrogantly corrupt. Because a hypocrite relies on lying, thinking that he could cheat his way out of any difficulty, God will give him two tongues of fire on the Day of Judgment. This is a horrid picture, but it very much represents such individuals.

God warns us about hypocrites in Surah Al-Baqarah: "And among men is he whose speech about the life of this world causes you to wonder, and he calls on Allah to witness as to what is in his heart. Yet, he is the fiercest in enmity. And whenever he gets the chance, he goes about the earth spreading mischief and destroying crops and livestock; though Allah does not love mischief-making. When it is said to him, guard against (the punishment of) Allah, pride carries him off to sin. Therefore, Hell is sufficient for him, and certainly it is an evil resting place."[42]

4. UNBELIEVER'S CHARACTER AND BEHAVIOR

The behavior of both believers and unbelievers was elaborated in the story of two men in Surah Al-Kahf. In this story, the unbeliever was ungrateful and arrogant, and he was punished by God for his attitude and behavior. As for the unbeliever: "He possessed much wealth. So he said to his companion, while he disputed with him: 'I have greater wealth than you and am mightier in followers.' Then he (and his companion) entered his garden while he was unjust to himself. He said: 'I do not think that this will ever perish, and I do not think the Hour will come. Even if I am returned to my Lord, I will most certainly find a returning place better than this.'"[43] "His wealth was (eventually) destroyed. Thus, he began to wring his hands for what he had spent on it, while it lay fallen down upon its roofs. All he could say was: 'Alas, would I have not associated anyone with my Lord.' There was no one besides Allah to help him, nor could he be of any help to himself. (Then he knew) that the only protection comes from Allah, the True One. He is the best to reward and the best to give success."[44]

4.1 Their Deeds will be of Intense Regret to Unbelievers

In many verses of the Qur'an, God describes the behavior of those who neither believe nor rely on God alone but associate others with Him in worship: "Yet there are men who take (for worship) others besides Allah, as equal. They love them as they should love Allah. But those of faith are overflowing in their love for Allah. If only the unrighteous could see, behold, they would see the penalty. To Allah belongs all power, and Allah will strongly enforce the penalty."[45] God tells us that the unbelievers will regret their behavior in the Hereafter, "When those who were followed shall renounce those who followed (them), and they see the chastisement and their ties are cut asunder, those who followed shall say: 'Had there been for us a return, then we would renounce them as they have renounced us.' Thus, will Allah show them their deeds to be intense regret to them, and they shall not come forth from the fire."[46]

The real aim of Islam is to help people to recognize their real, dignified position in the universe by freeing themselves from servitude to idols, other human beings, various objects of the universe, and even their own individual selfish desires. For this purpose, God advises that people should sincerely serve God and should not pollute their worship of God by serving anything else. After all, God says: "If you reject (Allah), truly Allah has no need of you."[47] After describing the behavior of unbelievers: "Then he sets up rivals with Allah, thus misleading others from His path,"[48] God asks: "Is one who worships devoutly during the hours of the night, prostrating himself or standing (in adoration), who takes heed of the Hereafter, and who places his hope in the mercy of his Lord (like one who does not)? Say: 'Are those equal, those who know and those who do not know?' It is those who are endued with understanding that receive admonition."[49] Clearly, the answer is that only believers will be guided to succeed.

4.2 Unbelievers Resist the Implementation of Divine Law

People are told in Surah Luqman: "Among men there are some people who take instead a frivolous discourse to lead astray from Allah's path without knowledge, who hold the call to the way of Allah to ridicule. A humiliating chastisement awaits them. And when Our verses are recited to such a person, he turns away in arrogance, as if he had not heard them, or as if there were deafness in both his ears. So give him tidings of a painful doom."[50] The implementation of divine law, no doubt will result in a just society that is prosperous, peaceful, and secure. Then why do the people ignore? God tells us: "They did not become divided until after knowledge had come to them out of envy (rivalry) among themselves."[51] They also want to benefit from the injustice done to others. Many of them are guilty of corruption and try to take advantage of others, paying no attention to other people's rights. According to the Qur'an they are those: (1) who are unjustly proud in the earth, (2) who do not believe in the meeting in the Hereafter,[52] (3) who missed prayers and (4) who followed after their selfish desires?[53]

God warns the unbelievers about their misconceptions and arrogance. Generally, corrupt people who occupied the place of leadership without any right and their followers think that this world is a purposeless place where they are not answerable to anyone. They believe there is no specific supreme entity, and they consider their own deities as the associates of God. They are not inclined to believe that the Qur'an is the word of the Lord. They have a strange, erroneous concept of apostleship on the basis of which they propose strange criteria in judging the Messenger's claim to it. In their evaluation, one great challenge to the truth of Islam is that their elders, important chiefs of their tribes and ethnic groups, and so-called government leaders do not accept Islam and that only a few young men, some poor folks, and slaves affirm faith in it. They think that resurrection, life after death, the rewards and punishments of the Hereafter are all fabrications whose occurrence is absolutely out of any possibility. However, God tells people:, "Of these (humankind and jinn), all have ranks according to their deeds, so that Allah may pay them back fully for their deeds, and they shall not be wronged."[54] On the day when unbelievers will be exposed to the fire of Hell, they will be told: "You did away with your good things in your life of the world, and you enjoyed them for a while. So today you will be rewarded with the punishment of abasement because you were unjustly proud in the land and because you transgressed."[55] Anas ibn Malik reported that Allah's Messenger said: "Verily, Allah does not treat a believer unjustly with regard to his virtues. He will confer upon him His blessing in this world and will give him reward in the Hereafter. As regards a non-believer, he will be made to taste the reward of what he has done for himself (his good deeds in this world) so much that when it will be the Hereafter, he will find no virtue for which he should be rewarded."[56]

4.3 Unbelievers of Accountability try to confuse People about God

God says in Surah Al-Hajj: "Yet, among men there is he who disputes about Allah without knowledge and follows every rebellious Satan. Against him it is written down that whoever takes him for a friend, he shall lead him astray and guide him to the chastisement of the burning fire."[57] Such ignorant people dispute about the Creator of the universe without even consulting the divine books. The discovery of the truth is not their intention. They know what the truth is. It is their arrogance and mischief-making nature that compel them to behave in this way to confuse others. God tells us about such people that they will be disgraced in both worlds: "And among people there is one who disputes about Allah without knowledge and without guidance and without an illuminating book, turning away haughtily that he may lead others away from the way of Allah; for him is disgrace in this world and on the Day of Resurrection. We will make him taste the punishment of burning. This is due to what your two hands have sent before, and because Allah is not in the least unjust to the servants."[58]

Such people are the followers of Satan and try to mislead others to immoral and inhuman behavior in the name of freedom, modernity, and progress, "Most surely the devils inspire doubts and objections into the hearts of their friends that they might dispute with you, and if you obey them, you shall most surely be polytheists."[59] God has warned people that such individuals have opposed each and every messenger of God and those men among people who tried to reform society. Therefore, one should not worry about them: "Allah did make for every prophet an enemy, evil ones from among men and jinn, inspiring each other with varnished falsehood to deceive. Had your Lord pleased, they would not have done it. Therefore, leave them and that which they forge. Let the hearts of those who do not believe in the Hereafter indulge in (their falsehoods); let them feel pleased about it, and let them earn what they are going to earn of evil."[60] God commanded the Messenger: "Say: 'Have you then considered that what you call upon besides Allah? Will they, if Allah desires to afflict me with harm, remove His harm? And if Allah desires to show me mercy, will they be able to withhold His mercy?' Say: 'Allah is sufficient for me; on Him do the reliant rely.'"[61]

NOTES

1. Qur'an 2:208.
2. Qur'an 6:112-113.
3. Qur'an 2:207.
4. Qur'an 11:7.
5. Qur'an 48:29.
6. Qur'an 29:3.
7. Qur'an 7:42.
8. Qur'an 32:16.
9. Qur'an 25:63-74.
10. Qur'an 2:200.
11. Qur'an 59:19.
12. Qur'an 2:201-202.
13. Qur'an 7:10.
14. Qur'an 5:66.
15. Qur'an 7:96.
16. Qur'an 5:87.
17. Qur'an 22:11.
18. Qur'an 22:12-13.
19. Qur'an 25:73.
20. Qur'an 41:3.
21. Qur'an 38:29.

22. Qur'an 39:18.

23. Qur'an 39:55.

24. Qur'an 35:29.

25. Qur'an 59:19.

26. Qur'an 2:8-10.

27. Qur'an 2:11-16.

28. Sahih Bukhari 3.43.639.

29. Qur'an 29:10-11.

30. Qur'an 9:75-77.

31. Qur'an 7:175-177.

32. Qur'an 3:188.

33. Qur'an 16:112.

34. Qur'an 11:102.

35. Qur'an 4:147.

36. Qur'an 11:101.

37. Qur'an 14:7.

38. Qur'an 7:144.

39. Qur'an 11:116-117.

40. Sahih Bukhari 4.56.699.

41. Abu Dawud 41.4855.

42. Qur'an 2:204-206.

43. Qur'an 18:34-36.

44. Qur'an 18:42-44.

45. Qur'an 2:165.

46. Qur'an 2:166-167.

47. Qur'an 39:7.

48. Qur'an 39:8.

49. Qur'an 39:9.

50. Qur'an 31:6-7.

51. Qur'an 42:14 & 45:17.

52. Qur'an 7:146-147.

53. Qur'an 19:59.

54. Qur'an 46:19.

55. Qur'an 46:20.

56. Sahih Muslim 39.6739.

57. Qur'an 22:3-4.

58. Qur'an 22:8-10.

59. Qur'an 6:121.

60. Qur'an 6:112-113.

61. Qur'an 39:38.

CHAPTER 7

HUMAN PERSONALITY THAT GOD LOVES
(God Loves Those Who Try to Excel)

GOD INVITES AND MOTIVATES humankind to His love by telling the Messenger in Surah Al-Imran: "Say: 'If you love Allah, then follow me; Allah will love you and forgive you your faults, and Allah is Forgiving, Merciful."[1] God says in Surah Al-Ahzab: "Indeed, there is for you, in the Messenger of Allah, a good example to follow."[2] Why is God again and again commanding people to accept the Messenger as a role model? One can find the answer in what the Messenger has himself stated: "I have been sent for the purpose of perfecting good morals."[3] In other words, the foremost purpose of his mission was to guide people to improve their character and behavior. His achievement as a role model was also confirmed by God Himself in Surah Al-Qalam: "Most surely, you conform (yourself, O Muhammad,) to sublime morality."[4] Again 'Abdullah ibn Amar said: "The Messenger of Allah was neither ill-mannered nor rude. He used to say that the better people among you are those who are best in their moral character."[5]

1. WHAT BRINGS THE BELIEVERS NEARER TO GOD?

Humankind has many physical, emotional, and moral weaknesses that, if not corrected, can hinder its growth and progress. Divine guidance is there to help remove these shortcomings. The Messenger of Islam worked ceaselessly to propagate this divine message to bring people under its influence and to strengthen the moral character of the people so that the world could really become an abode for humanity and not be a jungle inhabited by beasts.

1.1 Guidance and His Mercy are Only from God
Believers are aware that the Qur'an was revealed for the benefit of all

humankind. God's advice to Adam before he left Paradise was: "Get you down all from here; and if, as is sure, there comes to you guidance from me, whosoever follows My guidance, on them shall be no fear, nor shall they grieve."[6] God has also promised: "As for those who were led to the guidance, God increases them in their guidance and causes them to grow in their piety."[7] God's guidance is within the comprehension of each one of us. This encourages whoever wants to learn his obligations as God's trustee on earth. God reminds us again and again in Surah Al-Qamar: "We have indeed made the Qur'an easy to understand and remember; then is there any that will receive admonition?"[8] As members of humanity, we should say, "Yes," to God's invitation to this friendly advice. It is for our own good, both in this life and in the Hereafter. God tells people: "As for those who believe and do good deeds, We do not impose on any person a duty except to the extent of his ability. They are the dwellers of Paradise; in it they shall abide."[9]

1.2 Physical and Moral Strength

Islam is a faith that embodies the ideology and the basic principles from which Islamic laws and actions are derived. For this reason, action is firmly linked with faith in many verses of the Qur'an. In Surah Al-Asr, people are warned: "Man is a certain loser, save those who have faith and do righteous deeds."[10] In Surah Al-Baqarah, good news is given to the believers: "Give good tidings to those who believe and do good deeds that they shall reside in gardens beneath which rivers flow."[11] In Surah Al-Nahl, both men and women are reassured: "Whoever works righteousness, man or woman, and has faith, verily, to him will We give a new life, a life that is good and pure, and We will bestow on them their reward according to the best of their actions."[12]

How does Islam achieve unity between faith and action, and how does it relate faith in God and the observation of religious teachings to matters that are purely materialistic? In Islam, all individual efforts that are just and do not violate moral values and human rights during secular or materialistic activities are a form of worshipping God. God commands in Surah Al-Ahzab: "O you who believe! Be careful of your duty to Allah, and speak the truth. He will put your deeds into a right state for you and forgive you your faults, and whoever obeys Allah and His Messenger, he indeed achieves a mighty success."[13] How serious God is in supporting, strengthening, and protecting the believers is illustrated by a sacred Hadith narrated by Abu Huraira in which the Messenger said: "Allah said, 'I will declare war against him who shows hostility to my pious worshipper. The most beloved things with which My slave comes nearer to Me is doing what I have enjoined upon him, and My slave keeps on coming closer to Me through doing extra deeds besides what is obligatory, till I love him. So I then become his sense of hearing with which he hears, his sense of sight with which he sees, his hand with which he grips, and his leg with which he walks, and if he asks Me, I will give him, and if he asks My protection, I will protect him."[14]

1.3 Security and Prosperity are Only from God

God has appointed angels to look after believers who have true faith in God, steadfastly stand by their commitments, and strive strenuously to translate their belief into practice by worshiping God and doing good deeds. God tells us: "(As for) those who say: 'Our Lord is Allah,' then continue in the right way, the angels descend upon them, saying: 'Fear not, nor be grieved, and receive good news of the garden that you were promised.'"[15] The angels reassure them: "We are your guardians in this world's life and in the Hereafter, and you shall have therein what you desire, and you shall have therein what you ask for, a provision from the Forgiving, the Merciful."[16]

God does not change the good condition of a people as long as they remain good by not committing sins etc. People are asked to remember when your Lord proclaimed: "If you give thanks, I would certainly give to you more, and if you are ungrateful for My favors, My chastisement is truly severe."[17] "He gives you of all that you ask Him, and if you count Allah's favors, you will not be able to number them. Most surely, humankind is very unjust, very ungrateful."[18] However, if people commit sins and continue doing so for an extended period of time, that is bound to deteriorate the social conditions of the society in which they live, and then God's punishment comes due.

In order to maintain good conditions in a society, people who commit sins are strongly urged to reform themselves through repentance, which God out of His grace has bound Himself to accept. Repentance that is deeply felt by an individual indicates that he has undergone a total transformation that is associated with sincerely regretting past mistakes. Such a change of attitude when a person still enjoys good health and still aspires to a brighter future is normally accompanied by a genuine desire for self-purification and a resolve to follow a different way of life. In such a case: "Allah will, indeed, accept the repentance of only those who do evil out of ignorance and then repent shortly afterwards. It is they to whom Allah turns in His mercy. Allah is All-Knowing, Wise."[19] People's repentance improves their character and transforms them into hardworking, honest, and trustworthy individuals. When living together, such people will develop into a safe and prosperous community. God commands the Messenger: "Say: 'O people! I am only a plain warner to you. Then (as for) those who believe and do good, they shall have forgiveness and an honorable sustenance.'"[20] God's forgiveness and an honorable sustenance from Him translate into a peaceful and prosperous society.

1.4 God Helps His Friends to Succeed on Earth and in the Hereafter

God has cited several incidents from the lifetime of the Messenger to illustrate what kinds of behavior earn His friendship. He says in Surah Al-Maidah: "Whoever takes Allah and His Messenger and those who believe for a guardian, then surely the party of Allah is they that shall be triumphant."[21] In Surah Yunus, the believers are reassured: "Now surely the friends of Allah—they shall neither fear nor shall they grieve. Those who believe and guard against evil, they shall have good news in this world's life and in the Hereafter. There is no changing the words of Allah; that is the mighty achievement."[22] In Surah Al-Fath, God tells about the believers who swore allegiance to the Messenger: "Certainly, Allah was well-pleased with the believers when they swore allegiance to you under the tree, and He knew what was in their hearts, so He sent down tranquility upon them and rewarded them with a near victory."[23] Summarizing their general behavior, God says about believers: "You shall not find a people who believe in Allah and the Hereafter befriending those who act in opposition to Allah and His Messenger, even though they were their fathers, or their sons, or their brothers, or their kinsfolk. These are they into whose hearts He has impressed faith, and whom He has strengthened with an inspiration from Him, and He will cause them to enter gardens beneath which rivers flow, abiding therein. Allah is well-pleased with them, and they are well-pleased with Him. These are Allah's party; now surely, the party of Allah is the successful one."[24]

1.5 God is the Protecting Guardian of the Believers

God tells the Messenger and the believers in Surah Al-Rum: "We sent before you messengers to their people, so they came to them with clear arguments. Then We gave the punishment to those who were guilty; and helping the believers is ever incumbent on Us."[25] God assures believers of His help in Surah Al-Mumin: "We help Our messengers and those who believe in this world's life and on the day when the witnesses shall stand."[26] "O you who believe! If you help (the cause of) Allah, He will help you and make firm your feet."[27] He reminds in Surah Al-Fath: "Surely, We have given to you a clear victory. Allah will forgive your past and future shortcomings. He will complete His favors upon you and guide you to the straight way. Further, Allah will help you with a mighty help. He it is Who sent down tranquility into the hearts of the believers that they might have more faith added to their faith. Allah's are the forces of the heavens and the earth, and Allah is Knowing, Wise."[28] As stated in Surah Al-Baqarah: "Allah is the protector of those who believe. He brings them out of the darkness into the light. (As to) those who disbelieve, their patrons are devils who take them out of the light into the darkness; they are the inmates of the fire, in it they shall abide."[29]

1.6 None Despair of the Lord's Mercy except Unbelievers

Life on earth is a perpetual struggle between good and evil. God created humankind in a certain way and sent messengers with guidance to lead a happy human life. The messengers' role was to highlight what behavior is beneficent and avoids problems and misery. What they have conveyed is a complete message that outlines an integrated system devised by God, the Creator of humankind, Who knows what is appropriate and suitable for implementation in human life and what will bring real happiness. Thus, whoever obeys God's rules is a beneficiary. The benefit is immediate, as the rules were made to spare people affliction, contradiction, and confusion.

In Surah Yusuf, life struggle of Joseph provides guidance to humanity. The main traits of the story's characters reappear across time in the different people. One can find many similarities in the stories of: (1) Joseph and his brothers, (2) Moses and Pharaoh, (3) Muhammad and the Makkans, and (4) the people and corrupt governments of the present. From Surah Yusuf, people learn that during hardships, one should be patient and seek God's help, that God answers the prayers of His servants, and that none despair of God's help except unbelieving people. Joseph's father said: "O my sons! Go and inquire respecting Joseph and his brother, and despair not of Allah's mercy. Surely, none despair of Allah's mercy except the unbelieving people."[30] Since human efforts can avail nothing against God's will, one should not use evil means to help resolve one's difficulties.

Being in the best interest of humankind, both in this world and in the Hereafter, efforts to improve human character and behavior should continue irrespective of hardship and of opposition by people who are corrupt and unjust. God commands a person to bear with patience the hardships that one may have to face in the implementation of faith till God's judgment arrives and to avoid the impatience that caused suffering and affliction to the messenger Jonah. God commands in Surah Al-Qalam: "So wait patiently for the judgment of your Lord, and be not like the companion of the fish, who cried out in despair?"[31] God is always merciful; therefore, one should not be despairing of God's mercy. Also, consider the case of Abraham, who was given the good news of a son when he was of very old age. After his surprise at the news: "They (the angels) said: 'We give you good news with truth; therefore, be not of the despairing.' Abraham said: 'Who despairs of the mercy of his Lord except the misguided?'"[32]

2. GOD LOVES PEOPLE WHO PERFECT THEIR MORALS

The objective of Islamic worship is to reform people. Islamic forms of worship are not some sort of mystical exercises that link people with some unknown, mysterious being and that subject them to performing useless acts and meaningless movements. All Islamic compulsory forms of worship are designed as exercises and training to enable people to acquire correct morals and habits, to live righteously, and to adhere to these virtues throughout their individual lives under whatever circumstances. Besides worship, guidance has also been provided as to what is expected from people, what is their mission in life, what should be their accomplishments, and how they will be tried, evaluated, and rewarded. At various places in the Qur'an, God has told us about the kind of people He loves or does not love. Such character traits and human behaviors are highlighted in this section.

2.1 God Loves those who are Patient, Firm and Steadfast

In the ups and downs of life, when difficulties and hardships confront people, and when difficulties and sufferings become long, it is patience that keeps the believer resolute and safe from disappointment, desperation, and frustration. Patience is a basic quality with which a person needs to shape his life in this world and in the next. It is patience that prepares people to tolerate hardships and difficulties. It gives hope and makes people wait for positive results, however long that may take. Patience increases self-confidence and assures people that difficulties and hardships will eventually disappear and that success and prosperity will appear again. Therefore, the coming of relief should be awaited with patience, peace, and conviction. God commands believers in Surah Al-Baqarah: "Seek (Allah's) help through patience and prayer, and most surely it is a hard thing except for the humble ones."[33] The people who are patient are not short tempered and arrogant, but calm and humble.

God has stressed that no person can escape the tests and trials that are an integral part of life in this world. One should be alert and ready when hardships and difficulties appear. These hardships should not frighten people and make them disappointed or disheartened. God reminds believers in Surah Al-Imran that they are not alone in this struggle: "Many were the prophets on whose side fought a large number of people devoted to Allah. They never lost heart for all they had to suffer in Allah's way, nor did they weaken (in will) or give in. And Allah loves those who are firm and steadfast."[34]

2.2 God Loves those who Fight in His way in Ranks

In Surah An-Nisa, God promises help and reward to all those who fight in the way prescribed by God: "Whoever fights in the way of Allah, be he slain or be he victorious, on him We shall bestow a vast reward."[35] Furthermore, God commands the believers to fight in self-defense and for the defense of human rights. "Why you should not fight in the way of Allah for the sake of those helpless men, women, and children who, being weak, have been oppressed and are crying out, 'Our Lord! Deliver us from this habitation, whose inhabitants are unjust oppressors.'"[36] God also orders the believers to fight in self-defense with those hypocrites and disbelievers who initiate fighting with the believers: "Seize them wherever you find them and slay them. Do not take any of them as friends and helpers."[37] However, those hypocrites are excluded from attack who have joined a people with whom believers have a treaty. Likewise, those hypocrites who maintain a state of neutrality and are averse to fighting either against the believers or their own people are to be free from any attack from the believers. "Allah has left no cause for aggression against them if they leave you alone, refrain from fighting against you, and have a desire to make peace with you."[38] God commanded His Messenger to fight and urged the believers to do so because: "Whoever pleads a good cause will get a share from it, and whoever pleads an evil cause will get a share from it, for Allah keeps a strict watch over everything."[39] "(Since) death will come wherever one may be, even in fortified towers,"[40] the believers should not be afraid of death in this pursuit.

Since Islam is a religion of morality, believers are commanded to fight in self-defense like a firm and compact wall, but they are not in this pursuit to break their contracts, agreements, and treaties. In Surah Al-Saff, believers are told: "Surely, Allah loves those who fight in His way in ranks as if they were a firm and compact wall."[41] However, in Surah Al-Tawbah, believers are commanded not to initiate war by breaking contracts and agreements: "(But the treaties are) not dissolved with those of the idolaters with whom you made an agreement and who have not failed you in anything and have not backed up any one against you. So fulfill their agreement to the end of their term. Surely Allah loves those who are the righteous."[42] Believers are also commanded not to initiate fighting: "As long as they are true to you, be true to them. Surely, Allah loves those who keep their duty."[43]

2.3 God loves the Just who Act and Judge Equitably

It is mandatory in Islam that each person should try to establish justice under all circumstances. Neither a person's self-interest nor the self-interest of his parents, family, or relatives should come in the way of justice. Neither richness nor poverty should influence any judgment. One should not plead for the dishonest or sinful person. Efforts should be made to guard that blame or sin should not be associated with an innocent person. God commands believers to give trust into the care of those persons who are worthy of trust and to judge with justice among people. In Surah An-Nisa, God commands: "O you who believe, be maintainers of justice, bearers of witness for Allah's sake, though it may be against your own selves or (your) parents or near relatives. Whether he is rich or poor, Allah can best protect both. Therefore, do not follow your low desires lest you deviate, and if you swerve or turn aside, then surely Allah is aware of what you do."[44] The aim of divine guidance is to serve human interest, to help people build a happy life in a community characterized by justice. Justice must be achieved at all levels, within the family, the local community, the social hierarchy, and the political system. God's says in a sacred Hadith: "My servants, I have forbidden Myself injustice and made injustice forbidden to you. Therefore, do not act unjustly to one another."[45]

In several places in the Qur'an, God stresses the importance of justice by saying that He loves those who do justice and who judge and act equitably with both believers and unbelievers. In Surah Al-Maidah, believers are commanded: "O you who believe! Be upright for Allah, bearers of witness with justice, and let not hatred of a people incite you not to act equitably. Act equitably, that is nearer to piety, and be careful of your duty to Allah. Surely, Allah is aware of what you do."[46] God commands kindness and justice in dealing with the unbelievers who are not hostile to Islam. In Surah Al-Mumtahinah, believers are told: "Allah does not forbid you respecting those who have not made war against you on account of your religion, and who have not driven you forth from your homes, that you show them kindness and deal with them justly. Surely, Allah loves the doers of justice."[47] Even when it comes to those people who commit all sorts of sins, God commands us to judge them fairly. In Surah Al-Maidah, believers are told: "(They are) listeners of a lie, devourers of what is forbidden. Therefore, if they come to you, judge between them or turn aside from them. If you turn aside from them, they shall not harm you in any way. If you judge, judge between them with equity. Surely, Allah loves those who judge equitably."[48]

In Surah Al-Hujurat, God commands people to make peace between two fighting parties with justice: "And if two parties of the believers quarrel, make peace between them. But if one of them acts wrongfully towards the other, fight that who acts wrongfully until he returns to Allah's command. Then if it returns, make peace between them with justice, and act equitably. Surely, Allah loves those who act equitably."[49]

2.4 God loves the Pious Who are United and Trust Him

Religious activities should be carried out with the pure intention of helping people to become better individuals, which is in accord with the divine guidance. It should not be for creating disunity among the believers. People should be alert and should discourage hypocrites from propagating their version of Islam. God tells about such people in Surah Al-Tawbah: "There are those who put up a mosque by way of mischief and infidelity, to disunite the believers, and in preparation for one who warred against Allah and His Messenger aforetime. They will, indeed, swear that their intention is nothing but good, but Allah does declare that they are certainly liars."[50] God commands us: "Never stand you forth therein. There is a mosque whose foundation was laid from the first day on piety; it is more worthy of the standing forth (for prayer) therein. In it are men who love to be purified, and Allah loves those who make themselves pure."[51] God asks us to reflect and decide for ourselves: "Which then is best: he that lays his foundation on piety to Allah and His good pleasure, or he that lays his foundation on an undermined sand-cliff ready to crumble to pieces? And it does crumble to pieces with him into the fire of Hell, and Allah guides not people that do wrong."[52] Addressing the Messenger, God tells the believers that He loves those who always trust Him and His help: "Thus, it is due to mercy from Allah that you deal with them gently, and had you been rough, hardhearted, they would certainly have dispersed from around you. Therefore, forgive them, ask forgiveness for them, and consult with them in the affair. So when you have decided, then place your trust in Allah. Surely, Allah loves those who trust Him."[53]

2.5 God loves Trustworthy Worshippers who fulfill their Promises

A believer's journey in Islam has various distinct markers along the way. These markers highlight the stage of one's development and progress as a human. When people believe in Islam and worship God as set forth in the Qur'an and Sunnah, they should notice remarkable changes in their character and behavior. Such people are those who fulfill their promises: "Yea, whoever fulfills his promise and guards against evil—then surely Allah loves the God-fearing."[54] Such people are trustworthy and judge people with justice. In Surah Al-Nisa, God commands: "Surely, Allah commands you to make over trusts to their owners and that when you judge between people you judge with justice. Surely, Allah admonishes you with what is excellent. Surely, Allah is seeing, hearing."[55] God also tells us that such people are: "Those who faithfully observe their trusts and their covenants, and (those) who guard their prayers."[56] Since Allah admonishes with what is excellent, this should be reflected in people's character and behavior. As such, if people do not keep their trusts and promises, then certainly their belief and prayers need to be revisited.

2.6. God loves the Generous, Forgiving, and Kind who restrain their Anger

God commands the believers to spend in charity, control their anger, forgive people, and do good to others. This is because God loves those who do good deeds. In Surah Al-Baqarah, God commands: "Spend in the way of Allah, and cast not yourselves to destruction with your own hands, and do good to others. Surely, Allah loves the doers of good."[57] In Surah Al-Imran, God says the righteous are: "Those who spend (freely in charity), whether in prosperity or in adversity, who restrain anger, and who pardon people, for Allah loves those who do good deeds."[58]

Although God does not like those people who break their promises, agreements, and contracts, He commands the believers to forgive such deceitful people and overlook their misdeeds. In Surah Al-Maidah, we are informed and then commanded: "Because of their breach of their covenant, We cursed them and made their hearts grow hard. They change the words from their (right) places and forget a good part of the message that was sent to them, nor will you cease to find them, barring a few, ever bent on deceits. But forgive them (even those whom Allah has Himself cursed), and overlook (their misdeeds), for Allah loves those who are kind."[59]

3. GOD DOES NOT LOVE THOSE WHO REFUSE TO REFORM

God loves people, and why should not He love them? He has created them with His full attention, granted them capabilities that He has not given to any of His other creations, and provided them with His enormous bounties. The natural demand of His love is that people should reciprocate His love by listening to what He commands. However, if we are arrogant and do not care what He says or desires from us, if we refuse or waste His bounties or violate His laws by being unjust to others, and if we spread corruption in our communities while knowing very well that

God does not like this, then it is very natural for Him to leave us alone and forget about our welfare. God at various places in the Qur'an has described the kind of people He does not love. Such character traits and human behaviors are highlighted in this section.

3.1 God does not Love the denial of Faith, His Commands, or the Hereafter

If people desire God's love and His mercy, they should neither deny God's commands nor their accountability for their behavior and deeds in the Hereafter. We should know that we are being tested by what God has given us. To be successful in our test, God commands us to obey Him and the Messenger so that He may reward those who believe and do good deeds. In Surah Al-Imran, God tells the Messenger: "Say: 'Obey Allah and the Messenger;' but if they turn back, then surely Allah does not love those who reject faith."[60] Why should one obey God and His Messenger? God answers this in Surah Al-Rum: "That He may reward those who believe and do good out of His grace. Surely, He does not love those who reject faith."[61]

3.2 God does not Love the Arrogantly Boastful or Those who break their Treaties

God rewards people who believe in Him and do good deeds, both in this world and in the Hereafter. Then why do people still disbelieve? Is it people's ignorance and arrogance that blind their intellect? Is it because they refuse to know what is in their best interest and do not believe they will be held accountable for their behavior and deeds. God says in Surah Al-Nahl: "Your Allah is one Allah. As to those who do not believe in the Hereafter, their hearts refuse to know, and they are arrogant. Truly, Allah knows what they hide and what they manifest. Surely, He does not love the arrogant."[62] How does arrogance blind people's intellect? In Surah Al-Qasas, this is explained with an example of Qarun's behavior, "Qarun was of the people of Moses, but he rebelled against them. We had given him treasures, so much so that his hoards of wealth would have certainly weighed down a company of men possessed of great strength. When his people said to him: 'Do not exult—surely, Allah does not love the exultant, and seek by means of what Allah has given you a home in the next life, without neglecting your portion of this world. Do good (to others), as Allah has done good to you. Do not seek to make mischief in the land; surely, Allah does not love the mischief-makers.' He said: 'This has been given to me because of a certain knowledge which I have.' Did he not know that Allah had destroyed before him (whole) generations that were superior to him in strength and greater in the amount (of riches) they had collected? The wicked are not (always) asked about their acts of sin in this world."[63] In contrast to the behavior of Qarun, God advises people in Surah Al-Araf: "Call on your Lord humbly and secretly; surely, He does not love those who exceed the limits."[64]

People shouldn't be arrogant and boastful, treacherous, unfaithful, or ungrateful if they desire God's love and His mercy. People are commanded in Surah Al-Nisa: "Serve Allah, and do not associate anything with Him. Be good to your parents and relatives, and (be good) to the orphans, the needy, and your neighbors, whether near or far, and also to your companions around you and to wayfarers and those whom your right hands possess. Surely, Allah does not love him who is proud, boastful."[65] We are also commanded not to participate in harsh and heated argument, unless it is for securing justice or against injustice, "Allah does not love the public utterance of hurtful speech, unless (it be) by one to whom injustice has been done, and Allah is hearing, knowing."[66]

God tells us in Surah Al-Anfal that He does not love the treacherous who break their treaties: "But if you fear treachery on the part of a people, then throw back to them on terms of equality; surely, Allah does not love the treacherous."[67] In such cases, believers are assured of God's help: "Surely, Allah will defend those who believe. Surely, Allah does not love anyone who is unfaithful, ungrateful."[68] In Surah Hadid, God informs people that pleading for the dishonest, treacherous, or guilty is not going to be helpful and that gaining some benefit by unfair means will be futile. This is because: "No evil befalls on the earth or in yourselves, but is recorded in a decree before We bring it into existence. That is truly easy for Allah, in order that you may not grieve for what has escaped you or be exultant at what He has given you, and Allah does not love any arrogant boaster."[69]

3.3 God does not Love the refusal of His Bounties or the Exceeding of Limits

God has provided all good things of this world for the use of believers and unbelievers alike. In the Qur'an, God ask people: "Who is there to forbid the beauty that Allah has brought forth for His creatures and the good things from among the means of sustenance? Say: 'They are in the life of this world for those who believe (and) exclusively for them on the Day of Judgment.'"[70] This means that anyone who forbids beauty, adornments, luxuries, and comforts has no justification, as long as enjoying these does not involve anything forbidden.

When God bestows some blessings and comforts on one of His servants, He likes to see that person enjoying the blessing and acknowledging God's grace by doing good deeds to express his gratitude to God. If a person is given plenty of money, then God likes to see him giving his family a comfortable living, including a good house and plenty of provisions, without being wasteful and extravagant. However, God also loves to see that person giving out his Zakah and helping poor people and his community. Islam does not advocate a total rejection of life's comforts. On the contrary, a believer may enjoy these, provided that he acquires them in a legitimate way. Further, he must not become arrogant as a result of having such comforts. He should use them to show kindness to his neighbors and to the poor in the community. If he does, then these luxuries become a means of earning God's mercy.

3.4 God does not Love People's Contempt or Pleading for the Dishonest and Arrogant

The golden rule in relationships is that we should treat all people with respect but refuse to cooperate with those who are dishonest. We should neither treat people with contempt nor plead for the dishonest and arrogant. Dishonesty and arrogance have caused much loss and destruction on earth. It is arrogance that hinders people from admitting their mistakes, feeling sorry for their injustice, repenting, and trying not to repeat those mistakes. The friends of such people should not encourage them in their erratic behavior. Encouraging dishonest and arrogant behavior is not friendship, but a satanic behavior that should be discouraged for the benefit of all concerned. In this regard, the Qur'an records Luqman's advice to his son: "Do not turn your face away from people in contempt, nor go about in the land exulting overmuch. Surely, Allah does not love any self-conceited boaster."[71] God also commands in Surah Al-Nisa: "Do not plead for those who are dishonest to themselves; Allah does not love him who betrays trust and persists in sin."[72]

3.5 God does not Love Corruption in the Land or Tolerate Injustice

Most trouble in the world is caused by corruption and injustice. For peace and prosperity to exist, one should neither seek corruption in the land nor tolerate injustice. Unfortunately, however, there are some people who indulge in corruption and injustice to satisfy their selfish desires and to benefit from the injustice done to others. God commands people in Surah Al-Baqarah: "Do not eat up your property among yourselves for vanities or use it as bait for the judges, with intent that you may eat up wrongfully and knowingly a little of other people's property."[73]

True justice can only be achieved through the system that God has revealed and that He has tailored for the benefit of people. There is no one other than God, the Creator, Who knows what best suits people. God tells the believers in Surah Al-Imran: "As to those who believe and do good deeds, He will pay them fully their rewards; and Allah does not love the unjust."⁷⁴ As such, even when a wrong judgment is made because of false testimony, this wrong judgment will only bring eventual grief to the one knowingly benefited from it. It was narrated by Umm Salamah that the Messenger said: "I am only a human being, and opponents come to me to settle their claims. Maybe someone among you can present his case more eloquently than the other, whereby I may consider him true and give a verdict in his favor. So if I give the right of a Muslim to another by mistake, then it is really a portion of (Hell's) fire that he has the option to take or give up."⁷⁵

4. ENJOY THIS WORLD BY BEEING HONEST AND HUMBLE

God has shown in numerous ways that He loves people. That is why He commands only those things that are good for us. God says that we should serve Him and our families, neglecting neither! It is by serving God that we learn the importance of serving our family. We know that taking care of our family is a good thing to do. Who are the members of our family? They are our children, relatives, neighbors, countrymen, and the people all over the world. We have to work hard for their welfare and be just to all of them with whom we come into contact and have to deal. Additionally, we cannot forbid ourselves all the good things that God has made lawful for us. We have to try our best and fight to defend ourselves, our rights, and our values with patience and, at the same time, remain within permissible limits. This is required to save society from corruption and injustice. In case we accidently cross the limits, we have to mend our ways with repentance and good deeds. Islam does not distinguish between living the life for this world and living the life for the Hereafter. It expects its followers to live this life following all moral and ethical principles. How we live in this world will very much determine our life in the Hereafter.

4.1 Serve your Lord and your Family; Neglect Neither

People have been commanded to respect and honor God-given positions and responsibilities. It is God who created people and gave them spouses, children, parents, brothers and sisters, and all other relatives. He gave neighbors, friends, and servants; all these belong to one's family. People are to serve God and serve their family. No one should be proud of neglecting one's duties or be boastful of one's service. God commands this in Surah Al-Nisa: "Serve Allah, and do not associate anything with Him. Be good to your parents and relatives, and (be good) to the orphans, the needy, and your neighbors, whether near or far, and also to your companions around you and to wayfarers and those whom your right hands possess. Surely, Allah does not love him who is proud, boastful."[76] This verse virtually makes the whole of humanity our family. We have to respect each one of them and fulfill our obligations towards them to the best of our ability. God tells people in Surah Al-Araf: "As for those who believe and do good deeds, We do not impose on any person a duty except to the extent of its ability; they are the dwellers of Paradise; in it they shall abide."[77]

4.2 Do not forbid yourselves the Good things God has made Lawful

Islam informs us that it is a misconception to think that a different type of behavior is needed to earn and enjoy good things in life than is needed to help people to earn better life in the Hereafter. Islam expects its followers to earn and enjoy all the good things in life with legal, moral, and ethical means. This automatically earns people a good life in the Hereafter. God tells us in Surah Al-Maidah that the only thing we have to be careful for is not to exceed the limits: "O you who believe! Do not forbid yourselves the good things that Allah has made lawful for you, and do not exceed the limits. Surely, Allah does not love those who exceed the limits."[78] By telling us not to exceed the limits, God informs us that correct behavior is the one that includes less fortunate people in one's enjoyments and that does not act extravagantly. This is further explained in Surah Al-Anam: "He it is Who produces gardens, trellised and untrellised, and date palms and seed-produce of which the fruits are of various sorts, and olives and pomegranates, like and unlike; eat of its fruit when it bears fruit, and pay the (obligatory charity) due on it on the day of its reaping, and do not act extravagantly. Surely, He does not love the extravagant."[79] God does not forbid beautiful things in life. He commands us to dress beautifully and to eat and drink good things, but we should not waste and act extravagantly. In Surah Al-Araf, God commands people: "O children of Adam! Wear your beautiful apparel at every time of prayer, and eat and drink and be not extravagant. Surely, He does not love the extravagant."[80]

4.3 Do not lose Heart or fall into Despair, but Defend Yourself

God is just, and He does not love the unjust. Therefore, the believers are commanded to fight against the oppressors: "Permission to fight is given to those upon whom war is made because they are oppressed, and most surely Allah is well able to assist them."[81] Citing the example of what happened to the believers in the battle of Uhud, God tells us in Surah Al-Imran that believers should not lose heart or fall into despair: "So lose not heart, nor fall into despair, for you must gain mastery if you are believers. If a wound has afflicted you, a wound like it has also afflicted the (unbelieving) people. We bring these days to men by turns so that Allah may know those who believe and take witnesses from among you. Allah does not love the unjust."[82] In Surah Al-Shura, God commands the oppressed that they should defend themselves to stop the oppressor and his injustice: "Who, when a wrong is done to them, (are not cowed but) seek its redress. The recompense of evil is an evil like it, but he who forgives and makes amends, his reward lies with Allah. Surely, Allah does not love the unjust."[83]

4.4 Fight with those who Fight with you but exceed no Limits

God commands people to fight to defend themselves and against oppression within specified limits. God commands people in Surah Al-Baqarah: "Fight in the cause of Allah those who fight you, but do not transgress limits, for Allah does not love the aggressors."[84] "For all things prohibited, there is the law of equality: Whoever acts aggressively against you, inflict injury on him according to the injury he has inflicted on you; transgress you likewise against him. But fear Allah, and know that Allah is with those who restrain themselves."[85] "Retaliate only with the like of that with which you were afflicted. But if you are patient, it will certainly be best for those who are patient."[86] "Whoever defends himself after being oppressed cannot be blamed for his actions. The blame is only against those who oppress people, mistreat others, and insolently transgress beyond bounds through the land, defying right and justice. These shall have a painful punishment."[87] "Go forth and defend in Allah's way (with all your force), and be not just contented with this world's life, instead of the Hereafter. Be brave. If you do not go forth (to fight for your God-given rights), He will inflict you with a painful punishment and will replace you with other people who will go forth and defend in Allah's way."[88]

4.5 Have Faith in your Creator in this Struggle for the Truth

Remember that God commands believers in Surah Al-Ankabut: "Me alone should you serve. Surely, My earth is vast (therefore, migrate if needed)...Every person must taste death, then to Us shall be brought back (for accountability)...He will reward the workers...Who are patient (in their struggle and fight with patience), and rely on their Lord."[89] The believers have been encouraged to be sincere in faith and to make efforts in the cause of God, fulfilling all duties as His trustee and implementing His commands to develop just communities on earth. The believers have been told that there is only one way to success, both in this world and in the Hereafter, and that they should sincerely believe in God and

His Messenger and should exert their utmost in God's way with their selves and their wealth. As a reward, they will get God's help, relief from difficulties, and victory in the world. They will also earn immunity from God's punishment, forgiveness for their weaknesses, and eternal Paradise in the Hereafter. God tells the believers in Surah Al-Saff: "O you who believe! Shall I lead you to merchandise that will deliver you from a painful chastisement? You shall believe in Allah and His Messenger and struggle hard in Allah's way with your property and your lives; that is better for you, did you but know! He will forgive your faults and cause you to enter into gardens, beneath which rivers flow, and goodly dwellings in gardens of perpetuity; that is the mighty achievement. And yet another blessing that you love: help from Allah and a victory near at hand; and give good news to the believers."[90]

4.6 Improve your Character and Behavior by Repentance

Since people have free will, perfection of their character and behavior without divine guidance is not humanly possible. What Islam teaches is an attitude that leads to continual improvements in individual character and in society. Everyone errs, but when believers do, they seek God's forgiveness, which is forthcoming if the request is genuine. Human character is improved with every acknowledgment, regret, and effort not to repeat the mistake again. A human being may be in error throughout his life, but whenever he realizes his mistakes and repents. seeking God's forgiveness, God forgives him if he turns to Him in genuine repentance, even if he is the most wicked of humankind. God told the Messenger that when those come to you who believe: "Say: 'Peace be on you. Your Lord had inscribed for Himself (the rule of) mercy. Verily, if any of you did evil in ignorance, repented thereafter, and amended (his conduct), lo! He is forgiving, most merciful.'"[91] God also told the Messenger: "Say: 'O my servants who have transgressed against their souls! Despair not of the mercy of Allah, for Allah can forgive all sins, for He is the Forgiving, Most Merciful.'"[92]

NOTES

1. Qur'an 3:31.

2. Qur'an 33:21.

3. Malik's Muwatta 47.1.8.

4. Qur'an 68:4.

5. Sahih Bukhari 4.56.759.

6. Qur'an 2:38.

7. Qur'an 47:17.

8. Qur'an 54:17, 22, 32 & 40.

9. Qur'an 7:42.

10. Qur'an 103:2-3.

11. Qur'an 2:25.

12. Qur'an 16:97.

13. Qur'an 33:70-71.

14. Sahih Bukhari 8.76.509.

15. Qur'an 41:30.

16. Qur'an 41:31-32.

17. Qur'an 14:7.

18. Qur'an 14:34.

19. Qur'an 4:17.

20. Qur'an 22:49-50.

21. Qur'an 5:56.

22. Qur'an 10:62-64.

23. Qur'an 48:18.

24. Qur'an 58:22.

25. Qur'an 30:47.

26. Qur'an 40:51.

27. Qur'an 47:7.

28. Qur'an 48:1-4.

29. Qur'an 2:257.

30. Qur'an 12:87.

31. Qur'an 68:48.

32. Qur'an 15:55-56.

33. Qur'an 2:45.

34. Qur'an 3:146.

35. Qur'an 4:74.

36. Qur'an 4:75.

37. Qur'an 4:89.

38. Qur'an 4:90.

39. Qur'an 4:85.

40. Qur'an 4:78.

41. Qur'an 61:4.

42. Qur'an 9:4.

43. Qur'an 9:7.

44. Qur'an 4:135.

45. Sahih Muslim 32.6246.

46. Qur'an 5:8.

47. Qur'an 60:8.

48. Qur'an 5:42.

49. Qur'an 49:9.

50. Qur'an 9:107.

51. Qur'an 9:108.

52. Qur'an 9:109.

53. Qur'an 3:159.

54. Qur'an 3:76.

55. Qur'an 4:58.

56. Qur'an 23:8-9.

57. Qur'an 2:195.

58. Qur'an 3:134.

59. Qur'an 5:13.

60. Qur'an 3:32.

61. Qur'an 30:45.

62. Qur'an 16:22-23.

63. Qur'an 28:76-78.

64. Qur'an 7:55.

65. Qur'an 4:36.

66. Qur'an 4:148.

67. Qur'an 8:58.

68. Qur'an 22:38.

69. Qur'an 57:22-23.

70. Qur'an 7:32.

71. Qur'an 31:18.

72. Qur'an 4:107.

73. Qur'an 2:188.

74. Qur'an 3:57.

75. Sahih Bukhari 3.43.638.

76. Qur'an 4:36.

77. Qur'an 7:42.

78. Qur'an 5:87.

79. Qur'an 6:141.

80. Qur'an 7:31.

81. Qur'an 22:39.

82. Qur'an 3:139-140.

83. Qur'an 42:39-40.

84. Qur'an 2:190.

85. Qur'an 2:194.

86. Qur'an 16:126.

87. Qur'an 42:41-42.

88. Qur'an 9:38-39.

89. Qur'an 29:56-59.

90. Qur'an 61:10-13.

91. Qur'an 6:54.

92. Qur'an 39:53.

CHAPTER 8

DEVELOPMENT OF HUMAN CHARACTER
(Continual Improvement of Character)

GOD TELLS HUMANKIND TO reflect: "O humankind, do you not see that Allah has subjected to your use all things in the heavens and on earth and has made His bounties flow to you in exceeding measure, seen and unseen? Yet, there are among people those who dispute about Allah without knowledge and without guidance and without a Book to enlighten them!"[1] Why has God established people with authority on earth and provided all that they need for the fulfillment of life? God describes the purpose behind creation, saying: "Then We appointed you as rulers in the earth after them that We might see how you behave."[2] People have the assignment of being God's trustee on earth to evolve a system of life according to the dictates of their Lord, not according to the whims of their own selfish desires.

Therefore, God's trustees are those: "...who, should We establish them in the land, will keep up prayer and pay the poor-rate and enjoin good and forbid evil. The end of all matters rests with Allah."[3] This makes it obligatory on each one of us that we should keep up the prayers, pay Zakah, enjoin what is good and forbid what is evil. This is the only option we have if we want to succeed in life. Otherwise, our fate may not be any different than those fallen civilizations we read about in history. One should be beware of: "...and guard yourselves against a calamity that cannot fall exclusively on those of you who are wrongdoers, and know that Allah is severe in punishment."[4] "Truly, if the hypocrites, and those in whose hearts is a disease, and those who stir up sedition in the city, desist not, We shall certainly stir you up against them. Then will they not be able to stay in it as your neighbors for any length of time. They shall have a curse on them. Whenever they are found, they shall be seized and slain. Such has been the way of Allah with respect to those who have gone before, and you shall not find any change in the way of Allah."[5]

1. MISSION AND DESTINY OF HUMANKIND

According to the Qur'an, people are the master of the earth. They form a species different from animals, jinn, and angels. While Satan is disobedient to God, angels serve Him without any hesitation, while people can choose to do either. Hence, people are accountable for what they choose to do. They have been placed in charge of the earth and are required to build it. By building the earth, we mean building a happy human life, following God's guidance as explained by the prophets and messengers. God tells people that this is a test so that they may prove who among them can live a life to its best purpose and potential. God states in Surah Hud: "He is the One Who created the heavens and the earth in six days and – His throne was over the Waters – that He may try you, which of you is best in conduct."[6] In Surah Al-Mulk, we are told: "Blessed is He in Whose Hand is the dominion, and He is able to do all things, Who has created death and life that He may test you, which of you is best in deed."[7]

1.1 God gave Humankind Authority on Earth

God tells people in Surah Al-Araf: "Your Lord is Allah, Who created the heavens and the earth in six periods of time, and He is firm in power. He throws the veil of night over the day, which it pursues incessantly. He created the sun, the moon, and the stars (and) made (them) subservient to His command."[8] God then reminds people: "We assuredly established you with authority on earth and provided you therein with means for the fulfillment of your life. Small are the thanks that you give!"[9] God has provided all of us with sufficient means to live in prosperity in this world. We have to exploit and properly manage these natural resources for our benefit. An Islamic society built on hard work, truth, justice, and charity that is free of corruption, discrimination; exploitation, and oppression certainly provides all of the proper requirements for this effort.

1.2 People are to Serve God alone as His Trustees on Earth

God tells us: "I have only created jinn and humans that they may serve Me. I do not desire from them any sustenance, and I do not desire that they should feed Me."[10] Throughout Qur'an, there are numerous verses that highlight God's creation of humankind and humanity's objective in life. In Surah Al-Baqarah, we learn about our mission, the angels' concerns, and God's reply: "Just think when your Lord said to the angels: 'Lo! I am about to place a trustee on earth.' They said: 'Will You place on it one that will spread mischief and shed blood while we celebrate Your glory and extol Your holiness?' He said: 'Surely I know what you do not know.'"[11] What the angels did not know at that time was that God would provide humanity with divine guidance to properly discharge its duties. Initiating this process of guidance: "He (God) taught Adam all the names (wisdom, all what is right and what is wrong), then presented them to the angels. Then He said: 'Tell me the names of those if you are right.'"[12]

God commanded humankind: "You shall serve none but Him; this is the right religion, but most people do not know."[13] In Surah Al-Anam, God states the purpose of Adam's assignment: "He it is Who has placed you as viceroys on the earth and raised some of you above others by (various) grades so that He might try you by what He has given you."[14] The mission and destiny of humanity have been elaborated further in Surah Sad: "David! Surely, We have made you a ruler in the land, so judge between men with justice and do not follow (your) desire, lest it should lead you astray from the path of Allah. (As for) those who go astray from the path of Allah, they shall surely have a severe punishment because they forgot the Day of Reckoning."[15]

1.3 God has been motivating and helping People

Addressing the Messenger in Surah Bani Israel, God assures us of His help when people are struggling to accomplish their mission: "Their purpose was to scare you off the land in order to expel you, but in that case they would not have stayed (therein) after you, except for a little while. This has been Our way with the messengers We sent before you. You will not find any change in Our way."[16] As a way of motivating us and reassuring us of His help, God says in Surah Al-Araf: "Remember how He made you (A'ad) viceroys after Noah's folk and gave you growth of stature. Therefore, remember the benefits (you received) from Allah that you may be successful…Remember how He made you (Thamud) viceroys (rulers) after A'ad and gave you station in the earth. You choose castles in the plains and hew the mountains into dwellings. So remember the bounties of Allah, and do not evil, making mischief in the earth."[17]

1.4 Struggle and Patience are required to establish Justice

Human struggle and patience are the prerequisite to eliminate injustice from society. When the people of Moses complained about Pharaoh's injustice" "Moses said to his people: 'Ask help from Allah, and be patient. Surely, the land is Allah's. He causes such of His servants to inherit it as He pleases. The end is for those who guard against evil.' They (Moses' people) said: 'We suffered hurt before you came to us and since you have come to us.' Moses said: 'It may be that your Lord is going to destroy your adversary and make you viceroys in the earth that He may see how you behave.'"[18] Eventually God helped Moses' people because they struggled patiently: "We made the people who were deemed weak to inherit both the eastern and western land that We had blessed. The good word of your Lord was fulfilled in the children of Israel because they bore up sufferings patiently."[19]

1.5 God has been eliminating Unjust Communities

In Surah Hud, God tells about human behavior that brings destruction: "Certainly, We did destroy generations before you when they were unjust, and their messengers had come to them with clear arguments, and they would not believe; thus do We recompense the guilty people? Then We appointed you viceroys in the earth after them that We might see how you behave."²⁰ While Noah's people were destroyed, Noah and the believers were rescued: "But they rejected him (Noah), so We delivered him and those with him in the ark, and We made them rulers and drowned those who rejected Our revelation. See then what was the end of the (people) warned."²¹ Similarly, God delivered Abraham and Lot from their unjust communities: "We delivered him (Abraham) as well as Lot to the land that We had blessed for all people. We gave him Isaac and Jacob, a son's son, and We made (them) all good. We made them leaders, guiding by Our command, and We inspired them to do good deeds, to establish prayers, and to give Zakah. They worshipped Us alone."²²

2. DUTIES OF GOD'S TRUSTEE ON EARTH

God created people to appoint them as His trustees on earth. The creation was dramatically different from the creation of either angels or Satan, "Just think when your Lord said to the angels: 'Lo! I am about to place a trustee on earth.' They said: 'Will You place on it one that will spread mischief and shed blood while we celebrate Your glory and extol Your holiness?' He said: 'Surely I know what you do not know.'"²³ One could conclude from this conversation that God did not create people only for to worship Him, which the angels already did. The human mission is much broader than of angels. Various elements of human mission and the efforts needed to accomplish this are highlighted in this section.

Those who are the believers, they believe in and worship God, reform themselves, and do good deeds. The edifice of Islam has five sides to its structure. In other words, developing humanity to its potential as believers entails a five-step process: Firstly, the believers must have the desire and intention to succeed as God's trustee on earth. Since it is through knowledge and understanding that people believe and worship God, they must acquire religious knowledge. Secondly, the belief in and worshipping God cultivate God's love of us and motivate and help the believers to overcome their weaknesses of character. Thirdly, believers continually improve their character and behavior through repentance. Fourthly believers do not violate God's commands, and they do good deeds. Finally, believers enforce what is right and forbid what is wrong.

2.1 Managing Life According to Divine Law

One may question what sort of life we should lead. We have a choice at every moment in our lives. Should our lives be according to the divine laws and for what benefit? Our efforts in obeying certain rules in this world do not mean that we will be saved from suffering only in the Hereafter. Who benefits here on this earth? Does the benefit of our compliance accrue to someone else or to God? God does not benefit at all by our obedience or compliance with His rules; we do. In a sacred Hadith, agreed upon by Sahih Muslim, at-Tirmidhi, and ibn Majah, the Messenger quotes God as saying: "My servants, it is but your deeds that I reckon up for you and then recompense you for (in this world). Therefore, let him who finds good praise God, and let him who finds other than that blame no one but himself." [24]

Humankind has been created with certain physical, emotional, and moral needs. The implementation of divine law helps improve life on earth and makes people hardworking, honest, and just. Such people abhor exploitation, oppression, injustice, and corruption. Thus, whoever obeys God's rules is a beneficiary. The benefit is assured, as the rules are made to spare people from affliction, contradiction and confusion.

Our prayers and fasting do not benefit God in any way. Rather, our prayers benefit us by keeping us on our guard against temptation and falling to sin. Fasting also teaches self-discipline. In contrast, humankind suffers by not implementing God's laws, which does not harm God in any way. The choice is there. Do we do what is right and enjoy its benefits in this life, as well as in the Hereafter, or do we reject divine law and suffer the consequences of this rejection.

2.2 The Motivation for Continual Improvement

The perpetual availability of God's forgiveness and mercy is a very strong motivation for the continual improvement of human character and behavior. In Surah Al-Anaam, God tells the Messenger to encourage and motivate people to improve their individual character and behavior by turning to God in repentance and by doing good deeds: "When those who believe in Our revelations come to you, say: 'Peace be on you. Your Lord had inscribed for Himself (the rule of) mercy. Verily, if any of you did evil in ignorance, repented thereafter, and amended (his conduct), lo! He is forgiving, most merciful.'"[25] In Surah Al-Araf, God responds to Moses' prayer by saying: "(As for) those who took the calf (for a god), surely wrath from their Lord and disgrace in this world's life shall overtake them, and thus do We recompense the devisers of lies. (As for) those who do evil deeds, then repent after that and believe; your Lord after that is most surely forgiving, merciful."[26]

After an earthquake overtook him and his companions, Moses prayed, "'And ordain for us good in this world's life and in the Hereafter, for surely we turn to You (in repentance).' He (God) said: '(As for) My chastisement, I will afflict with it whom I please, but My mercy encompasses all things. I ordain it (specially) for those who guard against evil, pay the poor-rate, and believe in Our communications. (My mercy is specifically for) those who follow the Messenger, the unlettered prophet, whom they find written down with them in the Torah and the Gospel, who enjoins them good and forbids them evil. (The Messenger) makes lawful to them the good things and makes unlawful to them impure things. He removes from them their burden and the shackles that were upon them. So those who believe in him, honor him, help him, and follow the light that has been sent down with him, these are the ones who will be successful."[27]

3. HUMAN LIFE ON EARTH IS A TEST

The world we live in is a small corner of the universe. Our stay here is only a fraction of time, and our efforts during our stay are a trial by which we are being tested in every aspect of our character and behavior. This could be a test by way of poverty, affluence, or a mixture of both. Belief in God and trust in Him should result in behavior that is governed by the values and standards acceptable to God. As such, it is disgraceful that a great number of people do not get enough to eat and live in inhuman conditions. This is an indication that we are failing in our test. It is due to the fact that people are not following what God tells us, i.e., to believe in Him and do good deeds.

Life on this earth is full of problems and pleasures. As time passes and the problems begin to be solved, they appear to be much smaller than originally thought. Either the magnitude or importance of these problems was exaggerated, or the ability to deal with them was underestimated. Similarly, with the passage of time, the moments of great pleasure appear much smaller. This is because people tend to think of the present, of this moment, of now, and consider this life on earth as the only life we have. They forget that life on earth is a fraction of the life that has been bestowed upon us by God, a life that is to continue in the Hereafter.

3.1 Materialistic Cultures and Societies

The influence of materialistic ideology has adversely affected the way life on earth is being perceived. At present, especially in the West, material wealth is thought to be the source of all happiness. Everything is geared towards achieving the dream of getting rich. A person who gets wealthy quickly, applying whatever means are at his disposal, is perceived to be an extremely successful person. The draw of easy and fast wealth is always dangled before people's eyes. Lotteries are organized by governments; bookmakers flourish in business and pools are offered to the young and old. They all offer the same prize of elusive millions.

The majority of people in materialistic countries are good in their own way as individuals, and they may even be following several Islamic principles in their personal lives. However, as societies and governments, Western countries spend and continue to spend so much on weapons of mass destruction that there is insufficient money leftover for meeting humanitarian needs. Making matters still worse, these Western countries sell their weapons to Third-World countries who can ill-afford them and encourage them to make their countries experimental battlefields. This saps their resources and keeps them in continuing poverty.

3.2 Human Character, Behavior, and Society

Comparing the materialistic attitude with the noble character of the believer and with a society built on hard work, truth, justice, and charity that is free of corruption, discrimination, exploitation, and oppression, one can see that happiness in the life to come greatly depends on the efforts of believers to improve the life in this world. This is very important, and all of us, irrespective of our situation or status in life, should improve our behavior and try to help others in their struggle in life. Whether we suffer forever or are happy depends upon our deeds, and God administers absolute justice to all. As such, our actions determine our present and our future. The choices we make, knowing that all actions, good or bad, have appropriate consequences will forever impact us.

If we look at the condition of contemporary people, a large majority do not seem to have any specific purpose in life. It is our own fault, for we are neglecting to look into the main sources of faith to determine our duties and our mission in life, which is the development of the most human character, behavior, and society in this world.

4. DEVELOPMENT OF HUMAN CHARACTER AND SOCIETY

The Islamic concept of humankind gives this noble creature a very high position. It provides every facility needed to work up to its potentials. That ensures the best results of one's efforts. Indeed, it is through such willing contribution to the community effort by all individuals in a Muslim society that Islamic civilization made its mark on history and continued to lead humanity for centuries. Every time Islam is implemented, the same sort of marvelous results have been achieved. This assures us that the same could happen today if we, the Muslims, live in a way that implements Islam in our lives and in our society.

4.1 Basic Principals of Human Character and Behavior

Throughout the Qur'an, God explains and motivates people with basic principles, which if followed, help reform and improve their character and behavior. Some of these principles are outlined below:

1. "Surely Allah's guidance is the true guidance."[28] "They will have the reward of what they earn, as you will for what you do, and none shall be asked to answer for the other."[29]

2. "Everyone has a direction to which he should turn; therefore, hasten to do good works."[30]

3. "Good and evil cannot be equal. Repel evil with what is better."[31] "Repel evil by what is the best."[32]

4. "Allah does not love corruption."[33] "Were it not for Allah's repelling some with others, the earth would certainly be in a state of disorder."[34]

5. "Fulfill all obligations."[35] "Abandon sins, open and secret,"[36] "Seek means of nearness to Allah,"[37] "and take care of your own selves."[38]

6. "No person earns evil but against itself, and no bearer of burden shall bear the burden of another."[39]

7. "Help one another in goodness and piety, and do not help one another in sin and aggression."[40]

8. "Whoever believes in Allah and the Last Day and does good deeds: they shall have no fear, nor shall they grieve."[41]

9. "The bad and the good are not equal, though the abundance of the bad may please you."[42]

10. "Whoever brings a good deed, he shall have ten like it, and whoever brings an evil deed, he shall be recompensed only with the like of it."[43]

11. "Permission to fight is given to those upon whom war is made because they are oppressed, and most surely Allah is well able to assist them."[44]

12. Corruption, injustice, and mischief must be resisted: "Had there not been Allah's repelling some people by others, certainly there would have been pulled down cloisters and churches and synagogues and mosques in which Allah's name is much remembered."[45]

4.2 Righteousness, the Foundation of Human Character

What is righteousness? It is correct belief accompanied by good deeds. Righteous people think that: "Kind speech accompanied by forgiveness is better than charity followed by insulting words,"[46] and "Allah does not impose upon any person a duty but to the extent of one's ability."[47] God tells us that righteousness is correct belief, charity, keeping prayers, paying Zakah, fulfilling promises, and being patient during testing times: "It is not righteousness that you turn your faces towards east or west, but righteousness is to believe in Allah and the Last Day and the angels and the Book and the messengers, to spend of your substance out of love for Him for your kin, for orphans, for the needy, for the wayfarer, for those who ask, and for the ransom of slaves, to be steadfast in prayer and practice regular charity; to fulfill the contracts that you have made, and to be firm and patient in pain (or suffering) and adversity and throughout all periods of panic. Such are the people of truth, the God-fearing."[48]

There is no compulsion in religion, but God loves righteous people who are humble and strive hard in the way of God without any fear. God reminds believers in Surah Al-Maidah: "O Believers! Whoever from among you turns back from his religion, then Allah will bring a people (in place of you). He shall love them, and they shall love Him. They will be humble before the believers, yet mighty against the unbelievers, striving hard in Allah's way and not fearing the censure of any censurer. That is the grace of Allah; He gives it to whom He pleases."[49]

4.3 The Basic Principle of Dealings among Humankind

Duties toward God (haqooq Allah) cannot be over emphasized, but duties towards fellow human beings (haqooq ul abad), which are equally important, are unfortunately given a low position on the list of priorities in Muslim communities today, both at the individual and community levels. Yet, a good balance is the main characteristic of Islam and its code of living. Little importance has also been given to a high-priority objective of Islam, namely the elimination of injustice and corruption. Muslim voices that speak against injustice and corruption remain faint, particularly those of Muslim scholars. On the other hand, so much has been said and written about matters that cannot be described as being equally important to not being unjust to one's family, relatives, servants, employees, neighbors, or, indeed, fellow human being. We should always remember that God may forgive us all sins that relate to our duties toward Him, but He will not forgive us any sin against people until the wronged party himself is ready to forgive us. Hence, a balance between these two, haqooq Allah and haqooq ul abad, must be maintained before we can truly claim to lead an Islamic life. Since fraud and injustice cause so much corruption in society, we are commanded to give full measure when dealing with others. We are told that corrupt people are shameful and cursed. Various aspects of human dealings among people are further discussed below:

1. *Give Full Measure in your Dealings among Yourselves*: Truth and honesty, keeping promises, honoring trusts, fulfilling contracts, and

establishing justice are some important socioeconomic principles that assure the peace and prosperity of communities. Those who implement these in their lives benefit from them irrespective of whether they are believers or unbelievers. Thus, Anas bin Malik reported that Allah's Messenger told him: "When a non-believer does good, he is made to taste its reward in this world. As far as the believer is concerned, Allah stores (the reward) of his virtues for the Hereafter and provides him sustenance (in this world) in accordance with his obedience to Him."[50] Giving full measure with justice is the outcome of all socioeconomic principles mentioned above. There are several verses of the Qur'an that guide us when it comes to dealings among people. In Surah Al-Anam, God commands: "Do not approach the property of the orphan, except to improve it, until he attains his maturity, and give full measure and weight with justice. We do not impose on any person a duty except to the extent of his ability. When you speak, be just, even if a relative is concerned, and fulfill Allah's covenant. This He has enjoined you with that you may be mindful."[51]

God commands people through Shu'aib, one of His messengers, that they should give full measure, weight fairly, and not defraud people of their things: "And to the people of Madyan, We sent their brother Shu'aib. He said: 'O my people! Serve Allah; you have no god other than Him. Clear proof, indeed, has come to you from your Lord. Therefore, give full measure and weight, and do not diminish to men their things, and do not make mischief in the land after its reform. This is better for you if you are believers.'"[52] In Surah Hud, people are again reminded: "And to the people of Madyan, We sent their brother Shu'aib. He said: 'O my people! Serve Allah; you have no god other than Him. Do not give short measure and weight. Surely, I see you in prosperity now, but I fear for you the punishment of an all-encompassing day. O my people! Give full measure and weight with justice, and do not diminish the goods of others. Do not act corruptly in the land, making mischief. That which is left to you by God is best for you, if you are believers."[53]

2. *Fraud and Injustice cause Corruption*: Corruption is demeaning, inhuman, and a curse on human society, and corrupt people are an embodiment of laziness and dishonesty. Efforts, whether good or bad, have their consequences, and everything has a destiny. In Surah Al-Furqan, people are told: "He, Whose is the kingdom of the heavens and the earth, and Who did not take to Himself a son, and Who has no associate in the kingdom, and Who created everything, then ordained for it a destiny."[54]

It has been decreed for people: "Give full measure when you measure out, and weigh with a true balance. This is fair and better in the end."[55] In Surah Al-Shuara, God commands: "Give a full measure, and cause no loss (to others by fraud). Weigh with scales true and upright. Do not wrong men of their things, and do not act corruptly in the earth, making mischief."[56] In Surah Al-Qamar, God says: "Surely, We have created everything according to a measure."[57] Likewise, we are told in Surah Al-Rahman: "The heaven, He raised it high, and He has set up the balance (of justice) that you may not be inordinate with respect to the measure. Keep up the balance with equity, and do not make the measure deficient."[58]

3. *The Corrupt are not Successful but Cursed*: Does it not make sense that God has given us conscience and guidance for the sole purpose of reforming our dealings among ourselves? Are not law and justice a prerequisite for true humanity? God tells us in Surah Al-Hadid: "We sent aforetime our messengers with clear signs and sent down with them the Book and the balance (of right and wrong) that men may stand forth in justice."[59] In Surah Al-Talaq, it is confirmed that our livelihood does not depend on exploitation, injustice, and corruption. Rather, "He (God) provides for him from (sources) he never could imagine. If anyone puts

his trust in Allah, sufficient is (Allah) for him. Surely, Allah attains His purpose; Allah has set a measure for everything."[60] For this reason, God cursed and even destroyed unjust communities in the past. God tells us in Surah Al-Mutaffifin: "Woe to the defrauders, those who, when they have to receive by measure from men, exact full measure, but when they have to give by measure or weight to men, give less than due. Do they not think that they will be called to account on a mighty day, a day when mankind will stand before the Lord of the worlds?"[61]

4.4 Justice, the Structure of Human Society

In a sacred Hadith, the Messenger quotes God as saying: "My servants, I have forbidden Myself injustice and have made injustice forbidden among you. Therefore, do not act unjustly to one another." [62] Immediately after reminding them of their covenant with Him in Surah Al-Maidah, God commands the believers: "(O you who believe,) remember the favor of Allah on you and His covenant with which He bound you firmly when you said: 'We have heard, and we obey.' Be careful of your duty to Allah. Surely, Allah knows what is in the breasts."[63] God commands believers to be just in their dealings among themselves, "O you who believe, be upright for Allah, bearers of witness with justice, and let not hatred of a people incite you not to act equitably. Act equitably; that is nearer to piety."[64] God asks the Messenger to remind people in Surah Al-Araf: "My Lord has enjoined justice and that you set your whole selves (to Him) at every time of prayer and call on Him, making your devotion sincerely. As He brought you forth in the beginning, so shall you also return."[65] Addressing Jews and Christians, God tells them in Surah Al-Maidah that, if they had followed the law as given to them they would have been prosperous: "If they had kept up the Torah and the Gospel and that which was revealed to them from their Lord, they would certainly have been nourished from above them and from beneath their feet."[66] This verse confirms that the establishment of justice, judging people by what God has revealed, brings individual and collective prosperity. That is why God has revealed several books throughout history to guide humankind in the establishment of justice.

1. *Torah, the Book of Law for the Jews*: God tells about the Torah, the book of law for the Jews, in Surah Al-Maidah: "Surely, We revealed the Torah in which was guidance and light. With it, the prophets who submitted themselves to Allah judged (matters) for those who were Jews, and so did the religious leaders and scholars, because they were required to guard the book of Allah, and they were witnesses thereof. Therefore, fear not the people, but fear Me. Do not take a small price for My revelations, and whoever does not judge by what Allah has revealed, those are they that are the unbelievers."[67]

2. *The Gospel, the Book of Law for the Christians*: God tells about the Injeel (Gospel), the book of law for the Christians, in Surah Al-Maidah: "We sent after them in their footsteps Jesus, son of Mariam, verifying what was before him of the Torah, and We gave him the Injeel (Gospel), in which was guidance and light, verifying what was before it of the Torah. (The Gospel) was a source of guidance and admonition for those who guard against evil. The followers of the Injeel should have judged by what Allah revealed in it; and whoever did not judge by what Allah revealed, those are the transgressors."[68]

3. *Qur'an, the Final Book of Law for Humankind*: God also tells us about the Qur'an, the final book of law for humankind: "To you We sent the scripture in truth, confirming the scripture that came before it, and guarding it in safety. So judge between them by what Allah has revealed, and follow not their vain desires, diverging from the truth that has come to you. To each among you have we prescribed a law and an open way. If Allah had so willed, He would have made you a single people, but (His plan is) to test you in what He has given you. So strive as in a race in all virtues. The goal of you all is to Allah; it is He that will show you

the truth of the matters in which you dispute."[69] God commands: "Judge you between them by what Allah has revealed, and follow not their vain desires, but beware of them lest they beguile you from any of that (teaching) that Allah has sent down to you. If they turn away, be assured that for some of their crimes it is Allah's purpose to punish them, and truly most men are rebellious. Do they then seek after a judgment from (the days of) ignorance? But who, for a people whose faith is assured, can give better judgment than Allah?"[70]

NOTES

1. Qur'an 31:20.

2. Qur'an 10:14.

3. Qur'an 22:41.

4. Qur'an 8:55.

5. Qur'an 33:60-62.

6. Qur'an 11:7.

7. Qur'an 67:1-2.

8. Qur'an 7:54.

9. Qur'an 7:10.

10. Qur'an 51:56-57.

11. Qur'an 2:30.

12. Qur'an 2:31.

13. Qur'an 12:40.

14. Qur'an 6:165.

15. Qur'an 38:26.

16. Qur'an 17:76-77.

17. Qur'an 7:69 & 74.

18. Qur'an 7:128-129.

19. Qur'an 7:137.

20. Qur'an 10:13-14.

21. Qur'an 10:73.

22. Qur'an 21:71-73.

23. Qur'an 2:30.

24. Sahih Muslim 32.6246.

25. Qur'an 6:54.

26. Qur'an 7:152-153.

27. Qur'an 7:156-167.

28. Qur'an 2:120.

29. Qur'an 2:134 & 141.

30. Qur'an 2:148.

31. Qur'an 41:34.

32. Qur'an 23:96.

33. Qur'an 2:205.

34. Qur'an 2:251.

35. Qur'an 5:1.

36. Qur'an 6:120.

37. Qur'an 5:35.

38. Qur'an 5:105.

39. Qur'an 6:164.

40. Qur'an 5:2.

41. Qur'an 5:69.

42. Qur'an 5:100.

43. Qur'an 6:160.

44. Qur'an 22:39.

45. Qur'an 22:40.

46. Qur'an 2:263.

47. Qur'an 6:152.

48. Qur'an 2:177.

49. Qur'an 5:54.

50. Sahih Muslim 39.6740.

51. Qur'an 6:152.

52. Qur'an 7:85.

53. Qur'an 11:84-86.

54. Qur'an 25:2.

55. Qur'an 17:35.

56. Qur'an 26:181-183.

57. Qur'an 54:49.

58. Qur'an 55:7-9.

59. Qur'an 57:25.

60. Qur'an 65:3.

61. Qur'an 83:1-6.

62. Sahih Muslim 32.6246.

63. Qur'an 5:7.

64. Qur'an 5:8.

65. Qur'an 7:29.

66. Qur'an 5:66.

67. Qur'an 5:44.

68. Qur'an 5:46-47.

69. Qur'an 5:48.

70. Qur'an 5:49-50.

CHAPTER 9

PROTECTION OF HUMAN SOCIETY
(Continual Improvement of Society)

HISTORY TELLS US THAT every major social change that took place in the world was achieved at a very high cost in human misery and human lives. Humankind had managed very poorly without God's guidance. We continue to face endless misery; yet, we still resist acknowledging the basic truth that divine guidance is needed. In the sight of God, no one can legitimize one's gains or achievements by arrogance, false evidence, exploitation, bribes, and puppet governments installed by rigging elections and by manipulation of voters.

1. ELIMINATING SOCIAL INJUSTICE

Let everyone have what is due to them: "Give just weight and full measure. We do not charge a soul with more than it can bear."[1] This clearly applies to all socio-economic transactions and requires people to do their best to ensure that everyone gets what is due to him. Further, this verse provides a direct link between socio-economic transactions and faith. It is God Who gives this directive and Who urges people to give just weight and full measure. Therefore, commercial transactions have a very real link with divine servitude. This clarifies that faith has a direct relationship with all aspects of life. Ignorant societies, past and present, separate belief and worship from laws, human dealings, and transactions. The existence of this division was confirmed by Shu'aib's people when they questioned him: "Shu'aib, does your praying require you to demand of us that we give up all that our forefathers used to worship or that we refrain from doing whatever we please with our property?"[2] In this verse, the Qur'an makes the link between the rules governing financial and commercial transactions, on the one hand, and faith, on the other, in order to make it clear that Islam makes both faith and human dealings integral parts of itself.

1.1 People's Pursuit of a Just Socio-Economic System

Every past country had to go through much strife before appropriate welfare measures for its people could be introduced and implemented. These measures were the result of very hard struggles that were fought over long periods of time. This happened when capitalism took over from feudalism, and again it was the case at the time of the industrial revolution. The privileges that workers enjoy in Western countries today were not achieved through discussions between equals in meeting rooms. The same was the case when communism and socialism took over in certain countries. There was also a great deal of trouble in the years that followed the edifice of communism crumbling down. All these changes were episodes in people's pursuit of a just social system. However, a just social and economic system remains an elusive goal that is always opposed by tyranny and dictatorship, which may take the form of the power of capital or the dictatorship of a party or individuals.

There is simply no man-made system that has been able to eradicate social injustice, which is the result of people turning their backs on God's guidance and refusing to follow the divine principles that stress and demand for fair treatment among people. True social and economic justice can only be achieved through individual freedom and equality, coupled with general, technical, and religious education and respect for human rights. In other words, true justice can only be achieved through the implementation of God's commands. History tells us that humanity has managed very poorly when it turned its back on God's guidance. We continue to endure endless misery while resisting acknowledgment of the basic truth that such guidance is needed.

1.2 Justice is the Basis of All Human Interaction

The aim of divine guidance is to serve human interests and to help people build a happy life in a community characterized by justice. Justice must be achieved at all levels, within the family, the local community, the social hierarchy, and the political system. Besides, history proves that whenever people established their system on the basis of true divine guidance and applied God's law, their achievements were really great. The Islamic trust is to maintain justice, in its absolute sense, in every situation. It is an overall fairness that prevents aggression and oppression anywhere on earth. It guarantees justice between people, giving everyone, Muslim and non-Muslim, the same basic rights. In their entitlement to justice, all people, believers and unbelievers, are equal in God's sight. Similarly, relative and stranger, friend and foe, poor and rich are to be treated with absolute equality. This is something to be done as though one were dealing directly with God and for His sake. It is not for the sake of anyone else, for or against whom a testimony is given. Nor is it to serve the interests of any individual, group, or community. It is not something that takes into account the circumstances of any particular case. It is a testimony given for God's sake, free of any other desire, prejudice, interest, or consideration. What we should know is that it is not the system that creates justice, but the spirit behind the system, whatever form and shape it may take and regardless of the time and place where it is applied.

God's law is compatible with and suits the needs of every community at every level of civilization. Islam lays down certain principles that provide a framework within which human society can operate. Within that framework, we can choose to produce a social system that suits our individual circumstances. Islamic laws are the laws of nature, and there is nothing against nature revealed by God in the Qur'an. That makes it possible to be compatible with diverse traditions and cultures throughout the world. That is a great characteristic of Islamic law, which enables it to be applicable in all communities. There is, however, a main requirement for Islamic law to be properly applied. It should be applied as a complete whole, covering all aspects of human lives and society. In other words, Islamic law can only be properly applied in a truly Islamic community.

2. LEARNING TO MANAGE OUR AFFAIRS

Learning how to manage our affairs on earth is an obligation that people have to fulfill as God's trustee on earth. With knowledge comes understanding and then obedience. God commands in Surah Al-Alaq: "Read in the name of your Lord Who created—created man from a clot. Read, and your Lord is Most Honorable, Who taught (man to write) with the pen—taught man what he knew not."[3]

God's commands as given in the Qur'an are to be implemented both in individual lives and in the larger society. However, implementation can only come as a result of learning and understanding. How is it possible that someone who has not read the Qur'an or learnt any part of it can implement it? It cannot be done without reading the Qur'an and learning the meaning of its verses. Learning what God commands in the Qur'an and implementing those commands go hand in hand. The Qur'an is not meant for absent-minded reading that lacks understanding and implementation. Those who do not understand Arabic should learn to understand the meanings of the Qur'an in their own language. If a person who does not understand Arabic reads the Qur'an as an act of worship, he may be rewarded for his reading. However, it does not absolve believers from their duty to understand and implement the Qur'an in their own lives and in society.

2.1. All types of Education are needed for Human Excellence

The first thing God did after the creation was to teach Adam the "names of things," i.e., He gave Adam knowledge of good and evil and the willpower to implement his choice. This was Adam's orientation for his assignment as God's trustee on earth. Similarly, all children, both males and females, need a proper education to provide guidelines about what is expected from them in order for them to excel as true humans and as productive members of society. This makes it mandatory that men and women should be imparted both religious and secular types of education. Religious education is needed to inculcate the purpose of life and to develop the character, leadership traits, and wisdom required to set up a just society on earth. At the same time, professional education is needed to explore the universe for the prosperity of society, to improve the standard of living, and to earn an honest livelihood.

The Qur'an invites people to look around them in the universe and to try to discover its secrets. How can we do this unless we acquire appropriate knowledge? God has made everything in the universe subservient to us, and He wants us to use its natural resources to build human life. This is an assignment for humankind to complete. Therefore, education in all fields of knowledge is required to complete this assignment successfully. If the community is composed of ignorant people, then they have no hope of a good future. The task of an Islamic community is to provide a model of everything good in life. That can only be achieved through excellence in all fields of knowledge. This was how the early Muslim generations understood their task. They were able, as a result, to build a civilization that was unique in human history.

2.2 Belief in one God assures Human Freedom and Equality

The main purpose of divine law is to liberate humankind from submission to any authority other than that of God. In the sight of God, all individuals are equal. God tells us: "O people! Lo! We created you all from a male and a female and made you into nations and tribes that you may know one another. Lo! The noblest of you in the sight of Allah is the best in conduct. Lo! Allah knows and is aware."[4] Islam does not allow the hegemony of one philosophy, system, or nation over another. It wants the system laid down by God to replace the systems established by His creatures. It does not wish to establish a kingdom of anyone of God's servants, but to establish God's own kingdom. Hence, it has to move forward throughout the earth in order to liberate the whole of humankind, without discrimination between those who are within the land of Islam and those outside it. The whole earth is populated by humans that are being subjected to tyrannical authorities.

The freedom of humanity lies in the recognition of the inherent dignity and the equal and inalienable rights of all members of the human family. Only on this foundation of freedom, can justice and peace be achieved in the world. The disregard and contempt for human rights have resulted in barbarous acts that have outraged the conscience of humanity. The advent of a world in which people enjoy freedom of speech and belief, along with freedom from fear and want, coupled with individual respect and dignity that does not allow the domination of one philosophy, system, or nation over another, has been proclaimed as the highest aspiration of the common people. It seems essential that human rights should be protected by the rule of law and justice, in order to avoid people's rage and rebellion against injustice. Fundamental human rights, the equality of all humans, whether male or female, and the establishment of justice between people and between states is a prerequisite for the development of friendly relations among people and nations.

This has also been reaffirmed by the United Nations in their charter on fundamental human rights. This charter states: "The General Assembly proclaims this Universal Declaration of Human Rights as a common standard of achievement for all peoples and all nations, to the end that every individual and every organ of society, keeping this Declaration constantly in mind, shall strive by teaching and education to promote respect for these rights and freedoms and by progressive measures, national and international, to secure their universal and effective recognition and observance, both among the peoples of Member States themselves and among the peoples of territories under their jurisdiction." History tells us that this charter has not been implemented effectively and that some nations have used it politically (not honestly) to promote their superiority over others. The dignity and worth of people, the rights of men and women, social progress, and better standards of life cannot be achieved only by putting charters on paper. People have to implement these and other universal values honestly in their respective countries.

2.3 Good Moral Character and Behavior are Needed

The social conditions and the wellbeing of a community do not change themselves. People have to try and make efforts to change them. In Surah Al-Mulk, people are told that it is God, "Who has created life and death that He may try which of you is best in conduct."[5] God tells us about Himself: "He's the One Who made you successors in the land and raised some of you above others by various grades that He might try you by what He has given you."[6] What are the criteria for use in this trial? We once again find the answer in Surah Al-Hujurat where God tells us that the person who is best in character and behavior is the noblest among us: "O people! Lo! We created you all from a male and a female and made you into nations and tribes that you may know one another. Lo! The noblest of you in the sight of Allah is the best in conduct. Lo! Allah knows and is aware."[7]

2.4 God does not change a People's Lot unless They Change

God does not change a people's lot unless they change themselves. This is a universal law of nature that God has put in place. If people improve their character and behavior, they are protected and nourished. Otherwise, they live in corruption, and their lives are miserable. In other words, God provides protection and prosperity to those who follow His guidance. For example, God commands the angels to guard each person:

"For each person, there are angels in succession, before and behind him. They guard him by command of Allah. Allah does not change a people's lot unless they change what is in their hearts. But when once Allah intends punishment to a people (as a result of their own bad behavior and deeds), there is no averting it, and besides Him they have no protector."[8]

God does not change the good condition of a people as long as they remain good by not committing sins etc. On the other hand, none can stop God's punishment if people disbelieve and cause corruption. God says in Surah Ibrahim: "If you give thanks, I would certainly give to you more, and if you are ungrateful for My favors, My chastisement is truly severe."[9] "In the case of the people of Pharaoh and those before them, they disbelieved in Allah's revelations. Therefore, Allah destroyed them on account of their faults. Surely, Allah is strong, severe in requiting evil. This is because Allah has never changed a favor that He has conferred upon a people until they change their own condition."[10] "(This was Our) way with the messengers We sent before you. You will find no change in Our ways."[11] "(And this was) the practice of Allah among those who lived aforetime. No change will you find in the practice of Allah."[12] Given the above, if people desire to live in peace and prosperity, they have to reform themselves. This is because peace and prosperity are directly proportionate to the cumulative effect of people's moral character and good behavior. There is no alternative or an easy way out. This needs hard work, honesty, justice, dedication, and patience.

2.5 All People, good and bad, Suffer because of Corruption

All people, good and bad, suffer because of corruption, so if we do not do anything to stop discrimination, exploitation, oppression, and injustice in our societies, then everyone is going to suffer. This is about good governance. Addressing the believers: God commands in Surah Al-Anfal: "O you who believe! Answer the call of Allah and His Messenger when he calls you to that which gives you life…and guard yourselves against a chastisement that affects not in particular only those of you who do wrong."[13]

In a struggle between good and evil, honesty and corruption, justice and exploitation, freedom and slavery, the clear verdict is in favor of that which is good: "(O unbelievers)! If you demanded a judgment, the judgment has then, indeed, come to you. If you desist, it will be better for you. If you turn back (to your old bad behavior), We too shall turn back. Your forces shall avail you nothing, though they may be many, and know that Allah is with the believers."[14] God commands the Messenger and the believers: "Say to those who disbelieve that if they desist, that which is past shall be forgiven to them, but if they persist, then what happened to the ancients is already (awaiting them). Fight with them until there is no more persecution and Allah's religion prevails, but if they desist, then surely Allah sees what they do. If they refuse, then know that Allah is your patron, the best patron and the best helper."[15] God commands us to keep fighting for that in which we believe, and He assures us of His help in this perpetual struggle between good and evil.

2.6 The Corrupt get God's Respite for only a Limited Time

The corrupt can enjoy their corruption for only for a little while. God asks them in Surah Fatir if they are looking for the same fate as befell those evil communities who perished in the past: "They were arrogant in the land and planned evil, but evil plans shall not beset any but the men who make them. Now are they looking for the fate the ancients suffered? You shall not find any alteration in the course of Allah, and you shall not find any change in Allah's ways."[16] Again, God tells the corrupt to be ready and to know their fate: "Have they not traveled in the land and seen the nature of the consequence for those who were before them, even though those were mightier than these in power? Allah is not such that anything in the heavens or in the earth should escape Him. Surely, He is knowing and powerful."[17]

Why have the corrupt not yet been destroyed? God's answer to this is: "If Allah were to punish men according to what they deserve, He would not leave on the back of the earth a single living creature, but He gives them respite for a stated term. When their term expires, verily, Allah has in His sight all His servants."[18] "Such has been the course of Allah that has indeed run before, and you shall not find a change in Allah's course."[19] "My word shall not be changed, nor am I in the least unjust to the servants."[20] God tells us in Surah Ibrahim: "Do not think Allah to be heedless of what the unjust do. He only respites them to a day on which eyes will fixedly stare."[21]

3. INCULCATION OF CORE HUMAN VALUES

In present day Muslim countries, we normally know how to pray and to do other acts of worship. We love to visit Makkah and Madinah and to read the Qur'an, and we may even offer voluntary prayers and other types of worship. Seldom, however, do we care for human rights, social cooperation, and doing our duty well. We do not mind contravening laws or behaving arrogantly. Rarely do we differentiate between what is right and what is wrong, and few of us know how to live with respect and show good manners. Our social behavior needs much refinement. Islam has taught a great deal to the world in this area, but since the living of Islam went in decline in the Muslim world, so did our social behavior and our respect for other people's rights. It is true that we tend to give a great deal of emphasis to worship, but we uncouple our worship from the development of core human values. This is due to the fact that we tend to overlook numerous commands of God and Ahadith that make clear that our faith requires us to love for others what we love for ourselves. Islam teaches that a selfish attitude is wrong. It stresses that a believer should be one of a community where mutual love and compassion are paramount characteristics.

A review and analysis of the early history of Islam reveals how the Messenger managed the implementation of God's commands by developing a group of people with integrity of character who managed to establish a just human society on earth. To develop such social attitudes as Islam desires is a complex process, and the approach to achieve the desired goal must tackle all of its aspects at the same time. The issue is much too serious to be left to individuals, teachers, or parents. It requires a whole national and community effort.

3.1 Development and Propagation of Core Human Values

Human development is a must for community progress and cannot be achieved without certain core human values among its members. God tells us in Surah Al-Jumuah: "It is He Who has sent amongst the unlettered a messenger from among themselves, to rehearse to them His Signs, to sanctify them, and to instruct them in Scripture and Wisdom— although they had been, before, in manifest error"[22] In Makkah, we see the Messenger (1) teaching verses of the Qur'an, (2) purifying the people, (3) imparting knowledge, and (4) imparting wisdom. The objectives and the results of these activities at Makkah are highlighted below, and each one of us has to follow the footsteps of the Messenger to the best of our abilities, in order to reform ourselves and to help others in this pursuit.

Duties of the Messenger and Human Leaders	Objective	Impact
Recites to them Allah's revelations.	Develop faith in Allah and individual responsibility	Inculcate accountability for individual actions
Purifies them.	Develop character	Human development
Teaches the Book (Qur'an).	Provide religious guidelines	Set life's objectives
Teaches wisdom.	Religious and professional education for social and economic development	Develop religious and professional competency

3.2 Establishment of the Best Communities for Humankind

The core human values that were developed among the early followers of Islam were a prerequisite for establishing a just community at Madinah, and the same is true if we aspire to establish similar communities today. The end result of these efforts by early Muslims was what God declared: "You are the best of peoples, evolved for mankind, enjoining what is right, forbidding what is wrong, and believing in Allah."[23] For the protection of such a community, God commands: "Fight in the cause of Allah those who fight you, but do not transgress limits, for Allah loves not transgressors."[24] How were all of the core human values implemented and protected at Madinah? This is highlighted below

Items	Responsibilities	God's Commands	Areas of Human Activity
Protection of ideology	Piety and character	Have faith in Allah. Do and enjoin others to do what is right	Religious and professional education and practice
Protection of freedom	Individual and social responsibilities	Refrain from what is wrong	Establishing justice under all circumstances
Protection of society	Economical and political responsibilities	Forbid what is wrong (eradicate inequality, oppression, discrimination, corruption, and injustice)	Economic activity, trade Zakah, charity, taxation, and social and criminal justice
Protection of property	International relations and defense	Fight in the way of Allah with those who fight with you.	Treaties, army, and protection of the state

3.3 Corruption in Modern Islamic Communities

Efforts are required to improve the character and behavior of people, as well as the character and the working of the state. It is an individual's responsibility to elect honest and trustworthy people to the government who should be ready to account for their behavior, whether it is to the people or to God. Muslims cannot and should not be ruled by corrupt people or corrupt governments. Based on the Sunnah of the Messenger, the core protection areas that are required for the continual maintenance and progress of humankind, regardless of chronological era, are highlighted below:

No	Core Protection Areas	Required Implementation
1	Protection of life, liberty and prosperity	Equal access to food, shelter, and medical facilities
2	Protection of belief and freedom of belief	Comprehensive religious and professional education for all, male and female, poor and rich
3	Equal opportunity and freedom from discrimination and exploitation.	Implementation of justice under all circumstances and adoption of moral and social values
4	Protection of individual and state rights	Promoting good and forbidding evil
5	Protection of society and its institutions	Fighting against all types aggression and corruption

Individually and collectively, the development, implementation, protection, and improvement of these core values are obligatory for us, and we are all responsible for them in our own spheres of influence. Our efforts should be continuous and simultaneous, in order to ensure that the following are being taken care of at all times under all circumstances: (1) the basic necessities required for existence, (2) education to develop personal integrity and professionalism, (3) the inculcation of moral and social values, (4) the protection of individual and state rights, and (5) the protection of society and its institutions.

3.4 Morality is urgently needed in Our Governments

The importance of morality at an individual level is well-known. Without morality, humankind is just an animal taking care of its personal needs by whatever methods are available, whether legal or illegal. However, don't we also need morality at the public and collective level? According to Islam, the progress and survival of nations, the development of their civilization and culture, and the consolidation of their power and strength depend on morality. If people have good moral character, then all good qualities of leadership will be there in them. On the other hand, no nation can survive the immorality of their people, especially the immoral character of their leaders. This is because nations live as long as their morality lives, and when their moral character declines, they also decline. The Messenger said: "As you are, so will you have rulers over you."[25] The reality is that if the people are just their rulers will be just, and when people are corrupt their rulers will be corrupt. During corrupt times, one has to be patient until the situation improves, and such improvement can only happen through repentance that is followed with good deeds. It was narrated by 'Abdullah ibn Omar that the Messenger said: "A ruler is a shade of Allah on earth. Every oppressed person out of His servants takes shelter with him. When he administers justice, there is a reward for him, and there is gratitude on the part of the subjects. When he oppresses, there is sin on him, and there is then patience upon the subjects."[26]

This Hadith also confirms that the honor and respect of any community, nation, or government will depend on the moral values of its members. If a government is not serious about what God commands and the people are not satisfied with that, if the government does not decide matters justly, and if the government is not kind to the needy and does not honor its promises and covenant, then in such government Islam and the Qur'an are only words. Such a government, being devoid of all the basic values of Islam, deserves to be cursed from every corner of the universe. In a Hadith narrated by Aisha, Ummul Mu'minin: "The Messenger said: 'When Allah has a good purpose for a ruler, He appoints for him a sincere minister who reminds him if he forgets and helps him if he remembers. However, when Allah has a different purpose from that for him, He appoints for him an evil minister who does not remind him if he forgets and does not help him if he remembers.'"[27]

According to the law of nature that God has put in operation, He guards the justice-loving government, even if it is the government of the infidels, and destroys the tyrant government, even if it is the government of so-called Muslims. In the light of the Qur'an and Sunnah, morality is the perfect religion and also the perfect world. If any nation loses its honor in the eyes of God or commands no respect from the people, that happens because government lost its good moral character and became devoid of decent and honorable traits.

4. PRACTICING CORE HUMAN VALUES

A Hadith by At-Tirmidhi records four things that assure the protection of human character and society. The first two highlight honest and lawful earnings, while the third and fourth foster community feelings. These four requirements consist of the following: (1) when you steer away from what God has forbidden, you are among the most devoted of God's servants; (2) when you are content with what God has given you, you are the richest of people; (3) when you are kindly to your neighbor, you are a believer; and (4) when you wish for others what you wish for yourself, you are a Muslim.[28] When these four acts are practiced in a society, we have a community that is entirely different from all those on the face of the today's earth. There are some communities where some of these qualities exist in varying degrees, but there is hardly any approaching them in all aspects. Until we have a community where all these qualities are in full blossom, we cannot say there is a truly Islamic community. When these qualities are all lacking, then the community is not Islamic, even though all the people in that community have Muslim names and claim to believe in Islam. Therefore, we have to make arrangements for the continual propagation and adoption of these human values. This can be done by avoiding what is forbidden, nurturing community relations, enjoining good, and forbidding evil.

4.1 Avoiding what is Illegal, Unethical, and Forbidden

The Hadith narrated by At-Tirmidhi gives an idea of what Islamic life really means. Avoiding what is forbidden indicates true devotion to God. It is not demonstrated by simply offering prayers and fasting or by doing other religious duties more frequently. What is forbidden often has an appeal, and avoiding the forbidden requires the power of moral courage and some real effort, such as resistance to temptation and abandoning pleasure. When one does this for the sake of God, one is truly devoted to Him. Similarly, being content with what God has given is a test of richness. It shows that the lure of life's riches is secondary in one's thoughts. Moreover, it demonstrates that one only wants what comes to him in a lawful manner; if someone is patient and works hard, he will eventually get all that God has destined for him. What people get by theft, bribery, embezzlement, fraud, or similar methods constitutes an aggression against their fellow people or against the community at large. Provisions earned by unlawful means are neither blessed by nor pleasing to God. God commands us in Surah Al-Baqarah: "O people! Eat what is good and lawful on the earth, and do not follow in the footsteps of Satan. He truly is an outright enemy to you."[29]

4.2 Nurturing Friendship and Community Relations

Islam requires its followers to observe, by worship and normal social dealings, a specific Islamic behavior. A believer has a unique identity that is reflected in his manners and behavior. He is always polite, kind, and steering away from what is vulgar or obscene in words and actions. A believer is kind to others and always prefers what is likely to foster good relations with his fellow human beings. It is his duty to evaluate his dealings with others on a continual basis, in order to provide a good example of what Islam means in practice by living up to the requirements of his faith. A believer is an exponent of every virtue and refrains from everything that does not fit with the noble position God has given to humankind. He should bring out and enhance every good aspect in a human life and weaken every evil tendency. In the Hadith by At-Tirmidhi, as cited above, the character and the dealings of a Muslim are highlighted: when you are kindly to your neighbor, you are a believer;

and when you wish for others what you wish for yourself, you are a Muslim. The Messenger linked being a person of faith to being kind to neighbors. In addition, he attached the very idea of being a Muslim to wanting for others what one wants for oneself.

4.3 The People who are Best in Character form the Best Communities

People form the best communities when they believe in God and practice and encourage good behavior and deeds. Islam gives a correct concept of the universe and the relationship between the Creator and His creation. It also gives a correct concept of humankind, the purpose of its existence, and its true position in the universe. It is from this general concept that moral values and principles are derived. Believing in God is necessary in order that those who are hard working, honest, and just in their daily activities, and who encourage the same values in others, can proceed along their appointed course and bear all its difficulties and hardships. They have to face the tyranny of evil and the pressure of worldly desires. They also have to overcome complacency, weakness, and narrow ambitions. That is why in this struggle they have to be equipped with faith. Their support comes from God. If believers neglect the duties that make them the "Best Nation," then they lose the title and honor of being a best nation. God tells the believers in Surah Al-Imran: "You are the best of the nations raised up for (the benefit of) men; you enjoin what is right, forbid what is wrong, and believe in Allah. If the followers of the Book had believed, it would have been better for them. Of them, some are believers, and most of them are transgressors."[30]

4.4 Mobilization for Promoting Harmony and Justice

An Islamic community has to assign some of its members with the task of inviting to all that is good, enjoining the doing of what is right, and forbidding what is wrong. An Islamic community does not come into existence unless it has this essential quality by which it is distinguished from the rest of humankind. Its invitation to all that is good and its enjoining what is right and forbidding what is wrong, in addition to believing in God, give credence to its existence, without which it loses its Islamic identity. Several verses in Surah Al-Imran reflect the importance of promoting good and forbidding evil for the protection of human character and society: "From among you there should be a party who invite to good and enjoin what is right and forbid the wrong, and these it is that shall be successful."[31] "They (Muslims) believe in Allah and the Last Day, and they enjoin what is right and forbid the wrong, and they strive with one another in hastening to do good deeds, and those are among the good."[32] Enjoining what is right and forbidding what is wrong in an Islamic community is like multivitamins that people take to maintain their immune system. If an Islamic community does not exist, then the first priority should be to establish such community.

5. PROTECTING HUMAN VALUES AND SOCIETY

All efforts that believers make for the protection of human values are a struggle defined as Jihad. It could be a simple action, such as standing against any violation of human rights and of Islamic principles. This may require speaking out in public or writing articles or publishing books wherever Islamic principles are being ignored. It may also take the form of reminding people of their Islamic duties and motivating them to conduct their lives according to Islam. In extreme cases, it may entail fighting the enemies of Islam in battle to repel their aggression against the believers and their community. Fighting in Islam is a clearly defined individual right in certain circumstances, and the believers are permitted to fight for the cause of Allah with those who fight against them. If all else fails, fighting should be undertaken to protect people against persecution, coercion, corruption, and all efforts to force them to betray their faith or abandon it. However, fighting and warfare must not be defined by any human desire or motivation, including issues of nationalism and geopolitical ambition. War should not be pursued for glory, dominance, or material aggrandizement. It should not be pursued to gain new markets or to control other people's resources. It should not be pursued to give one class, race, or nation of people dominance over another.

5.1 The Equality and Freedom of Humankind

Most of the socio-political systems that exist today are man-made, and many of them promote the subjugation of one or another group or nation. However, no person or group of people has the right to dominate others. As such, the divine system should replace all those man-made systems that tend to cause people the humiliation of submission to other than the Creator Himself.

One may ask: "Since there is no compulsion admissible in matters of belief, why does Islam give permission to fight, and why has God bought the believers' lives and property with the promise of Paradise, so that they'll fight in His cause?" It is because the believers are committed to fight against tyranny and injustice. God's command of Jihad is same in all the divine books: the Torah, the Injeel (Gospel), and the Qur'an. God tells us in Surah Tawbah: "Surely, Allah has bought from the believers their persons and their property, and in return (He'll give them) Paradise. They will fight in Allah's way; they will slay and be slain— a promise that is binding on Him in the Torah, the Gospel, and the Qur'an. Who is more faithful to his covenant than Allah? Rejoice, therefore, in the pledge that you have made, and that is the mighty achievement."[33]

Jihad is to liberate people from the tyranny of the pharaohs of the world. Just like Moses and his people, the believers have to resist the tyranny of discrimination, exploitation, and corruption. If some people are being intimidated and persecuted, they should have a right to resist such treatment. God asks us: "And why should you not fight in the cause of Allah and of those who, being weak, are ill-treated (and oppressed)? (The oppressed are) men, women and children, whose cry is: 'Our Lord, rescue us from this town whose people are oppressors, and raise for us from You one who will protect, and raise for us from You one who will help!'"[34] Moses' Jihad against Pharaoh was not a war of aggression but a struggle for the liberation of Bani-Israil from the slavery of Pharaoh and his people. In any struggle, the possibility of killing and being killed is always there. Being a religion for all people, Islam aims to liberate people throughout the earth from submission to other people. As such, Islam always confronts tyrannical forces and systems that seek to subjugate people and dominate their lives. These systems are backed by regimes and powers of different sorts, which deprive people from a chance to listen to the Islamic message and to adopt it if they are convinced of its truth. They may even force people, in one way or another, to turn away from the Islamic message. That is the violation of the freedom of belief. For these reasons, Islam motivates people to move forward and fight such systems, but only if all available peaceful means of persuasion fail.

5.2 The Freedom of Individual Thought and Belief

Jihad aims to establish God's authority on earth in order to liberate humankind from submission to any authority other than that of God. This aspect of Jihad has nothing to do with fighting, as compulsion in faith is rigorously prohibited in Islam. In Surah Al-Baqarah, God says: "Let there be no compulsion in religion. Truth stands out clear from error. Whoever rejects evil and believes in Allah has grasped the most trustworthy support that never breaks."[35] People have clearly been told that the truth, if it is really true, does not need any compulsion to convince people of its truth. God tells us: "If it had been your Lord's will, they would all have believed—all who are on earth! Will you then compel people against their will to believe?"[36] Because truth is distinct from error, Islam came to declare and establish a universal principle of freedom of religion for all. This reflects the honor God has given to humankind and the high regard in which one's free will, thought, and emotions are held. God has reaffirmed in Surah Al-Furqan: "Had We willed, We would have raised up a separate warner in each habitation. So, (O Prophet,) do not yield to the disbelievers, but wage a strenuous Jihad against them with this (Qur'an)."[37] This shows God's determination to provide guidance to humankind without violating the freedom of choice that He Himself has granted to people. That is why God commanded the Messenger in this verse to wage Jihad against the unbelievers with the Qur'an, i.e., the word of God, not with the sword.

Freedom of belief is the basic right that recognizes people as human beings. To deny anyone this right is to deny him his humanity. Freedom of belief also implies the freedom to express and propagate one's belief without fear of threat or persecution; otherwise, that freedom is hollow and meaningless. In establishing a most sensible human and social system, Islam, undoubtedly the most enlightened view of life and the world, takes the lead in declaring freedom of religion as the most fundamental principle. It teaches its adherents that they are forbidden to compel or force others to embrace Islam. Islam absolutely forbids the use of force to convert people. Force was not used by the Messenger, even to reform the hypocrite. People converted to Islam because the implementation of its commands assures the welfare of humanity, both in this world as well as in the Hereafter.

5.3 The Protection and Safety of the People

Believers are allowed to fight with those who fight with them. What alternative do believers have if they are attacked because of their belief or for any other illegitimate reason? People have to fight an aggressor—even the animals do that. However, believers have not been allowed to initiate a fight or to be aggressors. God commands the believers: "Fight in the cause of Allah those who fight you, but do not transgress limits. God does not love aggressors."[38] The expression "aggressors" also includes those who attack non-combatants and peaceful, unarmed civilians. Aggression also entails exceeding the moral and ethical limits set by Islam for fighting a just war. These limits outlaw the atrocities perpetrated in wars outside Islam, past and present. Such atrocities are totally repugnant to believers and can never be sanctioned or committed by people who honor and fear God.

God commands the believers to fight in self-defense and for the defense of human rights. "And fight them on until there is no more tumult or oppression and there prevail justice and faith in Allah, altogether and everywhere. However; if they cease, verily Allah sees all that they do."[39] God also orders the believers to fight with those hypocrites and disbelievers who fight with them. However, those hypocrites are excluded who have joined a people with whom the believers have a treaty, as well as those who are averse to fighting either against the believers or against their own people. "God has left no cause for aggression against them, if they leave you alone, refrain from fighting against you and have a desire to make peace with you."40 God commands His Messenger to make efforts himself and to urge the Muslims to do so because, "Whoever pleads a good cause will get a share from it, and whoever pleads an evil cause will get a share from it, for Allah keeps a strict watch over everything."[41] Furthermore: "Wherever you are, death will find you out, even if you are in towers built up strong and high!"[42] Therefore, the believers should not be afraid of death in this pursuit.

5.4 The Elimination of Injustice and Corruption

Human society should be built on hard work, truth, justice and charity, and it should be free of corruption, discrimination, exploitation and oppression. If most of the people in a society are corrupt, and none are trying to improve, such a society will over time eventually be destroyed from within. Since God has discontinued sending messengers, corrupt people and communities may not be completely destroyed as in the past. However, God commands us: "Guard yourselves against a chastisement that cannot fall exclusively on those of you who are wrong-doers, and know that Allah is severe in punishment."[43] The ultimate objective of God's reward and punishment is to save humankind from evil. Evil is committed by one's capability of free choice, a capacity that should be regulated by education and discipline. History tells us that evil and corruption have destroyed many nations because they had false idols for worship, false standards of conduct and false goals of desire. People's efforts to reform their own character and behavior and their efforts to reform society are a part of Jihad. Rather, the efforts required to imple-ment Islamic principles within oneself and one's society and the efforts required to eradicate un-Islamic individual and social behavior are also Jihad.

Jihad is prescribed to establish justice, create functional economies, eradicate corruption, improve social services within a community and safeguard against internal digression and external oppression. God commands believers in Surah Al-Nisa: "O you who believe, be maintain-ers of justice, bearers of witness for Allah's sake, though it may be against your own selves or (your) parents or near relatives. Whether he is rich or poor, Allah can best protect both. Therefore, do not follow your low desires lest you deviate, and if you swerve or turn aside, then surely Allah is aware of what you do."[44] Believers are also commanded: "To fight until there is no more oppression and there prevail justice and faith in Allah. But if they cease oppression, then let there be no hostility."[45] God asks us why people shouldn't fight in the way of Allah for the sake of those help-less men, women and children who, being weak, have been oppressed? In a nutshell, Islam sanctions Jihad for war only to suppress tyranny and persecution and to guarantee freedom of belief for all. Specific situations for waging war and making peace are given in various places in the Qur'an. God tells us: "Warfare is prescribed for you, and you dislike it. But it may happen that you may hate a thing that is good for you, or it may happen that you may love a thing that is bad for you. Allah knows, and you know not."[46] Corruption, injustice and anarchy must be resisted in our communities at any cost: "Were it not for Allah's repelling some with others, the earth would certainly be in a state of disorder."[47]

NOTES

1. Qur'an 6:152.

2. Qur'an 11:87.

3. Qur'an 96:1-5.

4. Qur'an 49:13.

5. Qur'an 67:2.

6. Qur'an 6:165.

7. Qur'an 49:13.

8. Qur'an 13:11.

9. Qur'an 14:7.

10. Qur'an 8:52-53.

11. Qur'an 17:77.

12. Qur'an 33:62.

13. Qur'an 8:24-25.

14. Qur'an 8:19.

15. Qur'an 8:38-40.

16. Qur'an 35:43.

17. Qur'an 35:44.

18. Qur'an 35:45.

19. Qur'an 48:23.

20. Qur'an 50:29.

21. Qur'an 14:42.

22. Qur'an 62:2.

23. Qur'an 3:110.

24. Qur'an 2:190.

25. Al-Hadith, vol. II, no. 358w, p553.

26. Al-Hadith, vol. II, no. 367w, p567.

27. Abu Dawud 19.2926.

28. Al-Hadith, vol. I, no. 153, p252.

29. Qur'an 2:168.

30. Qur'an 3:110.

31. Qur'an 3:104.

32. Qur'an 3:114.

33. Qur'an 9:111.

34. Qur'an 4:75.

35. Qur'an 2:256.

36. Qur'an 10:99.

37. Qur'an 25:52.

38. Qur'an 2:190.

39. Qur'an 8:39.

40. Qur'an 4:90.

41. Qur'an 4:85.

42. Qur'an 4:78.

43. Qur'an 8:25.

44. Qur'an 4:135.

45. Qur'an 2:193.

46. Qur'an 2:216.

47. Qur'an 2:251.

CHAPTER 10

RELIGION IMPACTS THE HUMAN CHARACTER
(Educate Yourself to Be Moral)

IT IS MOST IMPORTANT to achieve harmony between faith, piety and implementation of the divine law in practical life, on the one hand, and work productivity and the fulfillment of the human mission on earth, on the other. It is this harmony that ensures the fulfillment of God's promise to people of earlier revelations, and indeed to all communities, that they will have abundance of provisions from all sources in this world and that they will be forgiven their sins and admitted into Paradise in the Hereafter. Thus, they have a paradise on earth and a paradise in Heaven. We must not forget, however, that the fundamental principles and the mainstays of the whole system are faith, piety and the implementation of the divine way in our own lives and in society. This, indeed, implies hard work, better productivity and development of human and material resources. Moreover, when a person maintains a constant link with God, all aspects of life bring about better enjoyment, enhance one's values and correct one's standards. This is the starting point from which everything else follows.

1. FAITH IS TO BE GOD CONSCIOUS AND HUMAN

People need to develop their character and behavior, along with their physical and mental maturity, to make themselves suitable as God's trustees. A complete description of the guidelines for what human conduct should be like is given in the Qur'an. These guidelines educate, and their implementation makes us disciplined. God tells us about the Qur'an in Surah Al-Baqarah: "This is the Book; in it is the guidance, without doubt, to those who fear Allah."[1] God then commands: "O people! Serve your Guardian-Lord, Who created you and those who came before you, that you may have the chance to learn righteousness."[2] Humanity needs guidelines and discipline to provide a better life on earth to all. The people who do not follow the guidelines create problems. God says about such people: "When it is said to them, 'Make not mischief on the earth,' they say, 'Why we only want to make peace!' Surely, they are the ones who make mischief, but they realize it not."[3]

1.1 Learn to be Human and God-Conscious

The purpose of education is to develop personal integrity and individual usefulness. After developing people's relationship with God, Islam helps build human character, refines human behavior and teaches how to deal with others. It is the Islamic religion that, through its obligations of belief, prayer, fasting, charity and pilgrimage, makes people conscientious of their accountability for their actions and develops patience, a quality of character that is very much needed to succeed in life. Hard work, integrity and contentment all go together in one's struggle in life.

1.2 Cultivate a Friendly Relationship with God

How can one cultivate a friendly relation with God? God tells us: "Prostrate to Allah, the Creator, if Him it is that you serve!"[4] Believers are those: (1) who say: "Our Lord is God," then continue in the right way; (2) invite people to God, do righteous deeds, and say, "I am a Muslim;" (3) know that goodness and evil are not equal and repel evil with what is better; (4) are patient and guard themselves; (5) seek refuge in God if Satan should ever tempt them to mischief; and (6) receive the protection of God's angels both in this world and in the Hereafter.[5]

1.3 Worship your Lord to Learn Righteousness

What is righteousness? It is correct belief and the doing of good deeds. God tells us in Surah Al-Baqarah: "Righteousness is to believe in Allah and the Last Day and the angels and the Book and the messengers, to spend of your substance out of love for Him for your kin, for orphans, for the needy, for the wayfarer, for those who ask, and for the ransom of slaves, to be steadfast in prayer and practice regular charity; to fulfill the contracts that you have made, and to be firm and patient in pain (or suffering) and adversity and throughout all periods of panic. Such are the people of truth, the God-fearing."[6] In addition, in Surah Al-Imran we are told that a person does not attain righteousness until he gives freely of that which he loves.[7]

1.4 God Develops His Trustees for their Betterment

God's angels assure the righteous people: "We are your guardians in this world's life and in the Hereafter, and you shall have therein what you desire, and you shall have therein what you ask for."[8] People should also remember that their Lord has proclaimed: "If you give thanks, I would certainly give to you more, and if you are ungrateful for My favors, My chastisement is truly severe."[9] People should not forget what God said to Moses when he desired to see Him: "O Moses! Surely I have chosen you above the people with My messages and by My speaking (to you); therefore, take hold of what I give to you, and be among the thankful."[10] God's commands motivate and help people to overcome their weaknesses and transform themselves into individuals of good moral character and behavior who are worthy of God's love and His mercy. God wants such people to be His trustees.

1.5 Believers Trust their Lord and Rely on Him

When people have earned God's love by being righteous and doing good deeds, they have no reason for not relying on God's help. Believers are commanded in Surah Ibrahim: "On Allah the believers should rely. What reason have we that we should not rely on Allah? He has, indeed, guided us in our ways, and certainly we will bear with patience your (unbelievers) persecution of us. Those who would rely (on something) should rely on Allah."[11] God has His Own divine ways to help those who put their trust in Him. God tells us in Surah Al-Talaq: "He (God) provides for him (the person who is mindful of God) from (sources) he never could imagine. If anyone puts his trust in Allah, sufficient is (Allah) for him."[12]

2. CHARACTERISTICS OF GOOD HUMAN BEHAVIOR

Morality is the most important aspect of human lives. It is human morality that determines and defines the quality of life on earth. One can even say that without good moral character humanity is bound to fail as God's trustee on earth, generating long-lasting negative consequences for itself and for others around it. That is why all of the elements of good moral character should be implemented. Islam has enumerated all these virtues and principles and has encouraged its followers to make them part of their lives. It was reported by Anas that whenever the Messenger addressed his followers, he invariably repeated this sentence: "The man has no faith who cannot keep trust, and the man who does not respect his promises has no religion."[13]

There are numerous sayings of the Messenger stressing the importance of good moral character. In one tradition, people asked Prophet Muhammad: "What is the best thing given to man?" He replied: "The best is moral character."[14] Masruq narrated that according to 'Abdullah bin 'Amr the Messenger said: "The best among you are those who have the best manners and character."[15] Aisha narrated that the Messenger said: "By his good character a believer will attain the degree of one who prays during the night and fasts during the day."[16] Abud Darda narrated that the Messenger said: "There is nothing heavier put on the scale of a believer on the Day of Judgment than good character."[17] Why was the Messenger stressing good moral character to the believers? This is due the fact that without good moral character, humankind ceases to be human and cannot deliver its responsibilities as God's trustee. Only trustworthy people can guard their trust.

2.1 Believers have Good Intentions and Conduct

People's good or bad actions are the outcome of their intentions. Believers have good intentions for everyone, and they confirm it by their behavior. The believer's intentions are always for piety to God and His pleasure. People are asked in Surah Al-Tawbah: "Which then is best: he that lays his foundation on piety to Allah and His good pleasure, or he that lays his foundation on an undermined sand-cliff ready to crumble to pieces?"[18] God tells us in Surah Al-Hujurat that in His sight, the noblest among people are those who are best in conduct: "O people! Lo! We created you all from a male and a female and made you into nations and tribes that you may know one another. Lo! The noblest of you in the sight of Allah is the best in conduct. Lo! Allah knows and is aware."[19]

There are many factors that motivate people to do a job in a better way. They can include self-promotion, greed for more wealth, the feelings of pride and self-importance, hypocrisy, and the desire for fame. Islam judges acts and deeds and decides their value on the basis of their intentions. For example, charity is usually an admirable act, but Islam does not value charity if it is given in a hypocritical way or for attaining fame. It should be given entirely for seeking the pleasure of God, as is described in Surah Al-Dahr: "They give food out of love for Him (God) to the poor and the orphan and the captive, (saying):'We feed you for the sake of Allah alone; no reward do we desire from you, nor thanks.'"[20] The same theme is reiterated in Surah Al-Layl: "But those most devoted to Allah...(are) those who spend their wealth for increase in self-purification and have in their minds no favor from anyone for which a reward is expected in return, except the seeking of the pleasure of his Lord, the Most High, and soon will they attain (complete) satisfaction."[21]

Even acts that are usually considered righteous, if carried out with wrong intention, become bad deeds. Such hypocrisy has been condemned in Surah Al-Maun: "So woe to the worshippers who are neglectful of their prayers, who (want but) to be seen (by men), but withhold even neighborly needs."[22] In short, prayers based on hypocrisy and without sincerity are of no value. Similarly if Zakah is paid for the benefit of a deserving person with an intention to seek God's pleasure, then it is acceptable; otherwise, it is wasted. God confirms this interpretation in Surah Al-Baqarah: "O you who believe! Do not make your charity worthless by reproach and injury, like him who spends his property to be seen by men and does not believe in Allah and the Last Day."[23] Otherwise beneficial deeds that are done without good intentions can neither achieve the pleasure of God nor benefit the worldly life. Abu Huraira reported that Allah's Messenger said: "Verily, Allah does not look to your faces and your wealth, but He looks to your heart and to your deeds."[24]

2.2 Believers are True in their Words and Deeds

God created the universe on the basis of love and commands people to build their lives on the foundation of truth. Humankind is instructed to be true in its words and dealings. God commands us in Surah Al-Tawbah: "O you who believe, fear Allah, and be with those who are true in word and deeds."[25] Also, in Surah Al-Hujurat, God tells about those who are the truthful: "The believers are only those who have believed in Allah and His Messenger and have never since doubted. They have struggled hard with their wealth and their lives in the way of Allah; such are the truthful ones."[26] This leaves no doubt that speaking the truth is one of the most important traits of the believers. It is the believers' duty to be truthful in every matter and to see every problem and affair through the glasses of truth. God tells people in Surah Al-Zumer: "He who brings the truth and he who confirms (and supports) it—such are the men who do right."[27]

Islamic society is developed on the foundation of truth, and mere conjectures and superstitions are opposed. Baseless things and imaginary stories are thrown out. Doubts and misgivings are not encouraged. This is because only strong and firm realities deserve to be highlighted. The Qur'an condemned those communities whose inhabitants followed conjectures, superstitions and spread corruption via misrepresentation of the truth. When referring to idols and to the female names given to the angels by the unbelievers, God tells us: "They are nothing but names you have made up—you and your fathers. Allah has not sent for (them to do) that. They follow nothing but conjecture and the low desires to which (their) souls incline…but they have no knowledge of it (the names of all the angels); they do not follow anything but conjecture, and surely conjecture does not at all avail against the truth."[28] The distinctive characteristics of the Islamic society at Madinah were truth, discipline, tolerance, and the use of good manners in speech. Falsehood, breaking promises, false accusations, and baseless things are the signs of breaking away from religion. To invent lies against God's religion is the worst evil. One who has the slightest relationship with God and His Messenger will never indulge in this kind of activity. It was narrated by Al-Mughira that he heard the Prophet saying: "Ascribing false things to me is not like ascribing false things to anyone else. Whoever intentionally tells a lie against me—then surely let him occupy his seat in Hell-fire."[29]

2.3 Believers Cultivate Truth in their Daily Lives

Islam commands that the importance of truth should be cultivated from childhood. People should not make false statements even in their jokes for the entertainment of people, thinking that there is nothing wrong if baseless information is given or false and imaginary events are related. Islam has prescribed that only those methods that are within the limits of truth are proper and permissible. God's Messenger said: "Woe to him who indulges in storytelling in order to make some people laugh, and for that he relies on falsehood. Woe to him."[30] Islam commands people to avoid exaggeration even in praising people. One should praise somebody only to the extent that is accurate. Exaggeration is a kind of falsehood that is forbidden.

Disregarding truth in giving evidence is the worst type of falsehood. When a person stands up to give evidence, he should state the truth regardless of the fact whether or not it hurts his close friend or a favorite person. No relationship or prejudice should make people deviate from the truth, nor should any greed or bribe make them waver in their stand. God commands believers in Surah Al-Nisa: "O you who believe, be maintainers of justice, bearers of witness for Allah's sake, though it may be against your own selves or (your) parents or near relatives. Whether he is rich or poor, Allah can best protect both. Therefore, do not follow your low desires lest you deviate, and if you swerve or turn aside, then surely Allah is aware of what you do."[31]

Modern marketing techniques are based on unlimited greed. The sellers desire the highest selling prices, while the buyer wants to buy for less. Some marketing people make erroneous and misleading statements in advertisements. Ignorant buyers may then believe whatever the seller says. Honesty does not permit taking undue advantage of people by charging unnecessarily high prices or concealing product defects. The trickery and deception that people see in advertisements are a type of falsehood in which people try to prove that what is false is actually true. Such misleading advertising is harmful to individuals and dangerous to society. If people are truthful in their speech and dealings, they will be sincere in their actions and behavior. Adopting truth in dealing with others also helps to improve peoples' character and behavior. God assures this in Surah Al-Ahzab: "O you who believe! Be careful of your duty to Allah, and speak the truth. He will put your deeds into a right state for you and forgive you your faults, and whoever obeys Allah and His Messenger, he indeed achieves a mighty success."[32]

2.4 Believers honor their Promises and Contracts

People should take special care in keeping their promises. When people keep promises, it confirms that they are true to their words and that they do not change in their stand. No society can progress on false promises. God considers fulfilling promises to be one of the attributes of the prophets. In Surah Maryam, it is said about Ismail: "Mention Ismail in the Book; surely, he was truthful in his promise, and he was a messenger, a prophet."[33]

Promises must be fulfilled, whether the other party is a believer or a non-believer. Morality and righteousness cannot be hypocritical, in that some people are treated with meanness while others are treated decently. Promises and covenants that are based on truth and straight dealing should be fulfilled, no matter who is the second party.

Believers should not compromise their promises and contracts. People often break their contracts due to the desire for temporary profit. Likewise, one nation makes an agreement with another nation, but greed for better advantages and other considerations compels it to break the agreement. Islam considers it highly objectionable that, just for temporary benefit, virtue is compromised by letting deception enter into dealings among people and nations. Islam makes it obligatory for individuals, as well as groups, to be honest, decent, and sincere. In all conditions of poverty or riches, victory or defeat, promises and contracts among individuals or countries must be safeguarded. In Surah Al-Baqarah and Surah Al-Maidah, God affirms: "Allah will not call you to account for (unrealistic) promises without forethought, but He will call you to account for the intentions in your hearts."[34]

There are a number of verses in the Qur'an that insist on fulfilling promises and that warn against indulging in disloyalty and breach of promises. In Surah Bani Israil, God commands people: "Fulfill your promises. Verily, you will be answerable for your promises,"[35] In Surah Al-

Nihl, the believers are commanded to honor covenants and oaths: "Fulfill the covenant of Allah when you have made one, and do not break the oaths after making them fast. You have, indeed, made Allah a surety for you; surely, Allah knows what you do."[36] God also commands people not to use their oaths and promises to mislead others: "And do not make your oaths a means of deceit between you, lest the foot that was stable might slip, causing you to taste the evil (consequences) of having hindered (others) from Allah's way, for yours would be an awful punishment. Nor sell the covenant of Allah for a miserable price, for with Allah is (a prize) far better for you, if you only knew."[37]

2.5 Believers are Trustworthy and deal with Justice

Islam expects from its followers that their hearts should be full of humanity under the wakeful guard of their conscience, thus ensuring people's rights. Believers should protect people from injustice, exploitation, and corruption. In Surah Al-Nisa, people are commanded: "Surely, Allah commands you to make over trusts to their owners and that when you judge between people you judge with justice."[38] As noted in Surah Al-Baqarah, testimony is also a trust; therefore, God commands people: "Do not conceal testimony, and whoever conceals it, his heart is surely sinful."[39] In Surah Al-Muminun, God describing the believers as: "Those who faithfully observe their trusts and their covenants, and (those) who guard their prayers—these are the heirs who will inherit Paradise."[40] From Islamic point of view, a trust means responsibility, and it entails the sense of having to appear before God and to account for one's actions.

People should make sure that they do not forget to honor their promises and contracts. If a person forgets his promises and covenants, how can he fulfill them? That is why some verses end with a note of admonition after giving a command to fulfill promises and contracts. In Surah Ta Ha, God says about Adam: "We had already beforehand taken the covenant of Adam, but he forgot, and We found on his part no firm resolve."⁴¹ In Surah Al-Anam, God commands us: "Fulfill the covenant of Allah; thus does He command you that you may remember."⁴² God clarifies that breach of promise and disloyalty destroy confidence, create disorder, sever relationships, reduce strength, and make individuals weak and low. People who break promises are advised in Surah Al-Nahl: "Be not like her who unravels her yarn, disintegrating it into pieces after she has spun it strongly, nor make your oaths to be means of mutual deceit so that one people might take greater advantage than another. Allah only tries you by this, and He will most certainly make clear on the Day of Resurrection the truth concerning the matters over which you differed."⁴³

2.6 Believers Guard the Deposits put in their Trust

An office or a position should be offered only to the deserving person who is able to shoulder its responsibilities and is capable of delivering the trust. Mere excellence in education or experience does not make a person suitable for some offices. A person may have good moral character and righteous behavior, but he is lacking professional capabilities and is not fit for the job. Prophet Yusuf (Joseph) did not offer his services as a treasurer in Egypt based only on his righteousness, but also on account of his learning and knowledge. We learn this in Surah Yusuf: "(Joseph) said: 'Place me over the treasures of the land; surely, I am a good keeper, knowing well.'"⁴⁴ On the other hand, a perfectly competent person could ruin his/her assignment by being corrupt and dishonest. Trust should be entrusted to those who can run things properly. By not offering assignments based on merit, one is committing a double crime. The initial crime is encouraging inefficiency and corruption. The second crime is discouraging hardworking, competent people who are not offered the opportunity. This leads future generations to corruption instead of to honesty and hard work. It was narrated by Abu Huraira that a man came to the Prophet and asked, "When will the Hour (the end of time) take place?" The Prophet said: "When honesty is lost, then wait for the Hour." He was again asked: "How will that be lost?" The Prophet said, "When the power or authority comes in the hands of unfit persons, then wait for the Hour."[45]

One should try one's best to live up to any trust given to him. An individual entrusted with an assignment should have a sincere desire to complete it satisfactorily. Performance of duty is a trust, while the misuse of office is the betrayal of trust. A public servant who is not trying to eliminate public hardships and injustice is deceitful and deserves to face the bad consequences of his inefficiency. Trust demands that one should not use one's position for self-promotion or for the benefit of one's relatives and friends. The use of public funds and facilities for personal use is a crime. Leaders should always be trustworthy. In Surah Al-Imran people are told: "No prophet could act unfaithfully, and he who acts unfaithfully shall have to restore what he misappropriated on the Day of Resurrection. Then shall every soul be paid back fully what it has earned, and they shall not be dealt with unjustly."[46] Islam forbids the exploitation of one's office and taking undue advantage from it. Islam is also very severe in closing down every avenue of injustice and of earning illegal wealth.

2.7 Believers Treat their Abilities as a Divine Trust

People should acknowledge and be thankful for the abilities with which God has blessed them. One's physical and mental capabilities, one's education and knowledge, and one's property and children are all God-given trusts. Therefore, these should not be a cause of arrogance and pride, but they should be utilized in His cause and in seeking His pleasure. If people suffer a loss in them, they should not complain. However, as long as they are in their possession, they should be treated and cared for like a trust. In Surah Al-Anfal the believers are reminded that they will be tried concerning their property and children: "O you

who believe! Be not unfaithful to Allah and the Messenger, nor knowingly be unfaithful to your trusts. And know that your property and your
children are a temptation and that Allah is He with Whom there is a
mighty reward."[47]

People are accountable for all deposits that are given to them for
safekeeping, and these trusts are to be returned on demand. In Surah An-
Nisa, God commands people: "Surely, Allah commands you to make over
trusts to their owners and that when you judge between people you judge
with justice. Surely, Allah admonishes you with what is excellent. Surely,
Allah is seeing, hearing."[48] It is confirmed that the Messenger used to
advise the believers to keep their promises and to pay back trusts.
'Abdullah bin 'Abbas narrated that the Messenger ordered that prayers be
established, the truth be spoken, and people be chaste, keep promises,
and pray back trusts. [49]

2.8 Believers are dignified in their Words and Speech

The ability to speak makes humankind superior to all other creatures
on earth. Islam has given special attention to speech, its style, its
etiquette, and its rules. The words that come out from peoples' mouths
disclose their intellect and moral nature. Islam has explained how people
should derive benefit from this blessing and how speech is to be used for
goodness and truth. An ability to avoid irrelevant and vain talk is a source
for success and a proof of perfection. In Surah Al-Munimun, keeping
aloof from vain talk is mentioned in between two essential duties of
believers, which gives an idea of its importance: "Successful indeed are
the believers, who are humble in their prayers, who avoid vain talk, who
engage in charity…"[50] In Surah Al-Furqan, people are told that the
believers are: "Those who do not bear witness to what is false, and when
they pass by what is vain, they pass by nobly."[51]

There are people who are never tired of talking and even talking
uselessly. God has not given people their tongues for senseless, absurd,

and vain talk. In Surah Al-Nisa people are told: "There is no good in most of their secret counsels, except if someone enjoins charity or goodness or reconciliation between people. Whoever does this (engaging in secret councils to promote charity, goodness, or reconciliation) seeking Allah's pleasure, We will give him a mighty reward."[52] Ill-mannered, hot-tempered, and offensive talkers are very difficult to deal with and should be avoided. God commands believers in Surah Al-Furqan: "The servants of (Allah) the Compassionate are those who walk on the earth in humility, and when the ignorant address them, they say, 'Peace.'"[53] Believers respect everyone, but that does not mean that people's bad behavior and offensive talk should be tolerated. Believers are told in Surah An-Nisa: "Allah does not love the public utterance of hurtful speech, unless (it be) by one to whom injustice has been done, and Allah is hearing, knowing. If you do good openly or keep it secret or forgive evil, lo! Allah is ever forgiving, powerful."[54] Believers are also discouraged from participating in controversial discussions and debate. Islam dislikes gatherings where people sit and waste their time and where people get involved in discussing the defects of others. Their purpose is to seek pleasure in the weaknesses of the others. God tells in Surah Al-Humazah: "Woe to every slanderer and defamer who has gathered wealth and arranged it. He thinks that his wealth will make him immortal. By no means! He will be sure to be thrown into that which breaks to pieces."[55] At present, such gatherings do occur in meeting halls, at dinner parties, on television, and even in mosques, which definitely should be discouraged.

2.9 Believers Say Something Good or Keep Silent

When a person has to speak, he should say something good and worthwhile or keep silent. He should teach himself decent and respectable conversation. It has been mentioned in Surah Al-Baqarah that the covenant that Moses took from Bani Israil included that they should speak with each other in good and worthwhile conversation: "And remember We took a covenant from the Children of Israel, saying, 'Worship none but Allah. Treat with kindness your parents and kindred and orphans and those in need. Speak fair to the people. Be steadfast in prayer, and practice regular charity.' Then did you turn back, except a few among you."[56] Good conversation impresses both friends and foes. It strengthens friendship and defeats all of Satan's whispers for sowing the seeds of discord among people. God commands the Messenger in Surah Bani Israil: "Say to My servants that they speak that which is best; surely, Satan sows dissensions among them; surely, Satan is an open enemy to man."[57]

If people talk gracefully with their enemies, their enmity will disappear, and their tempers will be cooled. God tells people in Surah Ha Mim Al-Sajdah: "Good and evil cannot be equal. Repel evil with what is better. Then between whom and you was enmity would be as if he were a warm friend."[58] Good words are a gift that are better than giving gifts in an indecent manner. In Surah Al-Baqarah people are told: "Kind speech accompanied by forgiveness is better than charity followed by insulting words."[59] God has commanded that we should discuss matters with the followers of other religions in the best possible manner. God commands believers in Surah Al-Ankabut: "Do not argue with the followers of the Book except by what is best, unless with those of them who act unjustly. Say: 'We believe in that which has been revealed to us and revealed to you. Our God and your God is one, and to Him do we submit.'"[60]

2.10 Believers Earn their Living with Honor and Dignity

Islam encourages everyone to work hard to earn one's livelihood. It also mandates that the government is responsible for helping people find jobs or establish a business. In Islam, work is equated with worship. Anas bin Malik narrated: "We were with the Messenger on a journey, and the only shade one could have was the shade made by one's own self. Those who fasted did not do any work, and those who did not fast (being exempt from fasting because of the journey) served the camels, brought the water to them, and treated the sick and wounded. So the Messenger said, 'Today, those who were not fasting took (all) the reward.'"[61] Anas bin Malik also narrated: "God's Apostle said, 'There is none among the Muslims who plants a tree or sows a seed, and then a bird or a person or an animal eats from it, but it is regarded as a charitable gift for him.'"[62] God called honest earning a "bounty of your Lord:" Ibn 'Abbas narrated: "Ukaz, Majanna, and Dhul-Majaz were marketplaces in the pre-Islamic period of ignorance. When Islam came, Muslims felt that marketing there might be a sin. So the divine inspiration came: 'There is no harm for you to seek the bounty of your Lord[63].' Ibn 'Abbas recited the verse in this way.[64]

In the struggle concerning one's earnings, avoiding what is forbidden indicates true belief in God and reliance on Him. There is no better food than what is acquired from lawful earnings. Highlighting the adverse consequences of consuming unlawful things, Abu Huraira reported God's Messenger as saying that God is pure, accepts only that which is pure, and commanded the believers as He commanded the messengers by saying: "O Messengers, eat of the good things, and do good deeds; verily, I am aware of what you do."[65] God also said: "O those who believe! Eat of the good things that We gave you."[66] The Prophet once made a mention of a person who travels widely, his hair disheveled and covered with dust. He lifts his hand towards the sky (and makes supplication): "O Lord, O Lord," but his diet is unlawful, his drink is unlawful, his clothes are unlawful, and his nourishment is unlawful. The Prophet then asked how this person's supplication can be accepted? [67]

2.11 Believers Abhor Charity or Begging for their Living

It is not permissible for a believer to live on charity or to beg, except in very limited cases. Samurah ibn Jundub narrated that the Prophet said: "Acts of begging are lacerations with which a man disfigures his face, so he who wishes may preserve his self-respect, and he who wishes may abandon it. But this does not apply to one who begs from a ruler or in a situation that makes it necessary."[68] Once, a man came to the Messenger, asking him for charity. He asked him whether he had any article of clothing or furniture in his home. The man was very poor, and he had a couple of articles that could not fetch much. The Messenger, nevertheless, asked him to bring them and asked his companions whether any of them would like to buy those two articles. One person bought them for a small amount. The Messenger divided the money in two halves, giving the man one-half to buy food for his children. With the other, he told him to buy an ax and a rope. Then he told him to go to the nearby mountain and collect firewood. When he made a bundle, he should take it to the market and sell it. The man continued this type of work for a fortnight, during which he did not come to see the Messenger. At the end of this period, the man came wearing a new dress and told the Messenger that he has been able to save a little amount of money. The Messenger said: "It is far better for any one of you to take an ax and go to the mountain to collect firewood than to ask people for charity, whether they give him what he asks for or decline to give."[69]

2.12 Charity is for Community Response to Emergencies

The Islamic economic system is based on individual development by education and training, equal opportunities, and social justice. Abundant jobs should be available for all community members. People who work should be able to earn enough money to meet their needs. However, the community should look after their poor and needy people, which should normally be a very small number. It is obligatory for rich people to pay their Zakah to deserving people. This is, indeed, something that should be undertaken by the Islamic state. When there is no central authority to collect Zakah and distribute it among its beneficiaries, then people should pay it individually.

There will always be some people in every community who are not able, for various reasons, to earn their livelihood, but they struggle on, preserving their modesty and personal dignity by not becoming a burden on anyone else. They do their utmost to hide their need and distress, and only a few people are able to detect and appreciate their hardship. In the Qur'an, God praises such poor people who conduct themselves with honor, giving the impression of being well off, and who do not ask other people to give them anything of what they have. Such people, who hide their needs, should be offered assistance privately and without offending their dignity. In Surah Al-Baqarah, God says: "(Alms are) for the poor who are confined in the way of Allah—they cannot go about in the land to earn their living. On account of (their) abstaining (from begging); the people thinks them to be rich. You may recognize them by their special mark; they do not beg from men importunately. Whatever good thing you spend, surely Allah knows it. (As for) those who spend their property by night and by day, secretly and openly, they shall have their reward from their Lord, and they shall have no fear, nor shall they grieve."[70]

3. PERSONAL RESPONSIBILITY AND ACCOUNTABILITY

Discrimination, exploitation, and corruption are directly proportionate to lack of belief in one's accountability for one's deeds and actions. Humankind, being God's trustee, has an assignment to complete during its life on earth. We are being supervised as how we perform our duties. Our life on earth is a test so that we may prove who amongst us can utilize one's life to its best purpose and potential. In Surah Al-Mulk, people are told that it is God, "Who has created life and death that He may try which of you is best in conduct."[71] God again reminds people in

Surah Al-Hujurat: "O people! Lo! We created you all from a male and a female and made you into nations and tribes that you may know one another. Lo! The noblest of you in the sight of Allah is the best in conduct. Lo! Allah knows and is aware."[72]

With regard to our responsibilities for which we are accountable, it was narrated by 'Abdullah bin 'Umar that he heard God's Messenger saying: "All of you are guardians and responsible for your wards and the things under your care. The Imam (ruler) is the guardian of his subjects and is responsible for them, and a man is the guardian of his family and is responsible for them. A woman is the guardian of her husband's house and is responsible for it. A servant is the guardian of his employer's belongings and is responsible for them…A man is the guardian of his father's property and is responsible for it. All of you are guardians and responsible for your wards and the things under your care."[73]

3.1 Individual Responsibility and Accountability

Humankind has not been born to be irresponsible in this world. We are accountable for our deeds, whether good or bad, and will have to face their good or bad consequences in this world and in the Hereafter. If we reflect a little, we will realize that our doubts and our astonishment about the Hereafter are absolutely baseless. How can our resurrection be impossible for that God Who created us in the first place from an insignificant sperm drop? We are reminded in Surah Fatir: "O people! Surely, the promise of Allah is true. Therefore, let not the life of this world deceive you, and let not Satan deceive you about Allah."[74] We are also reminded: "Whoever desires power, then all power belongs to Allah. To Him do ascend the good words (prayers), and (He) lifts up (the status of) good deeds. Those who plan evil deeds, they shall have a severe chastisement; and (as for) their plan, it shall perish."[75]

People are responsible for what they do, and none can bear the burden of another. They are only responsible to the extent of their abilities. God does not burden people beyond what He has given them. A number of rules that govern individual responsibility have been mentioned in the Qur'an. In Surah Yunus, God tells the Prophet to inform people that each person is only responsible for what he does: "Say: My work belongs to me and yours to you! You are free from responsibility for what I do, and I for what you do!"[76] Likewise, in Surah Bani Israel, God tells people: "Neither one can bear the burden of another, nor do We chastise until We raise a Messenger."[77] Still further, in Surah Al-Talaq, God tells people that they are only responsible to the extent of their abilities: "Let the people with means spend according to their means, and people whose resources are restricted, let them spend according to what Allah has given them. Allah puts no burden on any person beyond what He has given him."[78]

3.2 Believers are Honest and Strive Hard in Good Deeds

Believers are hard working, are not lazy, and diligently attend to their duties towards God and their duties towards His creation. They are honest in their dealings and do not fulfill their needs and desires by wrong ways. Such people are the servants of God. Their character and behavior is fully described in Surah Al-Furqan: "The servants of (Allah) the Compassionate are those who walk on the earth in humility, and when the ignorant address them, they say, 'Peace.' (God's servants are) those who pass their night in worship, prostrating and standing. They are the ones who say: 'Our Lord! Avert from us the wrath of Hell, for its wrath is indeed an affliction grievous. Evil, indeed, is it as an abode and as a place in which to rest.' When they spend, they are not extravagant and not miserly, but (they) hold a just (balance) between those (extremes). They invoke not, with Allah, any other god, nor do they slay such life as Allah made sacred, except for just cause, nor do they commit fornication. Any who does this (not only) meets punishment, (but) the penalty on the Day of Judgment will be doubled for him."[79] In Surah Luqman believers are told to be humble and moderate: "Do not turn your face away from people in contempt, nor go about in the land exulting overmuch. Surely, Allah does not love any self-conceited boaster. Be moderate in your stride, and lower your voice."[80] In Surah Al-Sajdah believers are described as follows regarding their attitude and behavior: "Their sides draw away from beds, they call upon their Lord in fear and in hope, and they spend out of what We have given them."[81]

Being human, people are liable to commit mistakes. In such situations, they call upon their Lord in fear and hope, repent, reform their behavior, and do good deeds. People are strongly encouraged to repent and reform. Otherwise, "The punishment shall be doubled to him on the Day of Resurrection. He shall abide there in abasement unless he repents, believes, and does good deeds, for then Allah changes the evil deeds to good ones, and Allah is forgiving, merciful. Whoever repents and does good has truly turned to Allah with an (acceptable) conversion. (God's true servants are) those who do not bear witness to what is false, and when they pass by what is vain, they pass by nobly When they are reminded of the communications of their Lord, do not fall down as if deaf and blind. They are the ones who say: 'O our Lord! Grant us in our wives and our offspring the joy of our eyes, and make us guides to those who guard against evil.'"[82]

3.3 Believers are Moderate in Expenditure and Charity

Those who believe prepare for the Hereafter. Their behavior has a two-fold characteristic: they recognize the claims of their Lord against them, and they fully realize that whatever has been bestowed on them by God, whether little or much, does not simply belong to them and their family. Instead, they feel that the needy also have a rightful claim on their wealth. The Qur'an speaks strongly against squandering or spending one's money in wrong ways. If one spends all of one's money for rightful purposes, one is not a squanderer. However, if one spends even a small amount in the wrong way, then one is. Thus, it is not the amount that one spends, but the purpose for which one spends.

Squanderers are indeed Satan's brothers because they spend their money for evil purposes and to finance their disobedience of God. In Surah Bani Israel, God commands: "Give to the near of kin his due and to the needy and the wayfarer. Do not squander wastefully. Surely the squanderers are the brothers of devils, and Satan was ever ungrateful to his Lord."[83] Showing us how not to squander money, the Qur'an orders moderation in all spending: "Make not your hand tied (like a miser's) to your neck, nor stretch it forth to its utmost reach, so that you become blameworthy and destitute."[84] In Surah Al-Furqan, it is again explained how to be moderate: "Be like those who, when they spend, are not extravagant and not miserly, but hold a just balance between these extremes."[85] God, in His perfect knowledge, commands people to be moderate, prohibiting both the extremes of miserliness and careless extravagance. In Surah Luqman, people are also commanded to be moderate in all other areas of their behavior: "Walk moderately, and speak softly…Do not turn your face away from people in contempt, nor go about in the land exulting overmuch. Surely, Allah does not love any self-conceited boaster."[86]

3.4 Believers Avoid Indecencies and False Accusations

God has urged His servants to take good care of their families, which are Islamic states in miniature. Good families make a good society that equates with purity, decency, and chastity. in Surah Al-Anam, they are forbidden to commit all types of indecency, whether openly or secretly: "Do not draw near to indecencies, those of them which are apparent and those which are concealed."[87] No family can survive and no community can prosper if they sink into shameful indecency, whether openly or secretly. Purity, cleanliness, and chastity are the basic essentials for healthy living of both the family and the community. Those who like to see the spreading of indecency throughout the community are the ones who try to weaken the structure of the family and to bring about society's collapse. Since all these indecencies have their own attraction and temptation, people are commanded not even to go near them. Staying away from them is the best way to avoid preliminaries and attractions that could weaken one's resolve. Islam believes in taking protective measures before there is any need to inflict punishments. It protects conscience by guarding emotions and feelings. God knows His creation best, and He helps protect them, for He is the Compassionate and the All-knowing.

In Surah An-Noor, both men and women have been instructed to lower their gaze and forbidden to cast glances: "Say to the believing men that they should lower their gaze and guard their private parts. That will make for greater purity for them...Say to the believing women that they should lower their gaze, guard their private parts, and not display their beauty and ornaments, except what must ordinarily appear thereof. They should also draw their veils over their bosoms and not display their beauty in public."[88] In Surah Al-Ahzab, the Messenger was commanded: "Say to your wives and your daughters and the believing women that they should let down upon them their outer garments. That is the easiest way for them to be known (as respectable), and thus they will not be given trouble."[89] Old women were given a concession from this restriction in Surah An-Nur: "(As for) women advanced in years who do not hope for a marriage, it is no sin for them if they put off their outer garments without displaying their ornaments, and if they restrain themselves it is better for them, for Allah hears and knows."[90]

3.5 Believers do not spread False Accusations or News

Surah An-Nur was revealed to strengthen the moral fabric of the Islamic community at Madinah, which had been shaken by the enormity of the slander of sexual impropriety that was maliciously leveled against the Messenger's wife. The believers were commanded to learn a lesson from this incident: "Those who brought forward the lie are a body among yourselves. Think it not to be an evil to you; on the contrary, it is good for you. To every man among them (the slanderers, will come the punishment) of the sin that he earned, and to him who took on himself the lead among them will be a grievous penalty. Why did not the believers, men and women, when you heard of the affair, put the best construction on it in their own minds and say, 'This (charge) is an obvious lie'?" [91] One should be very cautious about charges of adultery and should not spread them, but one should refute and suppress them immediately, especially when the accuser is a mean person while the accused is an innocent woman. God warns in Surah Al-Ahzab: "Those who speak evil things of the believing men and the believing women without their having earned it, they are guilty indeed of a false accusation and a manifest sin." [92] This should have been enough to convince someone that the accusation was not worth any consideration; rather, it was not even conceivable. For this reason, God commands believers in Surah Al-Hujurat: "O you who believe! If an evildoer comes to you with a report, look carefully into it, lest you harm a people in ignorance, then be sorry for what you have done." [93]

NOTES

1. Qur'an 2:2.

2. Qur'an 2:21.

3. Qur'an 2:11-12.

4. Qur'an 41:37.

5. Qur'an 41:30, 33-36, 31.

6. Qur'an 2:177.

7. Qur'an 3:92.

8. Qur'an 41:31.

9. Qur'an 14:7.

10. Qur'an 7:144.

11. Qur'an 14:11-12.

12. Qur'an 65:3.

13. Al-Hadith: vol. I, no. 162w, p. 475.

14. Al-Hadith: vol. I, no. 119w, p. 395.

15. Sahih Bukhari 8.73.56.

16. Abu Dawud 41.4780.

17. Abu Dawud 41.4781.

18. Qur'an 9:109.

19. Qur'an 49:13.

20. Qur'an 76:8-9.

21. Qur'an 92:17-21.

22. Qur'an 107:4-7.

23. Qur'an 2:264.

24. Sahih Muslim 32.6221.

25. Qur'an 9:119.

26. Qur'an 49:15.

27. Qur'an 39:33.

28. Qur'an 53:23 & 28.

29. Sahih Bukhari 2.23.378.

30. Al-Hadith: vol. I, no. 209a, p. 467.

31. Qur'an 4:135.

32. Qur'an 33:70-71.

33. Qur'an 19:54-55.

34. Qur'an 2:225 & 5:89.

35. Qur'an 17:34.

36. Qur'an 16:91.

37. Qur'an 16:94-95.

38. Qur'an 4:58.

39. Qur'an 2:283.

40. Qur'an 23:8-11.

41. Qur'an 20:115.

42. Qur'an 6:152.

43. Qur'an 16:92.

44. Qur'an 12:55.

45. Sahih Bukhari 1.3.56.

46. Qur'an 3:161.

47. Qur'an 8:27-28.

48. Qur'an 4:58.

49. Sahih Bukhari 3.48.846.

50. Qur'an 23:1-4.

51. Qur'an 25:72.

52. Qur'an 4:114.

53. Qur'an 25:63.

54. Qur'an 4:148-149.

55. Qur'an 104:1-4.

56. Qur'an 2:83.

57. Qur'an 17:53.

58. Qur'an 41:34.

59. Qur'an 2:263.

60. Qur'an 29:46.

61. Sahih Bukhari 4.52.140.

62. Sahih Bukhari 3.39.513.

63. Qur'an 2:198.

64. Sahih Bukhari 3.34.266.

65. Qur'an 23:51.

66. Qur'an 2:172.

67. Sahih Muslim 5.2214.

68. Abu Dawud 9.1635.

69. Abu Dawud 9.1637.

70. Qur'an 2:273-274.

71. Qur'an 67:2.

72. Qur'an 49:13.

73. Sahih Bukhari 2.13.18.

74. Qur'an 35:5.

75. Qur'an 35:10.

76. Qur'an 10:41.

77. Qur'an 17:15.

78. Qur'an 65:7.

79. Qur'an 25:63-69.

80. Qur'an 31:18-19.

81. Qur'an 32:16.

82. Qur'an 25:69-74.

83. Qur'an 17:26-27.

84. Qur'an 17:29.

85. Qur'an 25:67.

86. Qur'an 31:19 & 18.

87. Qur'an 6:120.

88. Qur'an 24:30-31.

89. Qur'an 33:59.

90. Qur'an 24:60.

91. Qur'an 24:11-12.

92. Qur'an 33:58.

93. Qur'an 49:6.

CHAPTER 11

BEHAVIOR THAT MAKES PEOPLE HUMAN
(Reform Yourself to Be Human)

THE UNIVERSE IS FUNCTIONING under God's sovereignty, and everything on the earth and in Heaven is subject to His command alone. God has established the entire system of the universe precisely and equitably on justice, and the nature of this system requires that those who dwell in it should adhere to justice within the bounds of their authority and should not disturb the balance. Relevant verses of Surah Ar-Rahman reflect the fact that justice is the law that governs the universe: "The sun and the moon follow a fixed rotation. Even the vegetation and the trees do prostrate. He raised the firmament high, and He made the balance (of justice) that you may not transgress the balance. So keep up the balance with equity, and do not make the measure deficient."[1] It has been narrated on the authority of 'Abdullah bin 'Umar that the Messenger of God said: "Behold! The dispensers of justice will be seated on the pulpits of light beside God, on the right side of the Merciful, Exalted, and Glorious. Either side of the Being is the right side, both being equally meritorious. (The dispensers of justice are) those who do justice in their rules, in matters relating to their families and in all that they undertake to do."[2]

One should know that faith, piety, worship, and the establishment of God's law in human life yield all their fruits in human life and give their benefits to the individual himself and to society. Islam lays strong emphasis on the fundamental principles and makes them the basis of all actions and activities. The reason for this is not that God gains anything from people's worship and piety; He does not. However, He knows that human life and affairs cannot be established on the right footing unless His method is followed. People may challenge themselves to reflect on each one of God's commands. They will find that each one of them is beneficial to one or the other aspect of individual and social life of this world.

1. HOW PEOPLE SHOULD DEAL AMONG THEMSELVES

People have been asked to respect and honor the God-given positions and responsibilities given to each one of us. It is God who created us as humankind and gave us our spouses and children, parents, brothers and sisters, and all other relatives. He gave us neighbors, friends, and servants. All these belong to one's family. We are to serve God and serve our family. One should neither be proud of neglecting one's duties nor be boastful of one's service. God commands this in Surah Al-Nisa: "Serve Allah, and do not associate anything with Him. Be good to your parents and relatives, and (be good) to the orphans, the needy, and your neighbors, whether near or far, and also to your companions around you and to wayfarers and those whom your right hands possess. Surely, Allah does not love him who is proud, boastful."³ This verse virtually makes the whole humankind our family. We have to recognize and respect their God-given roles in the human family and play our individual roles to the best of our abilities. To accomplish this we deal with each other with justice and fairness, treat others with kindness and affection, greet others with what is better, and honor their persons and their privacy.

1.1 Treat each other with Justice and Fairness

Being God's trustees, each one of us has specific duties and responsibilities to fulfill. Individuals have their own specific sphere of influence, and they are like the rulers within their respective areas. The Messenger defined seven classes of people who will enjoy God's shelter on Judgment Day. The first of these is a just ruler. It has been reported by Abu Huraira that the Messenger of God said: "Seven are (the persons) whom Allah will give protection with His shade on the Day when there would be no shade but that of Him, (and they are): a just ruler..."⁴

The divine command about being just is best illustrated in a sacred Hadith in which the Messenger quotes God as saying: "My servants, I have forbidden Myself injustice and have made injustice forbidden among you. Therefore, do not act unjustly to one another."[5] In the Qur'an, oppression or injustice is often equated with the denial of God. The importance of justice is very much stressed in several places in the Qur'an. God says: "We sent aforetime our messengers with clear signs and sent down with them the Book and the balance (of right and wrong) that men may stand forth in justice."[6] "Surely, Allah commands you to make over trusts to their owners and that when you judge between people you judge with justice."[7] "Give full measure, and weight with full justice...whenever you speak, speak truly, even if a near relative is concerned, and fulfill the covenant of Allah."[8] "Whoever pleads a good cause will get a share from it, and whoever pleads an evil cause will get a share from it, for Allah keeps a strict watch over everything."[9]

1.2 Treat each other with Kindness and Affection

God commands believers in Surah Al-Imran: "Be not like those who are divided among themselves and fall into disputations after receiving clear signs (instructions from Allah)."[10] There are instructions in the Qur'an for dealing with believers and non-believers. Believers deal gently among themselves and consult each other during the implementation of Islam. They forgive each other's faults and decide to go ahead in their own development and in the development of their community, while putting their trust in God. Believers neither conspire with unbelievers against each other nor give away their secrets. Believers should not obey the unbelievers in the matters of faith. God commands the believers: "O you who believe! If you obey the unbelievers, they will drive you back on your heels, and you will turn back (from faith) to your own loss."[11] Again God tells the Messenger: "Thus, it is due to mercy from Allah that you deal with them gently, and had you been rough, hardhearted, they would certainly have dispersed from around you. Therefore, forgive them, ask forgiveness for them, and consult with them in the affair. So when you have decided, then place your trust in Allah. Surely, Allah loves those who trust Him."[12] According to Islam, unity, justice, kindness, consultations, and trust in God trust should always govern people's mutual affairs.

1.3 Treat each other with Friendship and Respect

It is universally agreed that kindness wins people's hearts. People are normally grateful when they receive kind treatment, particularly from someone who has nothing to ask from them in return. A good person may wish to be kind to others as much as he can, but sometimes kindness may not come easily, particularly when one feels that the recipient does not appreciate it. However, a believer should be kind at all times. Islam has ordered that its followers should be kind to their relatives, even though they may have rejected Islam. Therefore, believing does not mean that the rights of the unbelieving relatives may be compromised. God commands in Surah Luqman: "We have enjoined on man (to be good) to his parents. His mother bears him in weakness upon weakness, and his weaning is in two years. Give thanks unto Me and unto your parents; to Me is the eventual coming. However, if they strive to make you join in worship with Me things of which you have no knowledge, obey them not. Yet, bear them company in this life with justice (and consideration), and follow the way of those who turn to me (in love). In the end, the return of you all is to Me, and I will tell you the truth of what you did."[13] The Messenger also insisted on treating the followers of the other religions kindly. It is narrated by Jarir bin 'Abdullah that the Prophet said: "He who is not merciful to others will not be treated mercifully."[14] This Hadith stresses that all people, irrespective of their religion, should be treated kindly.

1.4 Greet with what is better and Honor Individual Privacy

Muslims all over the world use the Islamic form of greeting, "Assalamo Alaikum" (peace be to you). The very wording helps generate a friendly and relaxed atmosphere. It is common in its shorter and longer forms to all Muslim communities wherever they happen to be. Thus, when two Muslims meet who are total strangers to each other, the moment they use this greeting, they immediately feel that they have common ground, even though they do not speak each other's language. The Islamic greeting has different versions, the shortest of which is the one mentioned above. The rule in Islam is that when offered a greeting, it should be returned with a better one or at least with its equal. God commands in the Qur'an that: "When a greeting is offered to you, reciprocate it with a greeting still more courteous or of equal courtesy. Allah takes careful account of all things."[15] It is narrated on the authority of 'Abdullah bin 'Amr that a man asked the Messenger of God which of the merits is superior in Islam. The Prophet responded: "That you provide food and extend greetings to one whom you know or do not know."[16]

The right to individual privacy is fundamental in Islam. People are forbidden to enter the houses of others without their permission. God commands believers in Surah Al-Nur: "Do not enter houses other than your own until you have asked permission and saluted those who (live) in them. That is the best (conduct) for you so you can heed (the importance of respecting privacy). If you find no one in the house, enter not until permission is given to you. If you are asked to leave, then leave, for that is the purest practice (to follow), and Allah knows what you are doing."[17] The sanctity of privacy in one's home is even enjoined for servants and children, including one's own. They are commanded not to enter the private rooms of any man or woman without permission, especially in the morning, at noon, and at night. In Surah Al-Nur, God commands: "O you who believe! Let those whom your right hands possess and those of you who have not attained to puberty ask permission of you three times: before the morning prayer, when you have disrobed for the noonday heat, and after the late-night prayer. These are three times of undress…But when the children among you have attained to puberty, let them seek permission, as do those senior to. Thus, Allah makes clear to you His communications, and Allah is knowing, wise."[18]

2. ELEMENTS OF BEHAVIOR THAT MAKE PEOPLE HUMAN

One's behavior as an individual and as a member of the society is very important in Islam. If people fulfill all their moral and socio-political obligations, they will be successful in this life and in the Hereafter. This will also make their community prosperous, peaceful, and secure. God tells the believers in Surah Al-Anfal: "O you who believe! Answer the call of Allah and His Messenger when he calls you to that which gives you life…and guard yourselves against a chastisement that affects not in particular only those of you who do wrong, and know that Allah is severe in punishment. Remember when you were few, deemed weak in the land, fearing lest people might carry you off by force, but He sheltered you and strengthened you with His aid and gave you of the good things that you may give thanks."[19] To guard against injustice, people must patiently and courageously struggle, be kind and generous to others, cooperate in good deeds, and support each other physically and morally during the difficulties and hardships of life. Since it is natural for people to make mistakes, it is essential for them to be tolerant and forgiving. Human fallibility makes it mandatory that people should be lenient and forgiving among themselves.

2.1 Believers' Courage Springs from Divine Reliance

God commands the believers in Surah Al-Furqan: "Put your trust in Him Who lives and dies not, and celebrate his praise. Enough is He to be acquainted with the faults of His servants."[20] Humankind, being weak by nature, has been created to work hard and to struggle in a hostile environment that is created by its own personal desires and by the jealousy of Satan. The misuse of the human faculty of free choice enhances the adverse consequences of human existence even more. Addressing humankind, God describes this situation like this: "Allah wishes to turn to you, but the wish of those who follow their lusts is that you should turn away (from Him)—far, far away. Allah wishes to lighten your (difficulties), for man was created weak."[21] For this reason, God arranged to guide humanity into the ways that will help people be successful in life. People who believe get their courage by their reliance on God. After describing the behavior of the hypocrites during and after the Battle of the Trench, God tells the Messenger in Surah Al-Ahzab: "Say: 'Running away will not do you any good if you are running from death or slaughter, for even if you did (get away), you would not be allowed to enjoy yourselves but a little while.' Say: 'Who is it that can protect you from Allah if He intends to harm you or intends mercy on you?' They will not find for themselves besides Allah any guardian or a helper."[22]

The believers are never discouraged by the propaganda of the hypocrites and unbelievers, but it always increases their faith. We are told of the believers' attitude in Surah Al-Imran, when a year after the battle of Uhud, there was a rumor that the Makkans were making extensive preparations to attack Madinah: "Men said to them: 'Surely people have gathered against you; therefore, fear them.' But this increased their faith, and they said: 'Allah is sufficient for us and a most excellent protector.'"[23] Then again at the time of the Battle of the Trench, the believers' response was, "When the believers saw the invading army, they said: 'This is what Allah and His Messenger promised us, and Allah and His Messenger spoke the truth.' It only increased them in faith and submission."[24]

2.2 Kindness to others earns God's Love and His Bounty

A believer should refrain from everything that might be helpful to the unbelievers during a conflict between the believers and unbelievers. However, the believers are encouraged to deal kindly and justly with those unbelievers who are not engaged in hostile activities against Islam or in the persecution of the believers. God tells the believers in Surah Al-Mumtahinah: "Allah does not forbid you respecting those who have not made war against you on account of your religion, and who have not driven you forth from your homes, that you show them kindness and deal with them justly. Surely, Allah loves the doers of justice."[25]

To succeed, one should neither oppress nor repulse others. God reminded the Messenger that He had been looking after him with kindness since his birth, that he was born an orphan, and that God made the best arrangement for his upbringing. The Prophet was unaware of the right way so God showed him the way. He was poor and was made rich by God. All this shows that the Prophet has been favored by God from the very beginning. Concluding Surah Al-Duha, God tells people how they should show their gratitude for His blessings on each one of them by not oppressing others, especially orphans and the poor, and by helping them as much as they can. "Did He not find you an orphan and give you shelter? Did He not find you unaware of the right way and guided you? Did He not find you in want and then enriched you? Therefore, as for the orphan, do not oppress him, and as for him who asks, do not repulse him."[26]

2.3 Neighbors have a claim on the People's Kindness

The Messenger was the best of neighbors, and he emphasized that neighbors have a claim on our kindness. He told the believers: "Gabriel continued to recommend me about treating the neighbors kindly and politely, so much so that I thought he would order me to make them as my heirs."[27] This means that the status of a neighbor should be viewed as comparable to that of a family member. Abu Shuraih narrated: "The Messenger said: 'By Allah, he does not believe! By Allah, he does not believe! By Allah, he does not believe!' It was said: 'Who is that, O Allah's Messenger?' He said: 'That person whose neighbor does not feel safe from his evil.'"[28] This Hadith confirms that neighbors, irrespective of their religion, should be treated like one's own relatives, and it also gives one an idea of how much emphasis Islam attaches to the rights of individuals, especially those who are near in relation or near in the community.

God commands in Surah Al-Araf: "Keep to forgiveness, enjoin kindness, and turn away from the ignorant."[29] By giving kindness to others, people become candidates for still more bounty from their Lord.

However, it is also the case that kindness is its own reward. God asks in Surah Al-Rahman: "Can the reward of goodness be any other than goodness?"[30] The answer to this question is found in Surah Al-Zumar: "For those who do good in this world is good …They shall have anything they wish from their Lord; that is the reward of those who act kindly."[31] In Surah Al-Qasas people are commanded: "Seek by means of what Allah has given you the future abode, and do not neglect your portion of this world. Do good to others as Allah has done good to you, and do not seek to make mischief in the land. Surely, Allah does not love the corrupt."[32] In Surah Yunus it has been confirmed: "For those who do good is a good (reward) and even more than that. Neither darkness nor shame will cover their faces. These will be the dwellers of Paradise; in it they shall abide."[33]

2.4 Generosity is an Essential Part of Human Conduct

Islam is a religion of charity, generosity, and philanthropy. It likes its followers to be generous and charitable. It advises believers to treat others kindly, act righteously, help their kinsmen, and do good and virtuous deeds. "If you give alms openly, it is well, and if you hide it and give it to the poor, it is better for you. This will do away with some of your evil deeds…Those who spend (in charity) of their goods by night and by day, in secret and in public, shall have their reward with their Lord. They shall have no fear, nor shall they grieve."[34]

It is expected that the believers will be moderate in meeting their needs and that they do not spend all their earnings only on their personal needs and wants. People should let others benefit from the blessings that have been bestowed on them. They should assign a part of their earnings for the help of the poor and needy. It was reported by Abu Umama that Allah's Messenger said: "O Adam's son! It is better for you if you spend your surplus (wealth), but if you withhold it, it is evil for you. There is, however, no reproach for you if you withhold means necessary for a living. Spend first for your family and dependents, and the raised hand is better than the lowered hand."³⁵ For this God commands believers in Surah Bani Israil: "Give to the near of kin his due and to the needy and the wayfarer. Do not squander wastefully. Surely the squanderers are the brothers of devils, and Satan was ever ungrateful to his Lord."³⁶ Believers have been advised to respect the sentiments of the needy, and their feelings should not be hurt. If there is nothing that can be given, then they should be refused in a kind and decent way: "If you are forced to turn away from them, seek hoped-for mercy from your Lord, (and) speak to them a gentle word."³⁷

2.5 Cooperation and Support are Human Characteristics

Mutual cooperation is is always needed in society. Since power and weakness, wealth and poverty exist side by side in human society, the strong should be kind to the weak, and the wealthy should help the poor and needy. This is required to achieve peace and security in society. God tells people in Surah Al-Furqan: "We have made some of you a trial for others; will you bear patiently? And your Lord is ever seeing."³⁸ A community can be successful only when the relationship among its members is friendly. No one should be so deprived as to face starvation or be so greedy as to be spending his wealth only for his own pleasures. Islam expects people to do righteous and virtuous deeds. They have been commanded to help each other and act righteously. The benefit of spending in the way of God is not only derived by the poor, but it also brings peace and satisfaction to the givers, who are protected from stinginess and jealousy. God reminds people in Surah Muhammad: "Behold! You are those who are called upon to spend in Allah's way, but among you are those who are miserly. Whoever is miserly, his miserliness is against his own self. Allah is Self-sufficient, and you have need (of Him). If you turn back, He will bring in your place another people who will not be like you."³⁹ Social injustice in a society can result from the miserliness of its rich people. This eventually leads to the destruction of the society; thus, "He will bring in your place another people."

2.6 Forgiveness is a Trait that is Human as well as Divine

Since people have numerous physical and emotional weaknesses, perfection of their character and behavior without divine guidance is not possible. What Islam teaches is an attitude that leads to continual improvement in individual character and society. God commands the Messenger in Surah Al-Anam: "When those who believe in Our revelations come to you, say: 'Peace be on you. Your Lord had inscribed for Himself (the rule of) mercy. Verily, if any of you did evil in ignorance, repented thereafter, and amended (his conduct), lo! He is forgiving, most merciful.'"[40] In Surah Al-Araf, God commands the believers to be forgiving and fair with people: "Hold to forgiveness; command what is right, but turn away from the ignorant, and if a slander from Satan afflicts you, seek refuge in Allah."[41]

The believers are commanded to forgive people if they like to be forgiven by God. In Surah Al-Imran, people have been told various ways that lead to Paradise. Forgiving other people is one of them: "Be quick in the race for forgiveness from your Lord and for a Garden whose width is that of the heavens and of the earth, prepared for the righteous. They spent (of that which Allah has given them) in ease and in adversity, restrained their anger, and forgave others. Allah loves the good."[42] As noted in the above verse, other deeds that can help us to receive God's mercy are restraining anger and giving in charity.

2.7 Human Fallibility Increases the Importance of Leniency

An excellent example to be followed is how the Messenger ignored and showed the leniency to the hypocrites of Madinah, especially during the incident in which the Messenger's wife was wrongly accused. During that incident, the Messenger and his companions were terribly distressed. They were in a great dilemma until at last the verses of Surah Nur were revealed that refuted the charges of the hypocrites, "Those who brought forward the lie are a body among yourselves. Think it not to be an evil to you; on the contrary, it is good for you. To every man among them (the slanderers, will come the punishment) of the sin that he earned, and to him who took on himself the lead among them will be a grievous penalty."[43] Involved in this tragic event of false accusation was a near relative of Abu Bakr, the father of the falsely accused wife of the Prophet. This relative had been living off of Abu Bakr's charity. Nonetheless, this person did not hesitate to accuse the chaste lady, whose father was sustaining him. He ignored Islamic teachings and did not care about the relationship. Abu Bakr was deeply hurt and swore that he would not give anything to this relative and would not show any kindness to him as he had in the past. Thereupon God commanded all those who expect His forgiveness to forgive each other: "Let not those of you who possess (wealth and status) among you swear against giving to the near of kin, the poor, and those who have fled in Allah's way. Pardon and overlook (their faults). Do you not want Allah to forgive you, too?"[44] Accordingly, Abu Bakr restarted helping his relative, saying: "I like Allah to forgive me."

3. MANAGING DESIRES WITH PATIENCE & FORGIVENESS

Patience and perseverance are frequently mentioned in the Qur'an. God commands in Surah Al-Imran: "O you who believe! Persevere in patience and constancy; vie in such perseverance; strengthen each other, and fear Allah that you may prosper."[45] God knows that enormous efforts are needed to ensure that proper behavior is maintained in the face of all temptations and motivations to abandon right conduct. This requires people to be on the alert and ready to give whatever sacrifice is required. For this effort, they need to be patient. They need patience to do good works and to abstain from sin, to fight those who are corrupt, to defeat their designs, and to bear with fortitude when victory seems to be delayed. They always need patience and perseverance when their objective seems to be very far away, falsehood seems to be very strong, and help seems to be not yet available. They need patience to face those who are dishonest, cunning, arrogant, and persistent in their rejection of the truth. Tolerance and forgiveness are those human values that are the direct outcome of patience. Believers are tolerant with people, irrespective of whether they are believers or unbelievers.

3.1 Prayers Help Believers Who Patiently Persevere

Patience may soon be exhausted when the period of suffering is long and strength seems to be decreasing. At such moments, individual strength needs to be renewed. Hence, prayer is needed to support patience. Prayer is a perpetual spring that renews believers' energy and gives them new strength. Believers are then able to persevere for as long as it takes to achieve their goals. Prayer also adds to their perseverance, contentment, confidence, and reassurance. When a weak person, and people usually are weak, faces a difficult task beyond his limited resources, faces the turmoil of evil, and finds temptations too strong, possible solutions too difficult, and resistance to tyranny and corruption too demanding, he needs to have a direct link with the source of all power, i.e., God. God encourages people to come to Him and commands the believers in Surah Al-Baqarah: "O you who believe! Seek assistance through patience and prayer, for Allah is with those who patiently persevere."[46]

When one's goal seems far away, despair starts creeping. Despair is most inevitable when one sees evil gaining in its strength, while good remains weak and marginalized, and no light seems visible at the end of the tunnel. At this stage, it is prayer that comes to rescue people. Prayer is the direct link with the Everlasting Power. Prayer is the ability to communicate with the Creator, and it is a source of more comfort than anyone needs. It is the source of spiritual strength that makes people physically strong. For this reason, whenever the Messenger experienced some hardship, or whenever he had to make an important decision, he prayed for a long time, in order to make his company with Allah more prolonged. Remembering God and asking for His forgiveness is another form of prayer that brings people patience and God's help during difficulties. 'Abdullah ibn 'Abbas reported that the Messenger of God said: "Whoever sticks to seeking forgiveness, Allah will create for him a way out from every difficulty and a relief from every anxiety, and He will supply him provision from where he could not think."[47]

3.2 Believers patiently await the Mercy of their Lord

When difficulties and hardships confront people in life, and when periods of suffering become long, it is patience that acts like a light for the believers that keep them safe from disappointment and frustration. Patience is a basic quality that believers need to shape their lives in this world. For this, the believers have to attend to all of their work and prepare themselves to face hardships and difficulties. One should try one's best as long it takes to overcome life's hurdles, and one should not run away from responsibilities, whatever they may be. No hardship or trouble should tempt one to indulge in what is illegal or immoral. One should not loose self-confidence and should not be overcome by the dark clouds appearing, even one after the others, but should be fully assured that these clouds of adversities and hardships will disappear with the help and mercy of God Who watches over people continuously. With God-given wisdom and foresight, the believer should face life's hardships with the hope of God's mercy since: "Who despairs of the mercy of his Lord but the unbelievers?"[48]

God has stressed that no person can escape tests and trials, so people should be alert and ready when these hardship and difficulties arrive. They should not be frightened, disappointed, or disheartened. God warns believers in Surah Al-Baqarah: "We will most certainly try you with somewhat of fear and hunger and loss of property and lives and fruits, and give good news to the patient."[49] God also advises people: "When a misfortune befalls you, say: 'Surely we belong to Allah, and to Him we shall surely return.'"⁵⁰ Remember that Luqman told his son: "Bear patiently that which befalls you; surely, these acts require courage."⁵¹

3.3 Courageous are the Patient who Forgive People

A believer is one who is patient in adversity and thankful for whatever may happen to him, knowing that it is all from God. He compares his fortunes with those of people who are in more difficult circumstances and thanks God for His blessings. Therefore, in difficulties and hardships, the first thing one should do is to have trust in God that He hears one's prayers and answers them in the best way.

Tolerance and forgiveness are two things that are the normal outcome of patience. Believers are tolerant of others, irrespective of whether the other is a believer or unbeliever. The believers are then told in Surah Ash-Shura: "If you show patience and forgive, that would truly be an exercise of courageous will and resolution in the conduct of affairs."⁵² Forgiving others and asking for forgiveness, both from God and His people, make one even more patient. It is arrogance, a behavior that is very much disliked by God that prevents people from forgiving others or asking for their forgiveness.

3.4 Believers are Friendly and Patient with Unbelievers

Dealings with unbelievers must always be cordial and friendly, provided they also treat the believers in the same way. Good relations with non-believers are encouraged in Islam. However, people who are hostile to Islam or try to ridicule its beliefs or practices are to be treated differently. Islam does not extend kindness to them, but instructs believers to stay away from them. Believers must not start hostility, but should not accept humiliation. Similarly in Surah Al-Anam, believers are commanded: "Do not abuse those whom they call upon besides Allah, lest exceeding the limits they should abuse Allah out of ignorance...If Allah had pleased, they would not have set up others with Him. We have neither appointed you a keeper over them nor placed them in your charge."[53] God commands the believers to be patient with the unbelievers in Surah Al-Ahqaf: "Therefore, bear up patiently, as did the messengers endowed with constancy, and be in no haste about the (unbelievers)"[54] God also commands the believers to be tolerant of what the unbelievers say in Surah Al-Muzzammil: "Have patience with what they (unbelievers) say, and leave them with noble (dignity)."[55] Believers, being motivated by their love to do good to all humanity, treat people with tolerance. They try to foil the evil schemes of others against them, but they do not scheme against anyone. They do not harbor grudges, although they take care not to fall victim to other people's grudges.

Believers often face aggression from unbelievers, an aggression that aims to turn believers away from their faith and from implementing it. Believers are, therefore, required to break down all barriers that prevent people from following divine guidance and its implementation. To achieve their aim, the believers are commanded in Surah Yunus: "Follow you the inspiration sent to you, and be patient until Allah does decide, for He is the best to decide."[56] In Surah Al-Baqarah, patience with the unbelievers is again emphasized in recounting the prayer said by the Israelites as they marched out to face Goliath and his Philistines: "Our Lord, bestow on us patience, make our steps firm, and assist us against the unbelieving people."[57]

3.5 Managing Desires with Patience and God's Mercy

People sometimes resort to wrong and illegal ways in moments of desperation. However, if they are patient and try their best, they will eventually be successful, for it is determination supported by patience that helps people manage selfish desires. God says in Surah Al-Rad: "Those who patiently persevere, seeking the countenance of their Lord, establish regular prayers, spend out of what We have given them for their sustenance, secretly and openly, and repel evil with what is good, for such there is the final attainment of the (eternal) home...Peace unto you for that you persevered in patience. How excellent is the final home!"[58] In Surah Al-Furqan, God gives the believers who are patient good news about their reward: "Those shall be rewarded with high places (in Paradise) because they were patient, and they shall be met therein with salutations and peace."[59]

The Islamic way of life is based on worshipping God, which provides support during the life journey of a believer, strengthens the spirit, and purifies the heart. If we believe in God and sincerely worship Him, then worship makes every obligation and its benefits acceptable to our hearts. It makes religious obligations and their benefits clear to us, thus sparing us from disobeying God's commands. On assigning his task to the Messenger, God said to him in Surah Al-Muzzammil: "O you wrapped up in your garments! Rise to pray in the night, but not all night—half of it or a little less or more. Recite the Qur'an in slow, measured tones. Soon We will send down to you a weighty message."[60] The preparation for receiving such words of surpassing gravity, for the hard task and the great role of God's Messenger, was simply worshiping at night and recitation of the Qur'an. Worship opens up people's hearts and strengthens their relation with God. God's friendship and His help make matters easy and provide limitless strength, confidence, and reassurance. It is not surprising, therefore, that God directs the believers to be patient, to persevere, and to resort to prayer when they face difficult tasks. God commands in Surah Al-Kahf: "Keep yourself content with those who call on their Lord morning and evening, desiring His goodwill. Let not your eyes pass from them, desiring the beauties of this world's life. Do not follow him whose heart We have made unmindful to Our remembrance, who follows his low desires beyond all bounds."[61]

3.6 Islamic Response to False News and Accusations is Patience

The Islamic requirements of always speaking the truth, not mixing truth with falsehood, and not knowingly concealing the truth are somewhat at variance with the concept of freedom of speech in secular societies. Their freedom of speech does not demand truth. Besides, no restrictions are imposed with regard to stereotyping people, backbiting, and sowing the seeds of suspicion. When listening to some news or advertisements in the Western, secular media, it is very difficult to differentiate between the true and the untrue or between biased and unbiased presentations. However, God demands authenticity and truth from people. In Surah Al-Hujurat believers are commanded: "O you who believe! If an evildoer comes to you with a report, look carefully into it, lest you harm a people in ignorance, then be sorry for what you have done."[62]

Since rules governing the freedom of speech differ in Islam, God advised the Messenger in Surah Yunus: "And let not their speech grieve you."[63] Instead, God tells the believers to concentrate on their own improvement. God tells the believers in Surah Al-Maidah that if they excel in the areas of importance, nobody can harm them: "O you who believe! Take care of your own selves; he who errs cannot hurt you when you are on the right way."[64] In Islam there is freedom of speech, but it needs to be free from things that are untrue. Abu Bakr said: "You people recite this verse, 'O you who believe! Take care of your own selves; he who errs cannot hurt you when you are on the right way,' and put it in its improper place…(Its proper implication is as) 'Amr ibn Hushaym's has: 'I heard the Messenger of God say: 'If acts of disobedience are done among any people and do not change them though they are able to do so, Allah will soon punish them all.'""[65]

NOTES

1. Qur'an 55:5-9.

2. Sahih Muslim 20.4493.

3. Qur'an 4:36.

4. Sahih Muslim 5.2248.

5. Sahih Muslim 32.6246.

6. Qur'an 57:25.

7. Qur'an 4:58.

8. Qur'an 6:152.

9. Qur'an 4:85.

10. Qur'an 3:105.

11. Qur'an 3:149.

12. Qur'an 3:159.

13. Qur'an 31:14-15.

14. Sahih Bukhari 8.73.42.

15. Qur'an 4:86.

16. Sahih Muslim1.63.

17. Qur'an 24:27-28.

18. Qur'an 24:58-59.

19. Qur'an 8:24-26.

20. Qur'an 25:58.

21. Qur'an 4:27-28.

22. Qur'an 33:16-17.

23. Qur'an 3:173.

24. Qur'an 33:22.

25. Qur'an 60:8.

26. Qur'an 93:6-10.

27. Sahih Bukhari 8.73.43.

28. Sahih Bukhari 8.73.45.

29. Qur'an 7:199.

30. Qur'an 55:60.

31. Qur'an 39:10 & 34.

32. Qur'an 28:77.

33. Qur'an 10:26.

34. Qur'an 2:271 & 274.

35. Sahih Muslim 5.2256.

36. Qur'an 17:26-27.

37. Qur'an 17:28.

38. Qur'an 25:20.

39. Qur'an 47:38.

40. Qur'an 6:54.

41. Qur'an 7:199-200.

42. Qur'an 3:133-134.

43. Qur'an 24:11.

44. Qur'an 24:22.

45. Qur'an 3:200.

46. Qur'an 2:153.

47. Al-Hadith vol. III, no. 97, p. 756.

48. Qur'an 15:56.

49. Qur'an 2:155.

50. Qur'an 2:156.

51. Qur'an 31:17.

52. Qur'an 42:43.

53. Qur'an 6:108 & 107.

54. Qur'an 46:35.

55. Qur'an 73:10.

56. Qur'an 10:109.

57. Qur'an 2:250.

58. Qur'an 13:22 & 24.

59. Qur'an 25:75.

60. Qur'an 73:1-5.

61. Qur'an 18:28.

62. Qur'an 49:6.

63. Qur'an 10:65.

64. Qur'an 5:105.

65. Abu Dawud 37.4324.

CHAPTER 12

ISLAMIC SOCIAL BEHAVIOR
(Living on Earth as Humans)

GOD ENQUIRES PEOPLE, "WHY were there not among the generations before you those possessing sense enough to have forbidden people from making mischief in the earth?...However, your Lord never destroys towns unjustly if their people acted well."[1] Resurrection and occurrence of the Hereafter are truths that inevitably have to take place. The people of past communities who denied accountability for their behavior and deeds and continued their sinful lives ultimately became subject to God's punishment, even in this world.

People are accountable for their social behavior. Islam demands unity, brotherhood, mutual help, and cooperation. We are commanded to respect the feelings and emotions of others. There are set rules for social gatherings, social work, and mutual discourse. Most importantly, believers are commanded to make peace between quarreling parties and to wish for others what they wish for themselves.

1. UNITY, MUTUAL RESPECT, AND COOPERATION

Islam desires that a society be built on unity, respect, and cooperation. Believers are commanded to be united for the promotion of peace and community development. They should encourage people in promoting justice, general welfare, mutual cooperation, and respect for the feelings and emotions of others.

1.1 Believers are a Party united for Peace and Progress

A group of dedicated people of good moral character and behavior is required for the implementation of any socio-political system. The responsibility for the implementation of Islam is assigned to the Islamic community. All believers should be united in this community. In Surah

Al-Imran, God commands the believers: "Hold fast all together by the rope of Allah, and be not disunited...Do not be like those who are divided amongst themselves and fall into disputations after receiving clear signs (instructions from Allah)."[2] Believers deal gently among themselves and consult each other during the implementation of Islam. They forgive each other's faults and decide to go ahead for the implementation of Islam while putting their trust in God.

What attitude should the believers adopt in the case where two groups fall into mutual fighting? God affirms that the believers are brothers one to another. As such, the believers are commanded to make peace when people are fighting. This obligation of the believers is described in Surah Al-Hujurat: "And if two parties of the believers quarrel, make peace between them. But if one of them acts wrongfully towards the other, fight that who acts wrongfully until he returns to Allah's command. Then if it returns, make peace between them with justice, and act equitably. Surely, Allah loves those who act equitably. The believers are but brethren; therefore, make peace between your brethren, and be careful of your duty to Allah that you may receive mercy."[3] The general rule to remember is: "Say: 'Peace be on you. Your Lord had inscribed for Himself (the rule of) mercy. Verily, if any of you did evil in ignorance, repented thereafter, and amended (his conduct), lo! He is forgiving, most merciful.'"[4] Peacemaking is of tremendous importance in an Islamic society. Even the secret councils that are forbidden under normal circumstances become legal if they are for peacemaking, "There is no good in most of their secret counsels, except if someone enjoins charity or goodness or reconciliation between people. Whoever does this (engaging in secret councils to promote charity, goodness, or reconciliation) seeking Allah's pleasure, We will give him a mighty reward."[5]

1.2 Believers Respect People, their Feelings, and their Emotions

Believers have been commanded to safeguard against the evils that spoil mutual relationships. Mocking and taunting each other, calling others by nicknames, creating suspicions, spying into other people's affairs, and back biting are evils that are not only sins in themselves, but they also cause corruption in society. God mentioned these evils individually and forbids them as unlawful in Surah Al-Hujurat: "O you who believe! Let not some men among you laugh at others. It may be that the (latter) are better than the (former). And do not let some women laugh at others, for it may be that the (latter) are better than the (former). Do not defame nor be sarcastic to each other, and do not call each other by (offensive) nicknames. Ill-seeming is it to use an insulting nickname for someone after he has become a believer. Whoever does not desist is doing wrong."[6]

There are people who laugh at honest and hardworking believers. Their disgraceful, humiliating, and dishonest behavior and evil deeds will meet with a most dire end in the Hereafter as a result of their bad conduct. God says in Surah Al-Mutaffifin: "Those in sin used to laugh at those who believed. They winked at one another (in mockery) when they passed by them, and when they returned to their own followers, they returned joking."[7] The believers, on the other hand, will feel comforted when they see their fate in the Hereafter: "So on this day, those who believe shall laugh at the unbelievers from high thrones. Surely, the unbelievers are paid back for what they did."[8]

1.3 Suspicion and Spying on Others is not Allowed in Islam

Since truth has lost its importance in the present world, everybody is suspects and spies in others. Some governments have even made it legal to spy on its citizens. In contrast to this state of affairs, God says in the Qur'an: "O you who believe! Avoid suspicion as much (as possible), for in some cases is a sin. Do not spy on one another or backbite one another. Would any of you like to eat the flesh of his dead brother? Surely, you would loathe it. Remain God-fearing, for Allah accepts repentance and is Merciful."[9] This verse establishes certain rules that apply within human society and that protect the integrity and freedom of individuals, while at the same time teaching people how to cleanse their feelings and consciences.

Islam does not stop at this point in educating people's hearts and minds. The verse also establishes a principle that applies to mutual dealings among people. It protects individual rights, so that people may not be punished or tried on the basis of suspicion. Abu Huraira reported God's Messenger as saying: "Avoid suspicion, for suspicion is the gravest lie in talk, and do not be inquisitive about one another, and do not spy upon one another."[10] This means that people remain innocent, enjoying all their rights, freedom, and status, until it is absolutely clear that they have committed some offense. It is not sufficient that they are suspected of having committed something, in order to pursue them with the aim of establishing whether they are guilty. This verse also shows the limits to which Islam goes in protecting people's freedom, integrity, rights, and status. Islam achieves this in real life, after it establishes it in people's hearts and consciences. How does this compare with what even the best democratic countries boast of in terms of protecting human rights? I leave this to the readers to reflect and judge.

2. COMMUNITY SERVICE AND COMMUNICATIONS

In any good community, there are norms of mutual help and social behavior. In the Qur'an, the general attitude of the believers and the hypocrites has been described to enable every believer to discriminate between the two. The community is always bound together by adopting certain disciplinary measures that tend to increase its strength and to discourage people from creating mischief. In Surah An-Noor, God commands the believers to take permission before leaving from a community project in which they are participating: "Only those are believers who believe in Allah and His Messenger. When they are with him on a matter requiring collective action, they do not depart until they have asked for his leave. Those who ask for your leave are those who believe in Allah and His Messenger; so when they ask for your leave for some business of theirs, give leave to those of them whom you will, and ask Allah for their forgiveness: for Allah is forgiving, merciful."[11] Islam commands its followers not to get involved in scheming for sinful plots or revolt. They should show courtesy at public meetings and social visits. In their conversations, they should be polite, truthful and not engaging in false arguments and discourse.

2.1 Participation in Secret Counsels for Sin and Revolt

God knows everything, and the unbelievers have been warned about their hidden malice in greeting the Messenger and about their secret whisperings and consultations, by which they conspired and intrigued against the Messenger. In their arrogance, the unbelievers asked: "Why does not Allah punish us for what we say?" However, they will certainly be punished in Hell. In Surah Al-Mujadila, God talks about the unbelievers holding secret counsels for sin and revolt: "Do you not see that Allah knows whatever is in the heavens and whatever is on the earth? Nowhere is there a secret counsel among three persons without Him being the fourth of them, nor (among) five except He is the sixth, nor less than that nor more but He is with them whereever they are. He will inform them of what they did on the Day of Resurrection; surely, Allah knows all things. Have you not seen those who were forbidden secret counsels? Yet, they return to what they were forbidden. They hold secret counsels for sin and revolt and disobedience to the Messenger. When they come to you, they greet you with a greeting with which Allah does not greet you, and they say to themselves: "Why does not Allah punish us for what we say?"

Hell is enough for them; they shall enter it, and evil is the resort."[12]

After reaffirming that the whisperings of the hypocrites could do them no harm, the believers were told that they should go on doing their duty with full trust in God. Unlike the behavior of the unbelievers, the believers were further advised that when they talk secretly, they should not talk about sin, transgression, and disobedience to the Messenger, but of goodness and piety. God commanded the believers in Surah Al-Mujadalah: "O you who believe! When you confer together in private, do not discuss sin, revolt, or disobedience to the Messenger. Rather, talk about goodness and mindfulness (of God). Be careful of your duty (to God) to Whom you will be brought back. Secret counsels are only the work of Satan that he may cause grief to the believers, but he cannot hurt them in the least, except with Allah's permission, and on Allah let the believers rely."[13]

2.2 Show of Courtesy at Public Meetings and Social Visit

The believers have also been given instructions to eradicate certain social evils that were prevalent among people at the time of the Prophet, even as they are today. People sitting in an assembly did not even show the courtesy to squeeze in so as to make room for latecomers. This used to be a frequent occurrence in the Messenger's assemblies. However, believers should not behave selfishly and narrow-mindedly in their assemblies, but they should accommodate newcomers with an open heart: "O you who believe! When you are told to make room for one another in your assemblies, then make room, for then Allah will make room for you. When it is said: 'Rise up,' then rise up. Allah will exalt those of you who believe and those who are given knowledge in high degrees, and Allah is aware of what you do."[14] Likewise, when people go to visit others, they should not prolong their visits, realizing that it may cause hardship to the people they are visiting.

Believers have been told that, in general, all meetings are confidential except those in which some illegal activity is taking place. It was narrated by Jabir ibn 'Abdullah that the Prophet said: "Meetings are confidential except three: those for the purpose of shedding blood unlawfully, committing fornication, or acquiring property unjustly."[15] People have also been advised to avoid sitting on paths and holding meetings there. "Abu Sa'id Khudri reported Allah's Messenger as saying: 'Avoid sitting on the paths.' They said: 'Allah's Messenger, we cannot help but hold our meetings (in these paths) and discuss matters (there).' Thereupon Allah's Messenger said: 'If you insist on holding meets, then give the path its due right.' They said: 'What are its due rights?' Upon this he said: 'Lowering the gaze, refraining from doing harm, exchanging of greetings, commanding of good, and forbidding from evil.'"[16]

2.3 Believers are Polite and Converse in the Best Possible Ways

Our duties toward God cannot be over emphasized, but our duties toward our fellow human beings, which are equally important, are generally given a lower priority in the minds of believers, both at the individual and community levels. Yet, a good balance is the main characteristic of Islam and its code of living. Our duties and dealings include all types of people, believers and unbelievers alike. We are commanded in Surah Al-Ankabut that we should not dispute about religion with Jews and Christians. It should be discussed in a best possible way. "Do not argue with the followers of the Book except by what is best, unless with those of them who act unjustly. Say: 'We believe in that which has been revealed to us and revealed to you. Our God and your God is one, and to Him do we submit.'"[17]

If good and polite conversation is not possible with a particular person or group, because he or they are making fun of or misrepresenting Islam, then one should politely withdraw from him or them. In Surah Al-Anam, believers are advised: "When you see those who enter into false discourse about Our revelations, withdraw from them until they enter into some other discourse. If Satan causes you to forget, then after recollection, do not sit with the unjust people. On their account, no responsibility falls on the righteous, but (their duty) is to remind them, that they may (learn to) fear Allah. Leave alone those who have taken their religion for play and an idle sport, and who are deceived by this world's life. Remind them that every soul destroys itself by its own course of action."[18]

3. SOME FINAL THOUGHTS

God commands believers to wish for others as they wish for themselves. This thought and feeling initiate a fury of activities that help establish all that is good and eliminate those things that are harmful to the welfare of the people. Eventually, people's proper belief and cumulative righteous activities can make an entire community Islamic. Previous communities suffered because they ignored the importance of enjoining the doing of what is right and of forbidding what is wrong. "Abdullah ibn Masud reported God's Messenger as saying: 'The first defect that permeated Banu Isra'il was that a man (of them) met another man and said: 'O so-and-so, fear Allah, and abandon what you are doing, for it is not lawful for you.' He then met him the next day, and that did not refrain him from eating with him, drinking with him, and sitting with him. When they did so, Allah mingled their hearts with one another.' He (the Prophet) then recited the verse: 'Curses were pronounced on those among the children of Isra'il who rejected faith by the tongue of David and of Jesus the son of Mary'...up to 'wrongdoers.' (Qur'an 5:78) He then said; 'By no means, I swear by Allah, you must enjoin what is good and prohibit what is evil, prevent the wrongdoer, bend him into conformity with what is right, and restrict him to what is right.'"[19]

When people's character and behavior keep deteriorating, and when corruption is on the rise, some corrective measures need to be taken to save the community from destruction. Amirah al-Kindi narrated that the

Messenger said: "When a sin is committed on earth, a person who witnesses it and denounces it is the same as one who has not seen it. But the one who has been absent and approves of it is considered like one who has taken part in it."[20] It is, therefore, a matter of utmost importance that people repent, do good deeds, and avoid what is bad for human individuals and society. The entire Islamic code is for the benefit of the people; it either prevents harm or brings benefit. When God addresses the believers in the Qur'an, you will find either something good that people are encouraged to do or something evil that they are required to avoid or a combination of both. Compliance of God's commands is the only way if we wish to receive His mercy and not His punishment.

NOTES

1. Qur'an 11:116-117.
2. Qur'an 3:103 & 105.
3. Qur'an 49:9-10.
4. Qur'an 6:54.
5. Qur'an 4:114.
6. Qur'an 49:11.
7. Qur'an 83:29-31.
8. Qur'an 83:34-36.
9. Qur'an 49:12.
10. Sahih Muslim 32.6214.
11. Qur'an 24:62.
12. Qur'an 58:7-8.
13. Qur'an 58:9-10.
14. Qur'an 58:11.
15. Abu Dawud 41.4851.

16. Sahih Muslim 26.5376.

17. Qur'an 29:46.

18. Qur'an 6:68-70.

19. Qur'an 49:13.

20. Qur'an 49:15.

21. Abu Dawud 37.4322.

22. Abu Dawud 37:4331.

Books Cited or Recommended

Akbar, Muhammad (trans.). *The Meaning of Holy Qur'an* by
Syed Abu Ala Maududi.
> Lahore: Islamic Publications (Pvt) Limited, 2000.

'Ali, 'Abdullah Yusuf. *The Meaning of Holy Qur'an.*
> Beltville, Maryland: Amana Publications, 11th ed., 2009.
> www.usc.edu/schools/college/crcc/engagement/resources/texts/

Al-Ghazali, *Muhammad. Muslim's Character.*
> Riyadh, Saudi Arabia: Mubarat Sk. Hassan Tahir Al-Islmiah.

Al-Muhtaj, Sheikh 'Abdullah Bin Muhammad. *Insan*, (Urdu).
> Riyadh, Saudi Arabia: Darussalam, 1998.

At-Tarjumana, A'isha 'Abdarahman and Johnson, Ya'qub, (trans.).
Malik's Muwatta
> www.usc.edu/schools/college/crcc/engagement/resources/texts/

Hasan Prof. Ahmad, (trans.). *Sunan Abu-Dawud*
> www.usc.edu/schools/college/crcc/engagement/resources/texts/

Irving, Thomas Ballantine, Ahmed, Khurshid and Ahsan, Muhammad
Manazir.
> *The Qur'an Basic Teaching (s).*
> Leicester, England: The Islamic Foundation, 1994.

Karim, Maulana Fazlul. *Al-Hadith*, trans.Mishkat-ul-Masabih.
> New Delhi: Islamic Book Service, 2006.

Khan, Dr. Muhammad Muhsin and al-Hilali, Dr. Taqi-ud-Din.
The Noble Qur'an.
Riyadh, Saudi Arabia: Darussalam, 1996.

Khan, Dr. Muhammad Muhsin (trans.). *Sahih Bukhari.*
www.usc.edu/schools/college/crcc/engagement/resources/texts/).

Maududi, Syed Abul Ala, (trans. Ansari, Zafar Iqbal). *Towards Understanding the Qur'an.*
Leicester, England: The Islamic Foundation, 2006.

Pickthall, Muhammad Marmaduke. *Holy Qur'an.*

www.usc.edu/schools/college/crcc/engagement/resources/texts/).

Salahi, Adil, (ed.). *Our Dialogue.*
www.ourdialogue.com.

Siddique, Abdul Hamid, (trans.). *Sahih Muslim.*
www.usc.edu/schools/college/crcc/engagement/resources/texts/).

Shakir, Muhammad Habib. *The Qur'an.*

www.usc.edu/schools/college/crcc/engagement/resources/texts/).

Tantavi, Sheikh Ali. *Introduction to Islam.*
Lahore, Pakistan: Qur'an Ahsan Tareek, 2004.

Yusuf, Hamza. *Purification of the Heart.*
www.starlatch.com: Starlatch Press, 2004.